BALL PEEN HAMMER

:01
First Second
NEW YORK & LONDON

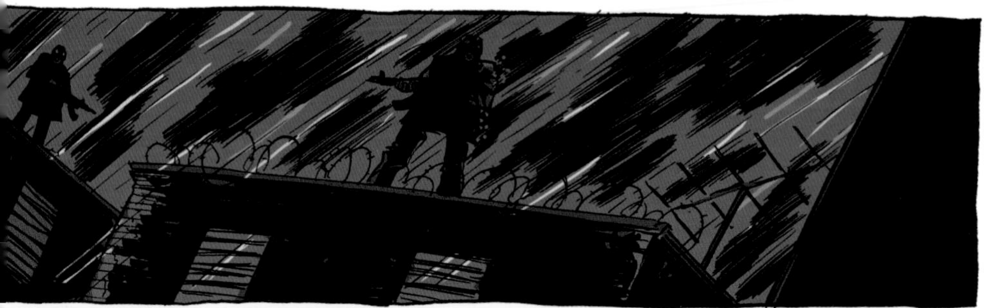

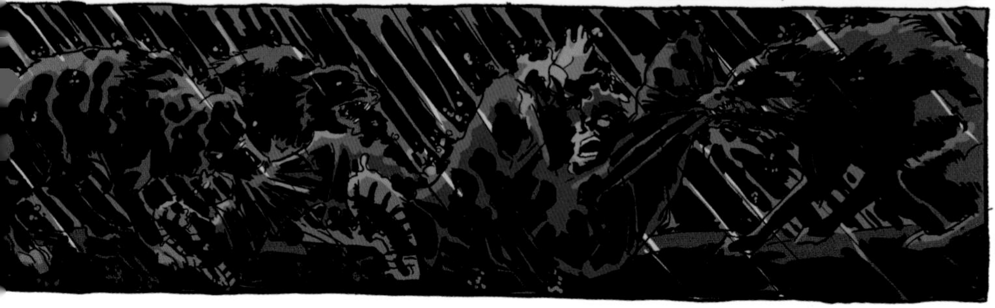

BALL PEEN HAMMER

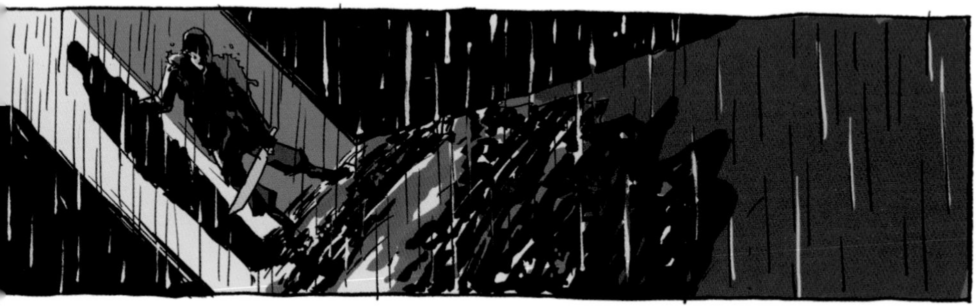

adam rapp & george o'connor

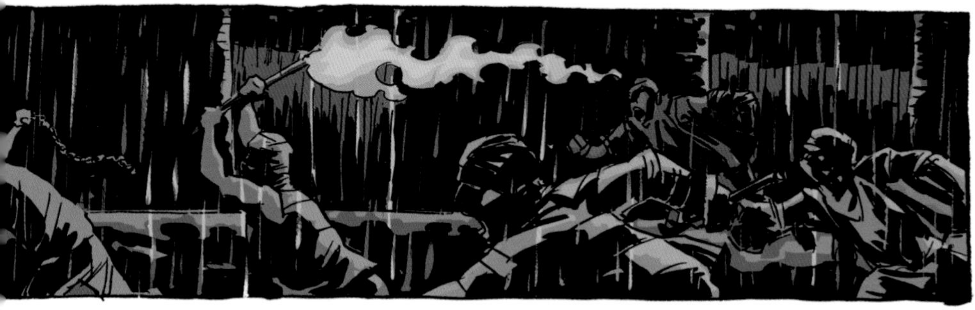

color by hilary sycamore

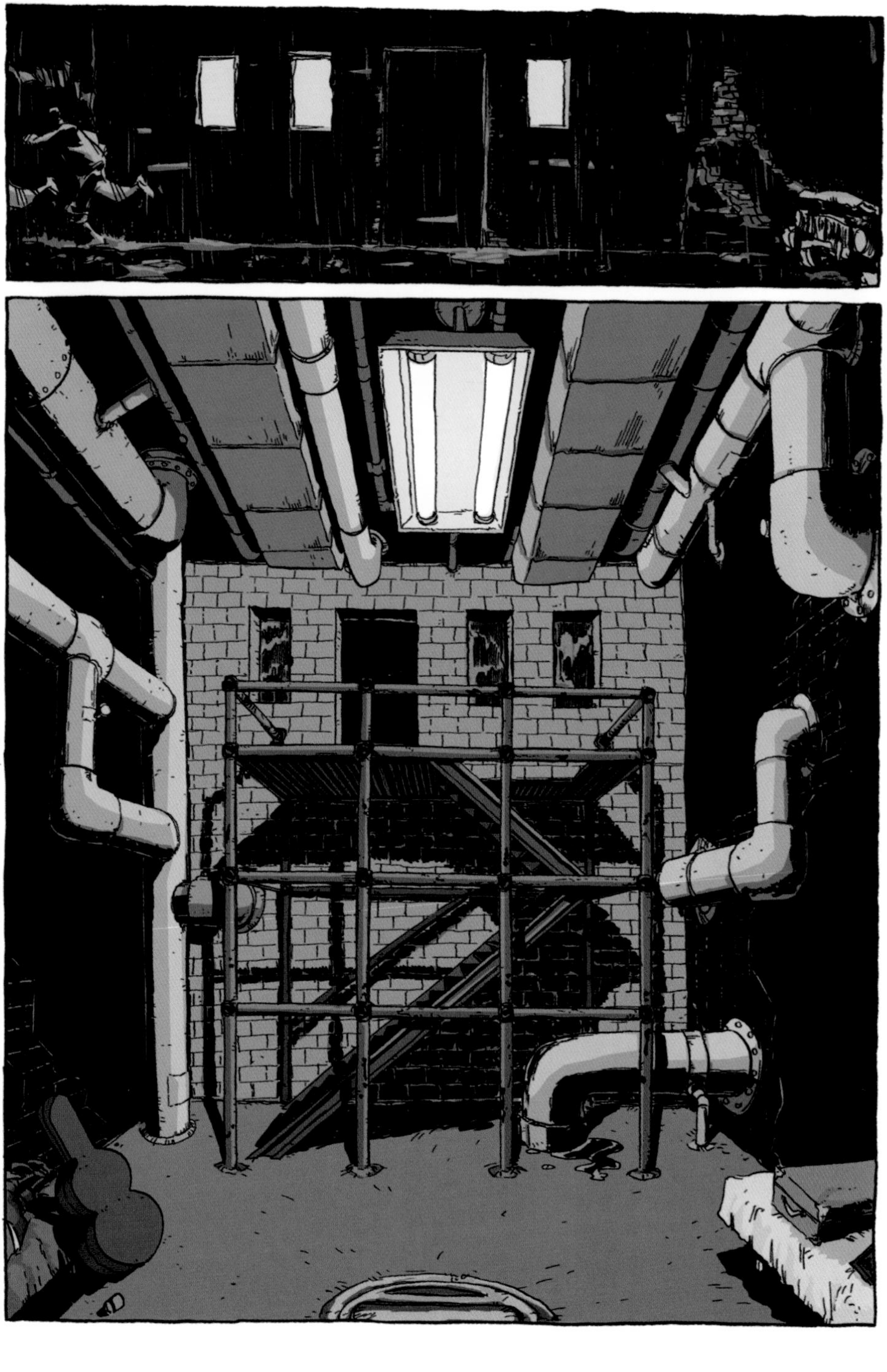

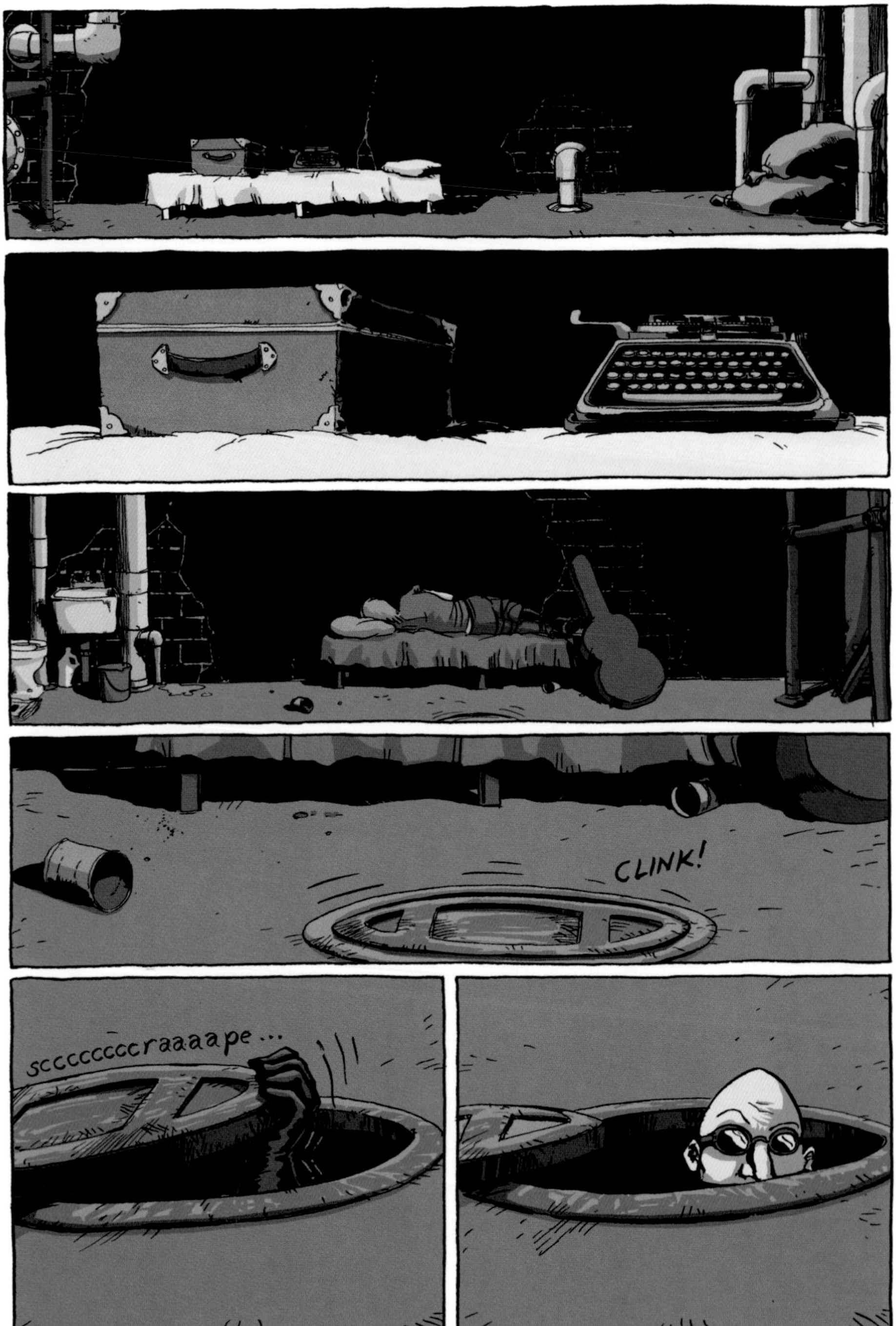
CLINK!
scccccccraaaape...

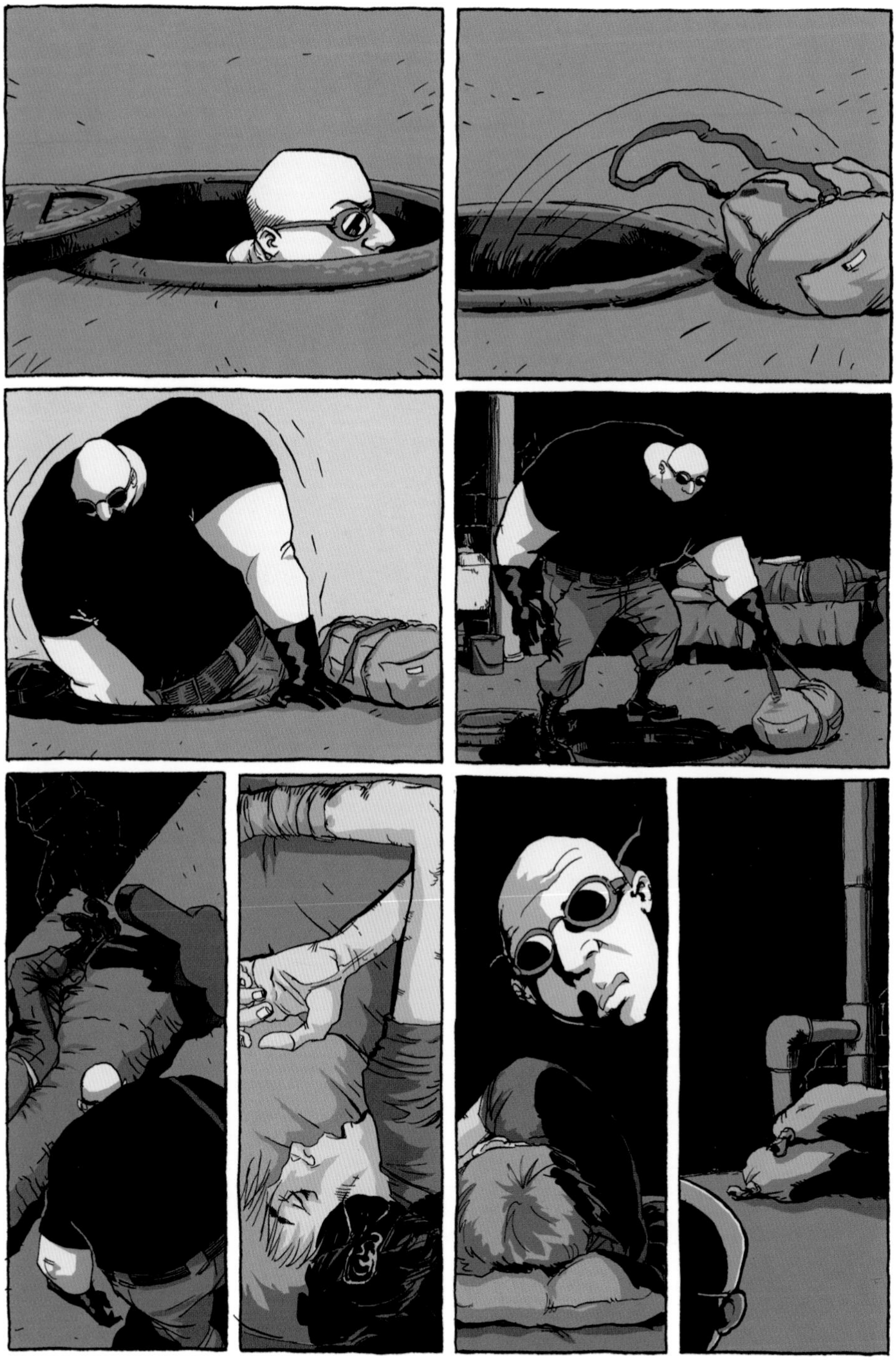

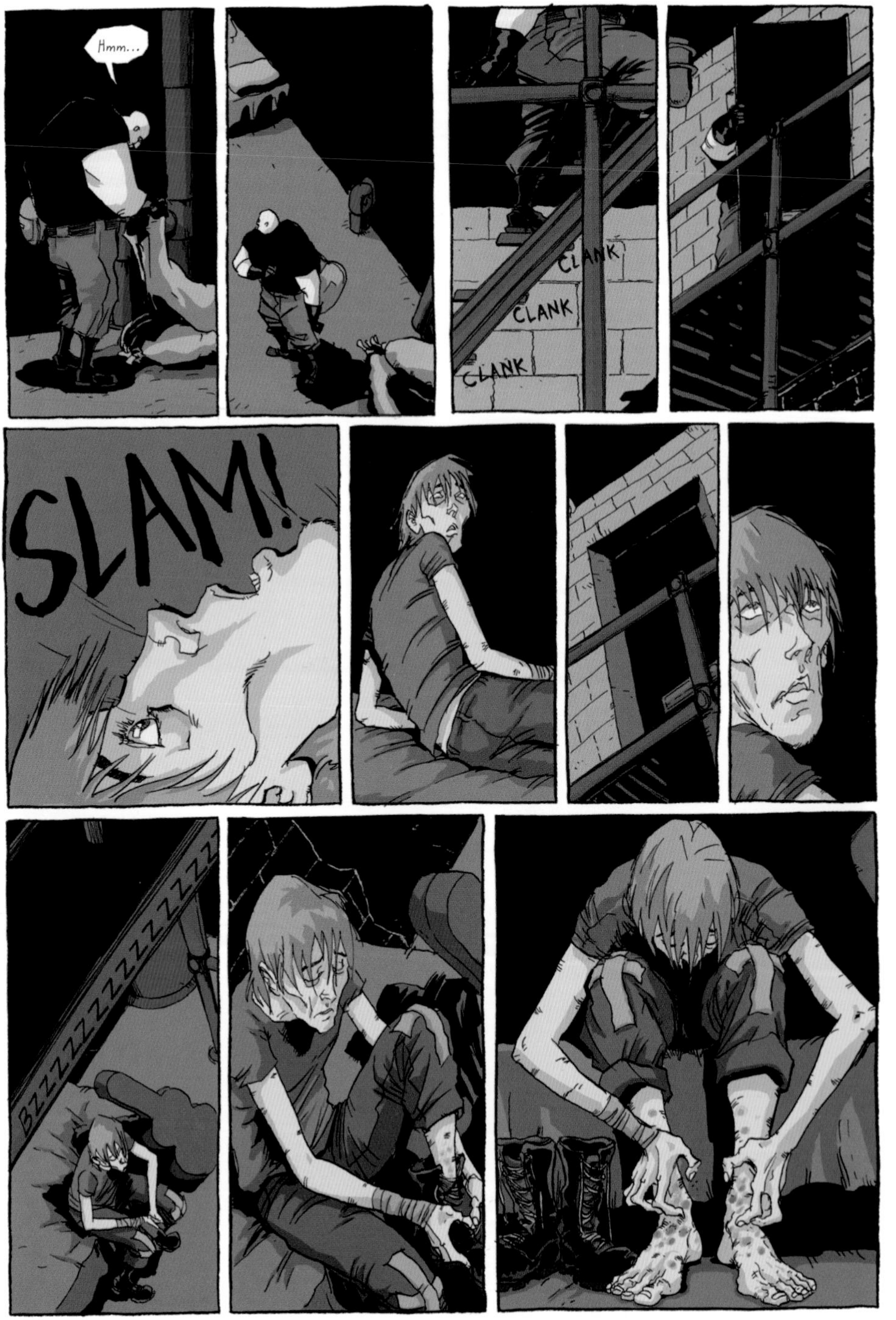
Hmm...
CLANK
CLANK
CLANK
SLAM!
BZZZZZZZZZZZZZZZ

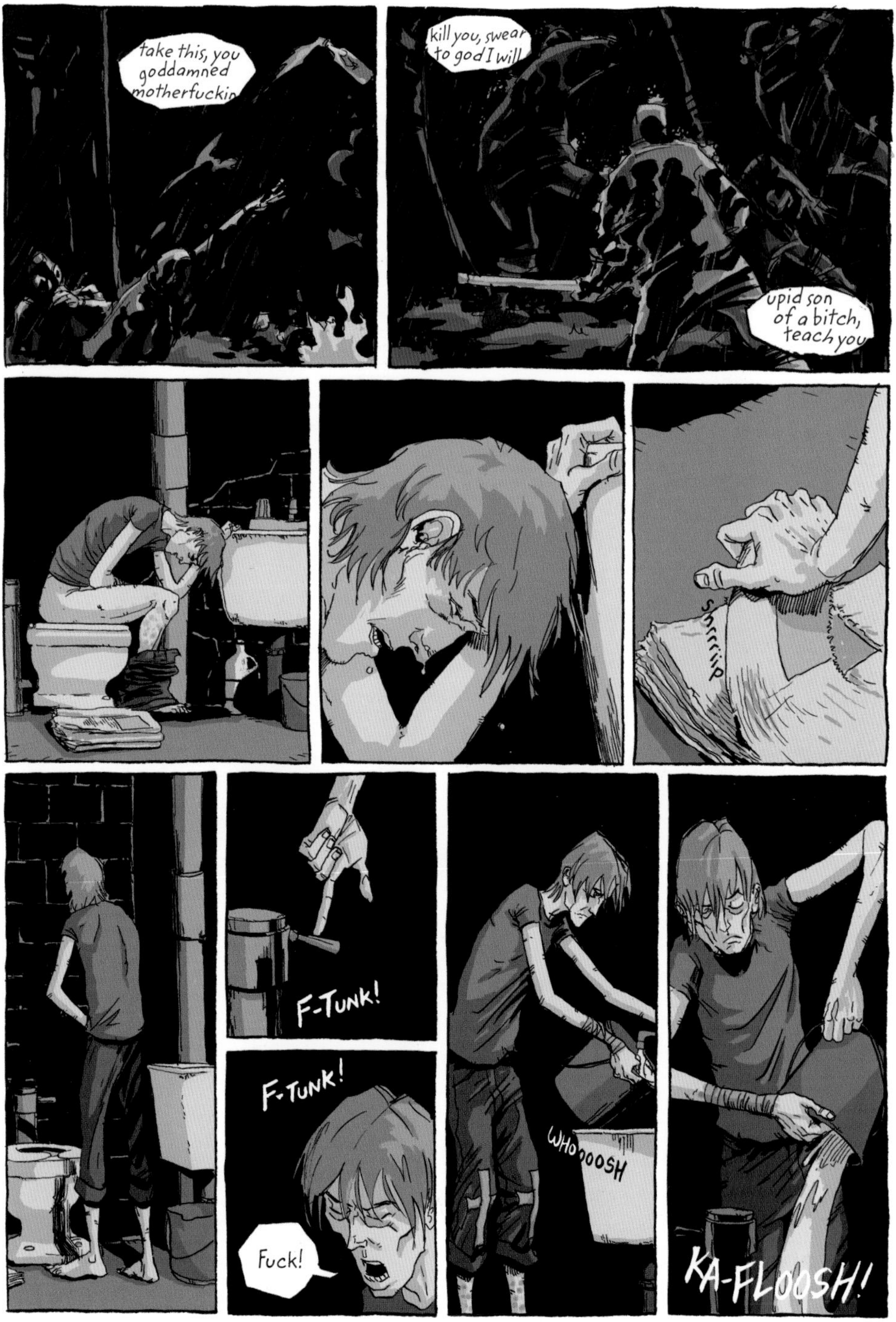
take this, you goddamned motherfuckin
kill you, swear to god I will
upid son of a bitch, teach you
Snrrriip
F-TUNK!
F-TUNK!
Fuck!
WHOOOOSH
KA-FLOOSH!

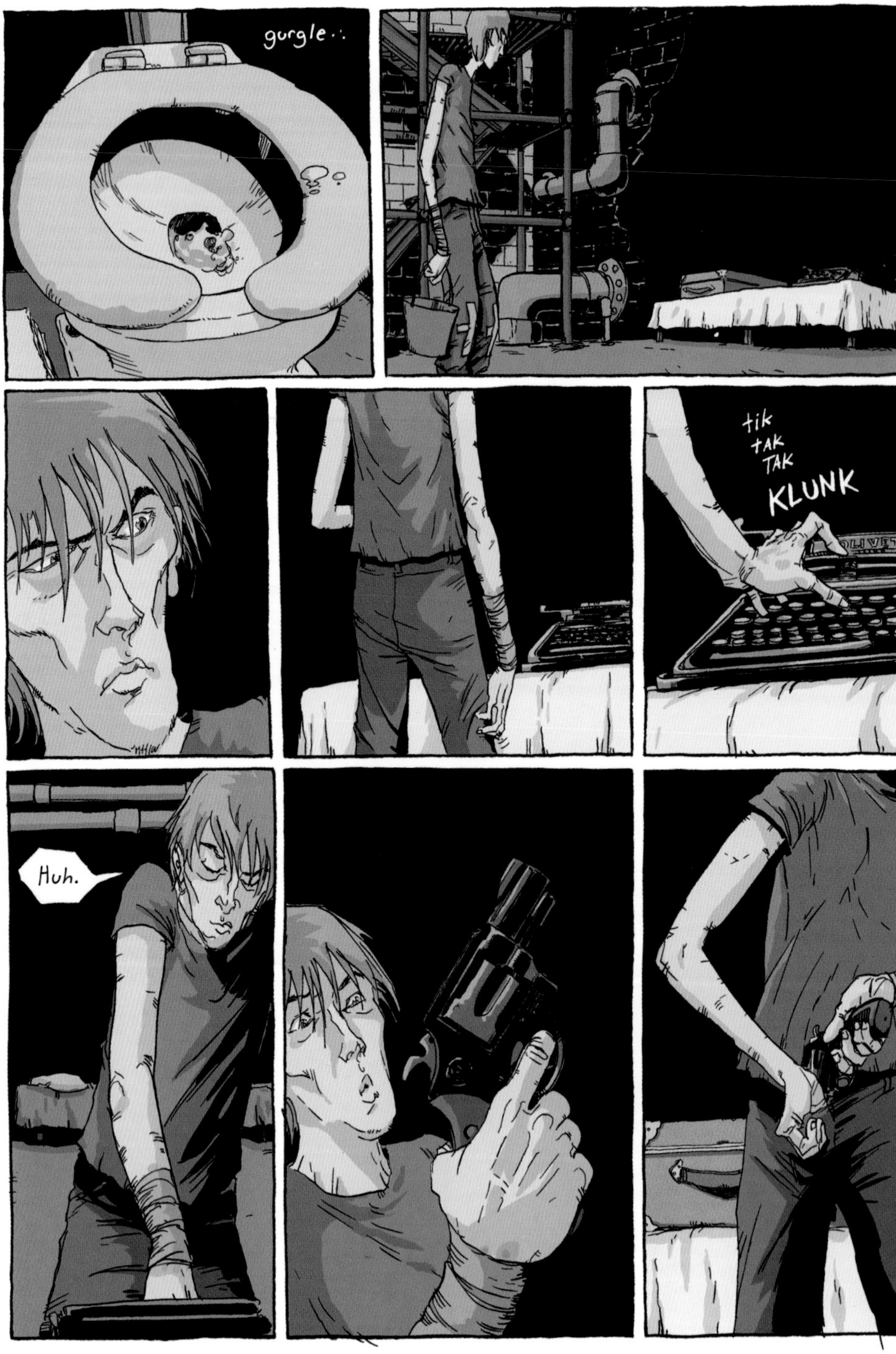
gurgle . .
tik
tak
tak
KLUNK
Huh.

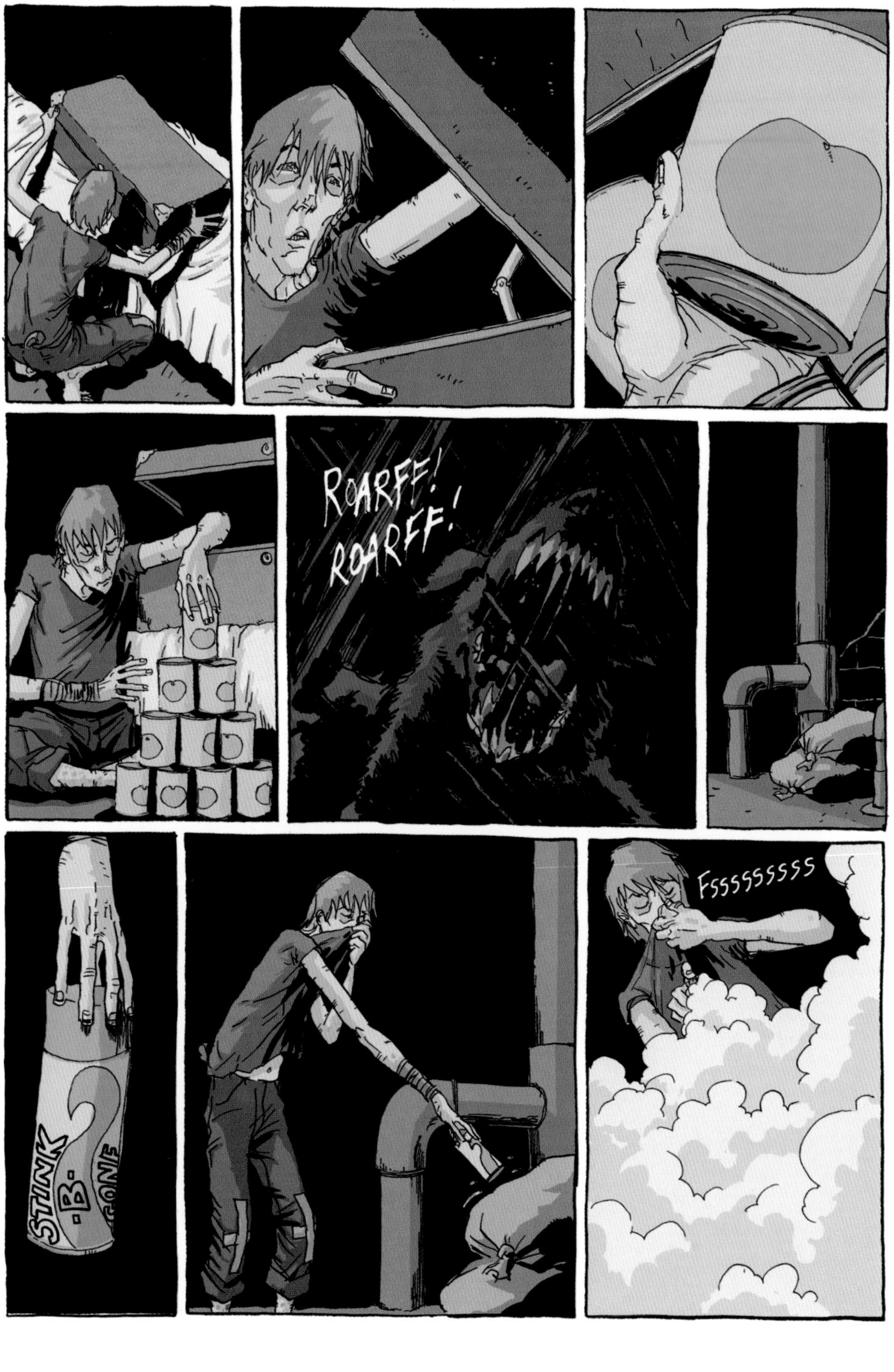
ROARFF!
ROARFF!
STINK-B-GONE
Fsssssssss

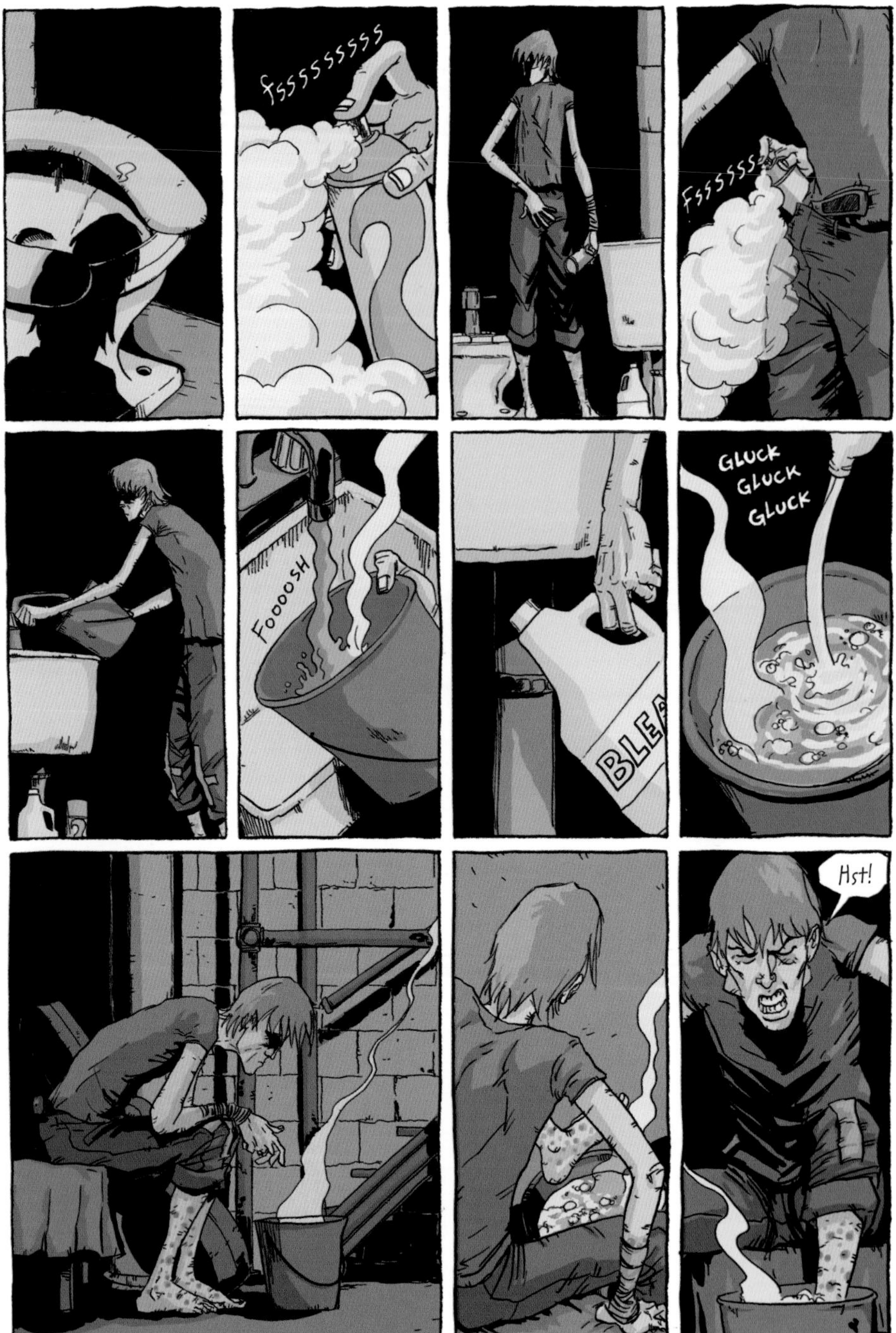
fsssssssss
Fssssss
FOOOOSH
BLEA
GLUCK
GLUCK
GLUCK
Hst!

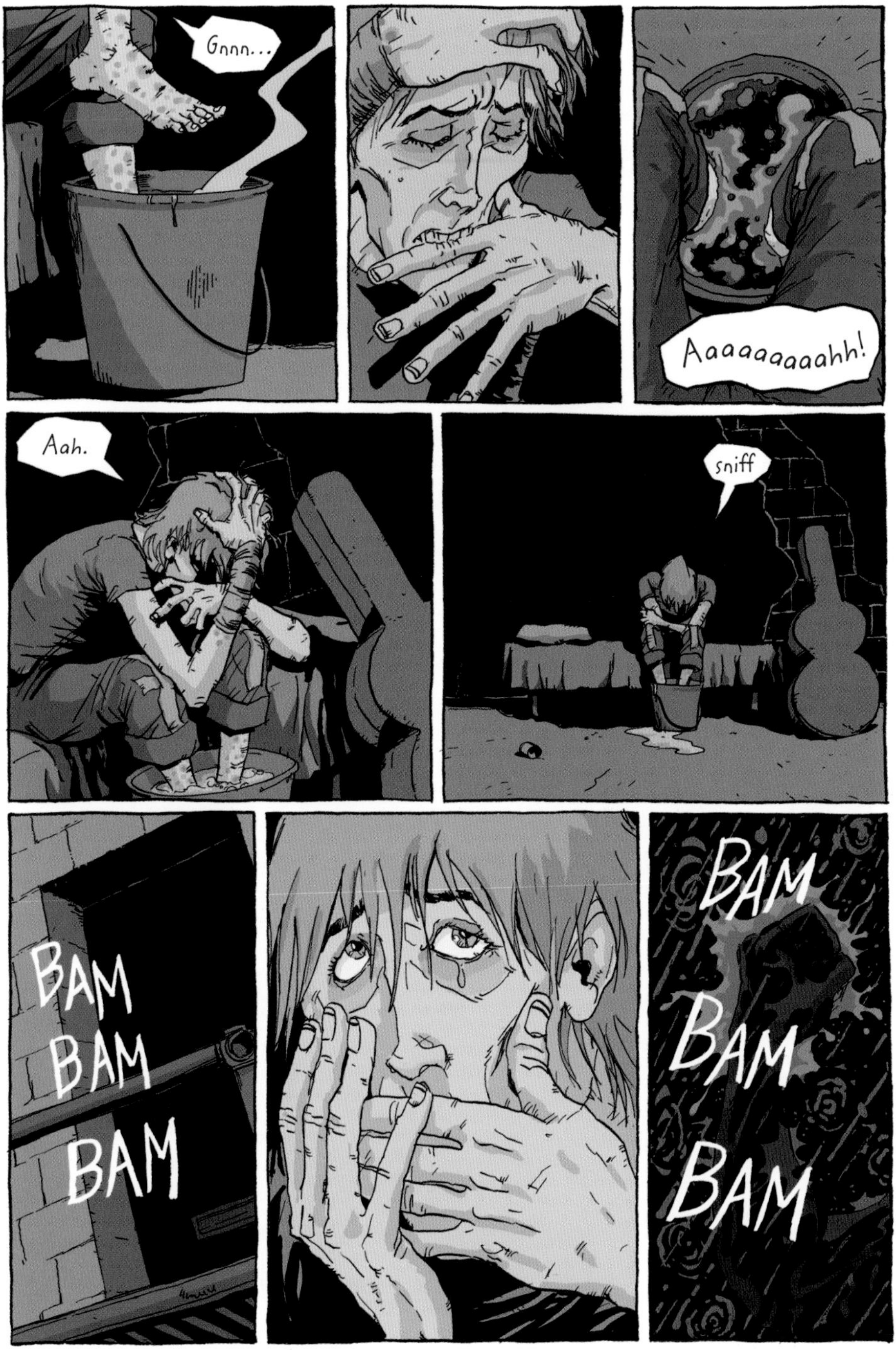
Gnnn...
Aaaaaaaaahh!
Aah.
sniff
BAM
BAM
BAM
BAM
BAM
BAM

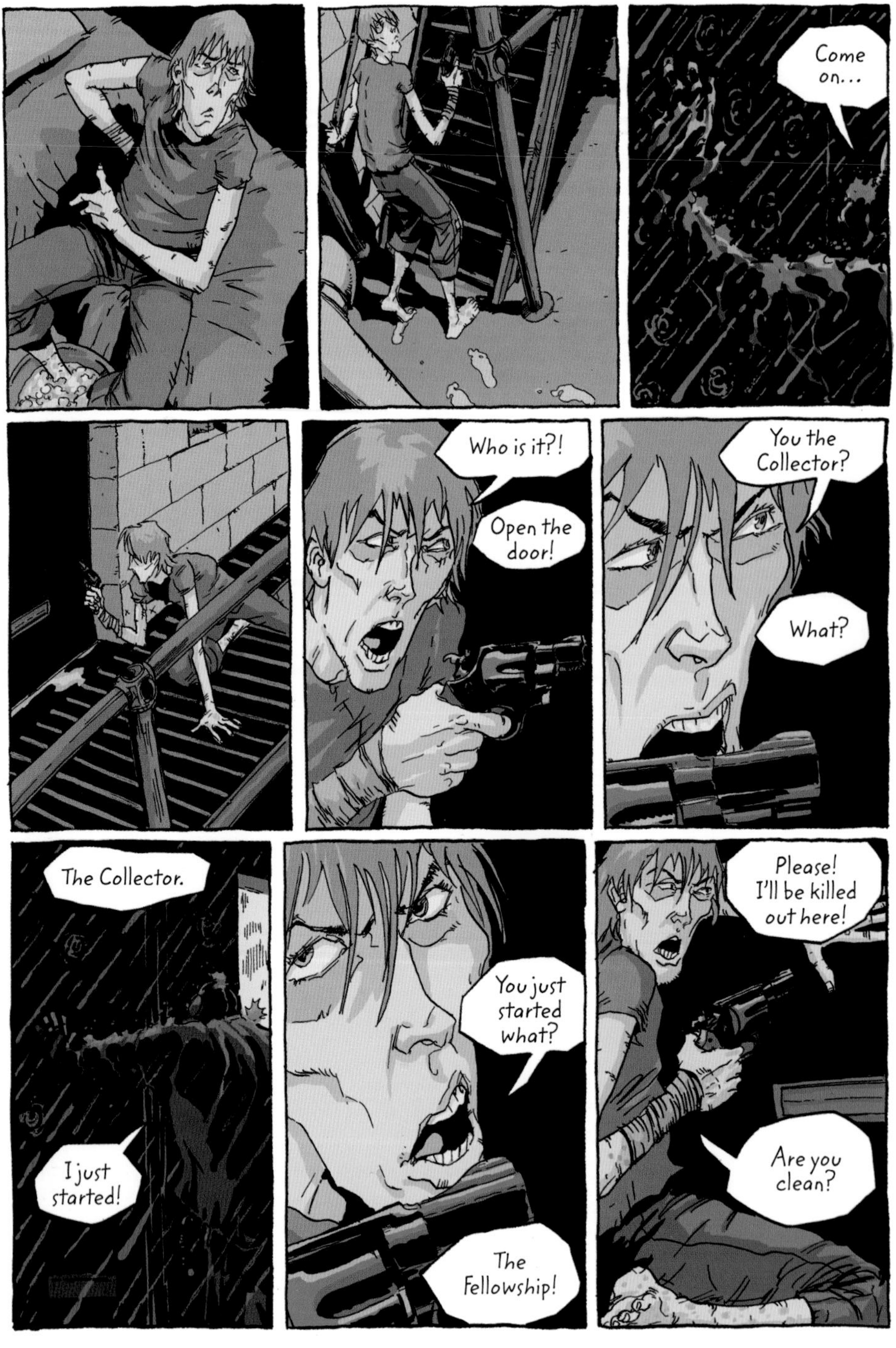

Come on...
Who is it?!
Open the door!
You the Collector?
What?
The Collector.
I just started!
You just started what?
The Fellowship!
Please! I'll be killed out here!
Are you clean?

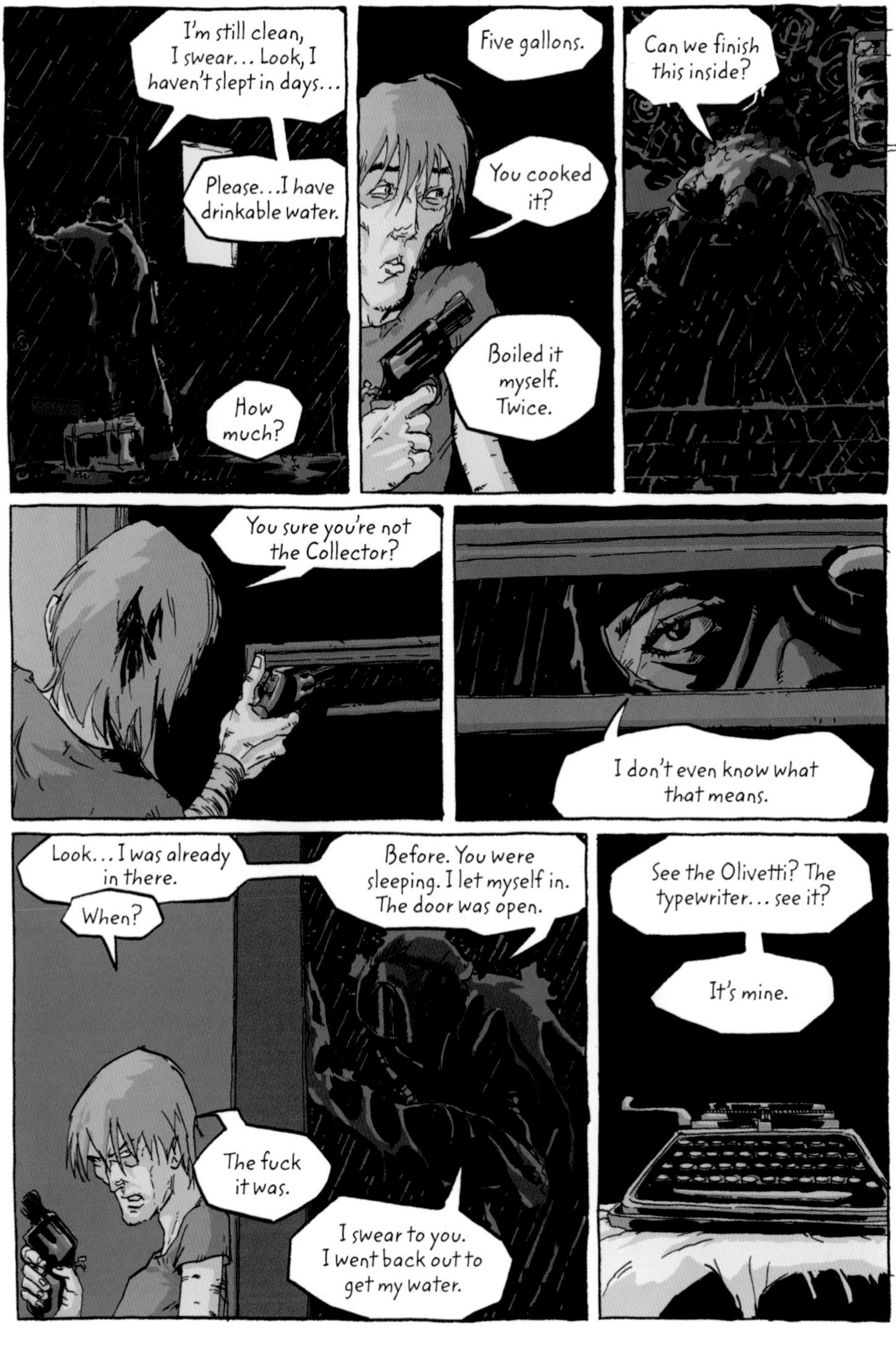
I'm still clean, I swear... Look, I haven't slept in days...
Please...I have drinkable water.
How much?
Five gallons.
You cooked it?
Boiled it myself. Twice.
Can we finish this inside?
You sure you're not the Collector?
I don't even know what that means.
Look... I was already in there.
When?
Before. You were sleeping. I let myself in. The door was open.
The fuck it was.
I swear to you. I went back out to get my water.
See the Olivetti? The typewriter... see it?
It's mine.

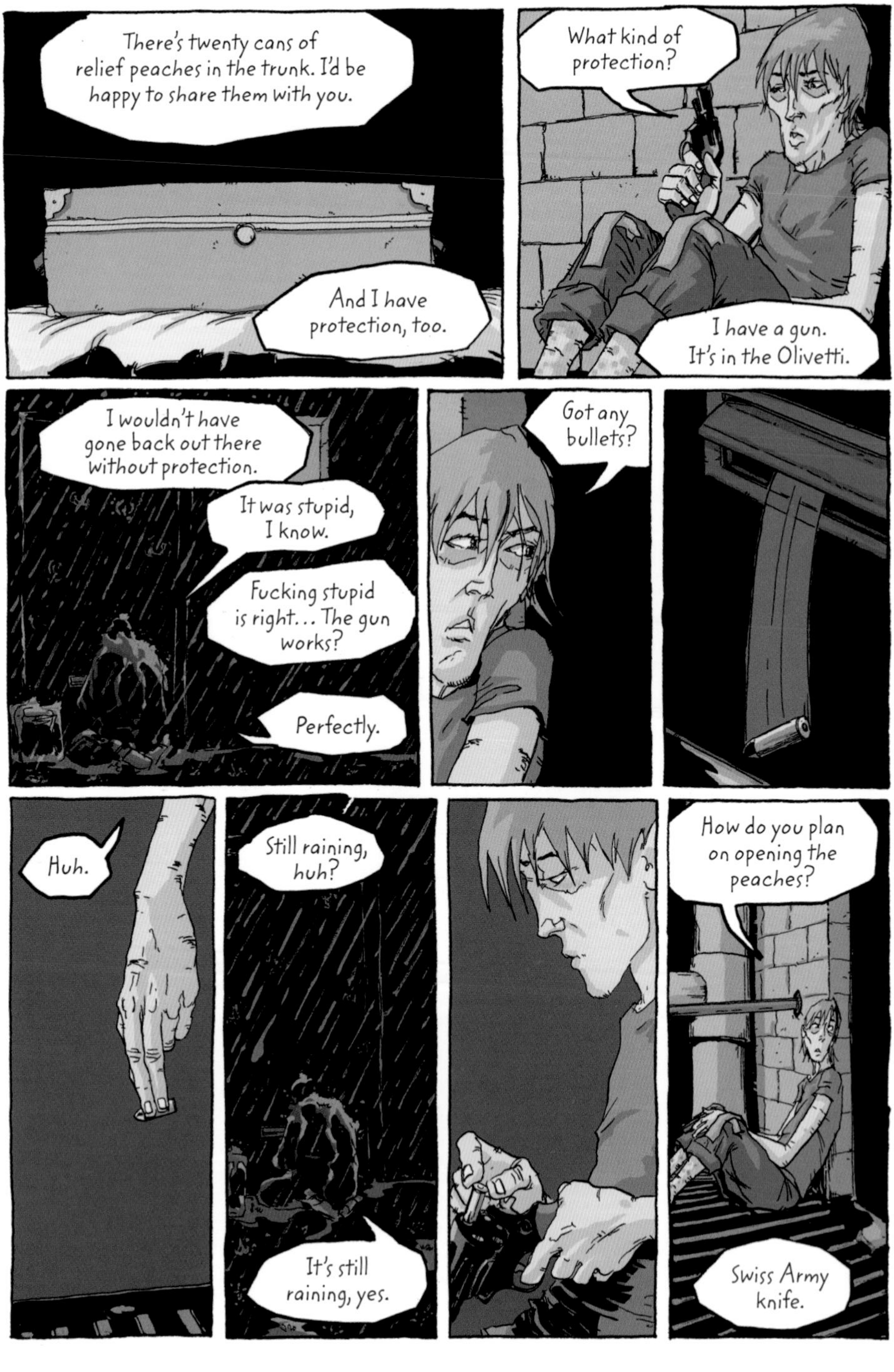
There's twenty cans of relief peaches in the trunk. I'd be happy to share them with you.
And I have protection, too.
What kind of protection?
I have a gun. It's in the Olivetti.
I wouldn't have gone back out there without protection.
It was stupid, I know.
Fucking stupid is right... The gun works?
Perfectly.
Got any bullets?
Huh.
Still raining, huh?
It's still raining, yes.
How do you plan on opening the peaches?
Swiss Army knife.

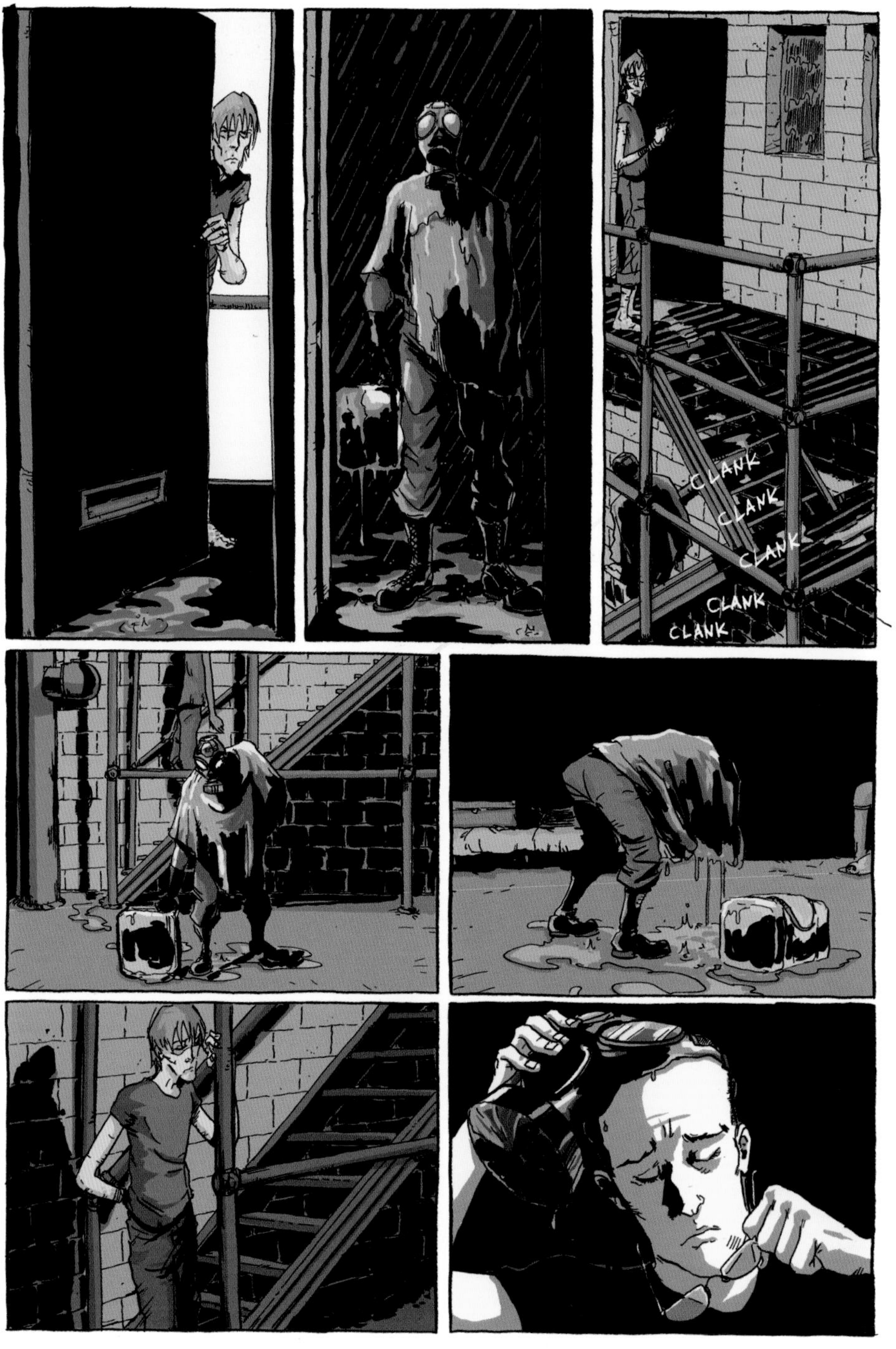
CLANK
CLANK
CLANK
CLANK
CLANK

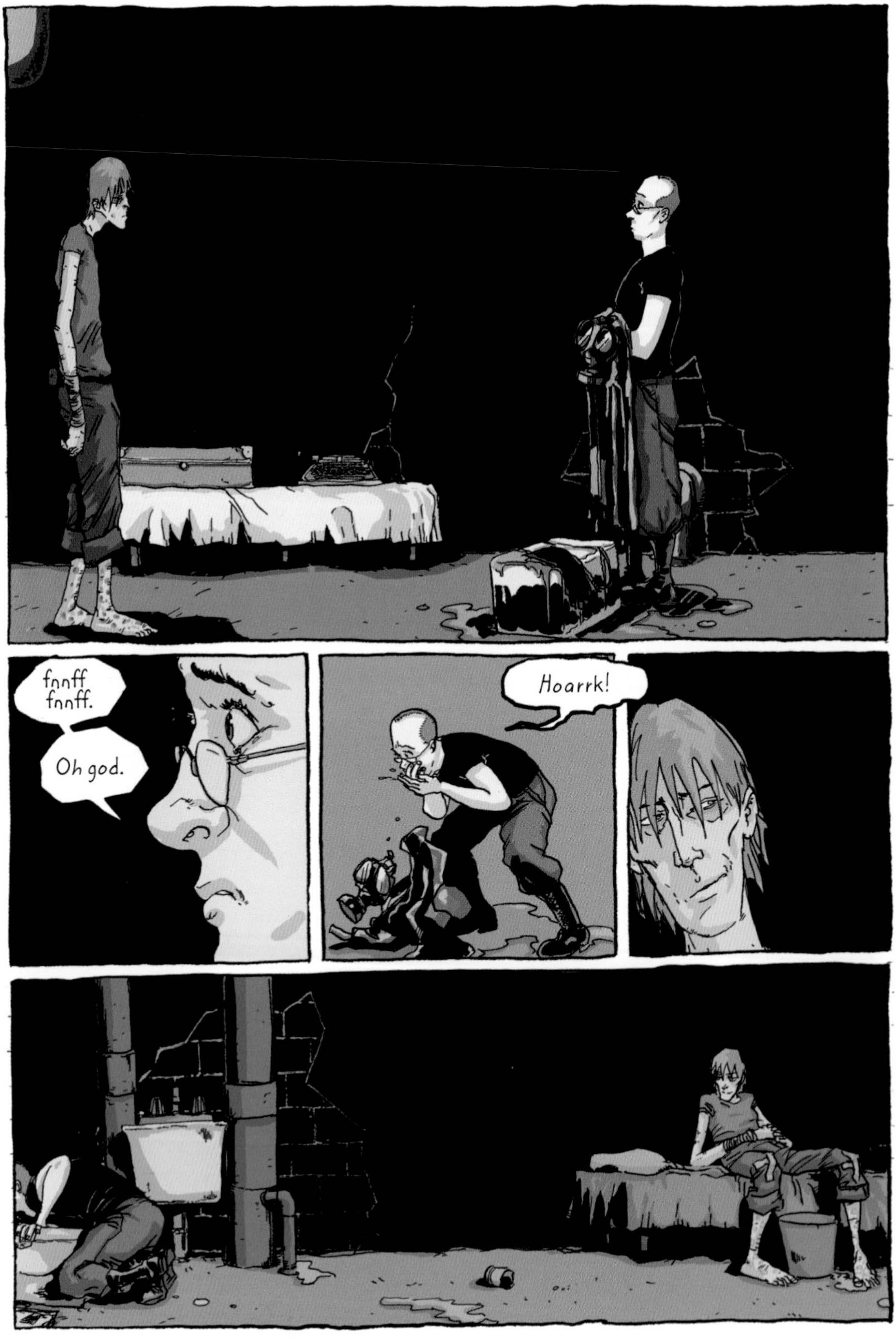
fnnff
fnnff.
Oh god.
Hoarrk!

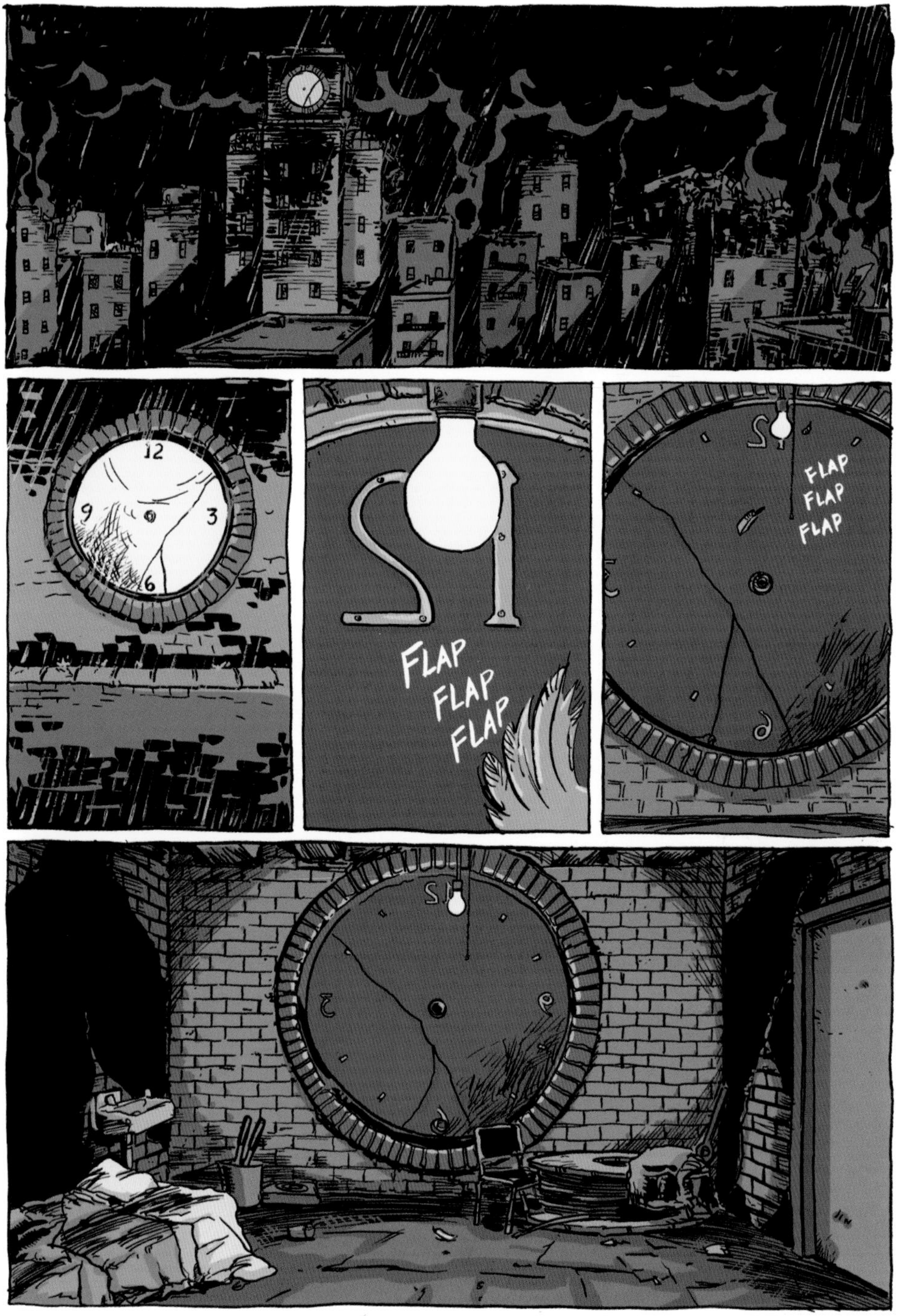
FLAP
FLAP
FLAP
FLAP
FLAP
FLAP

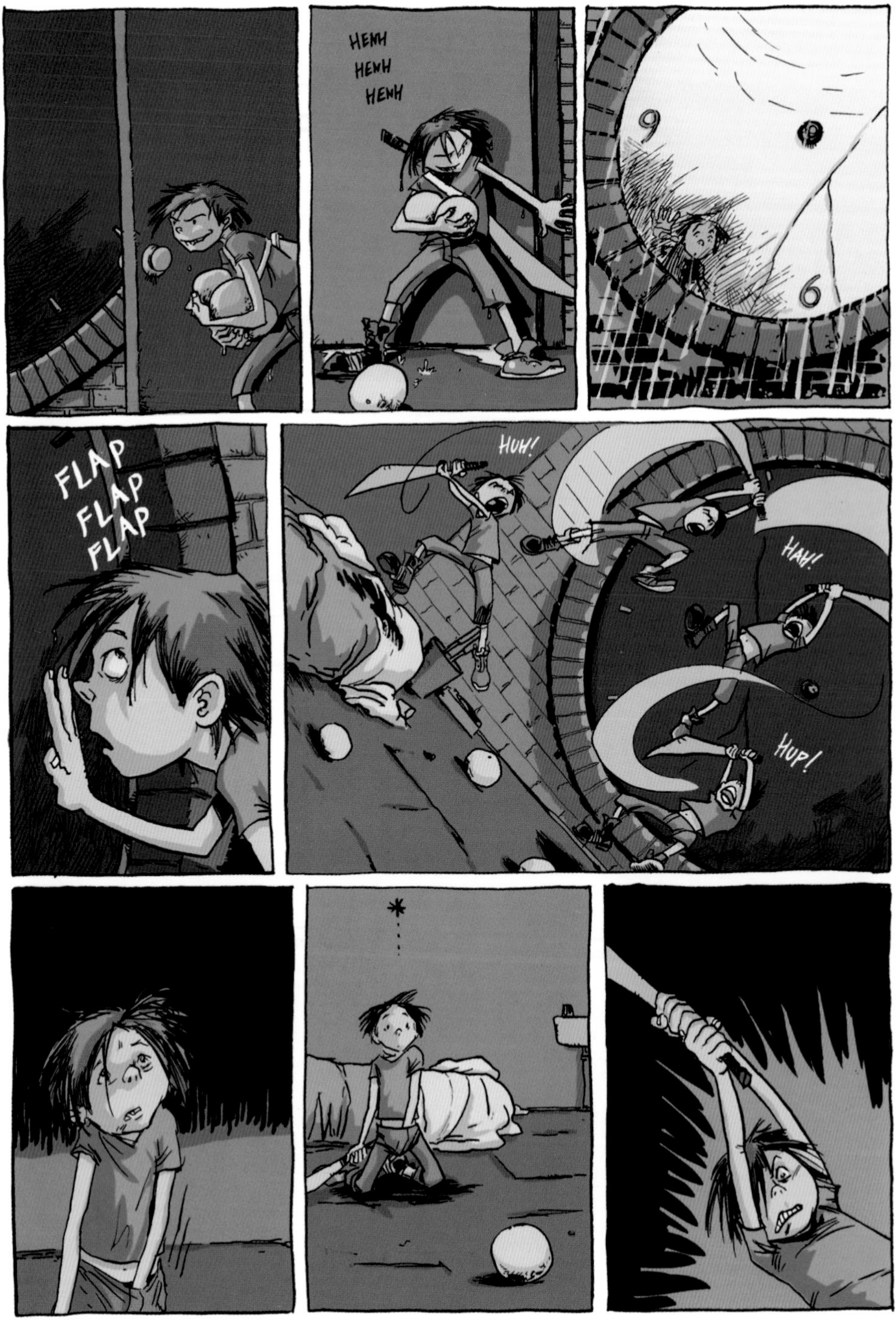
HENH
HENH
HENH
FLAP
FLAP
FLAP
HUH!
HAH!
HUP!

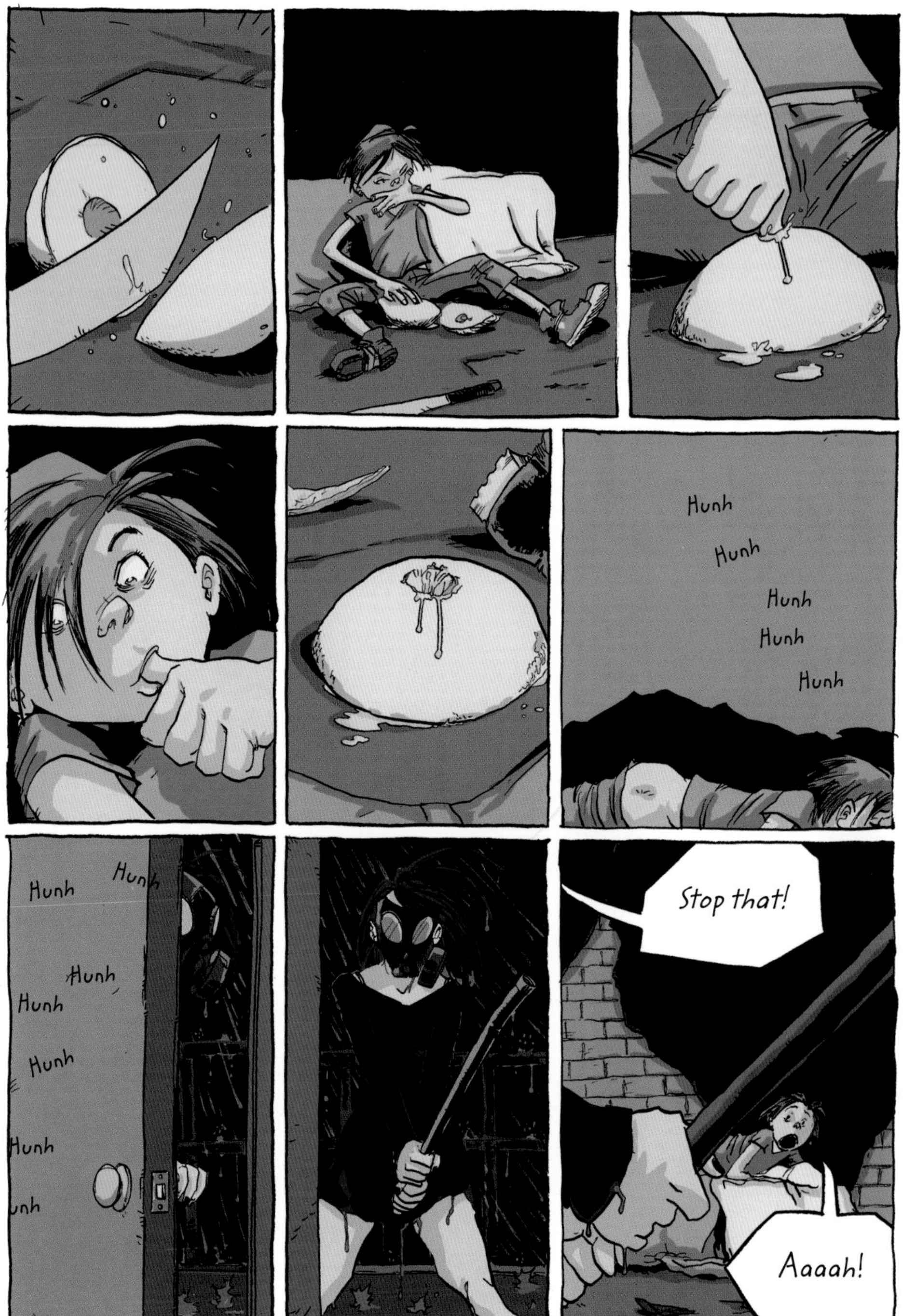
Hunh
Hunh
Hunh
Hunh
Hunh
Hunh
Hunh
Hunh
Hunh
Hunh
Hunh
unh
Stop that!
Aaaah!

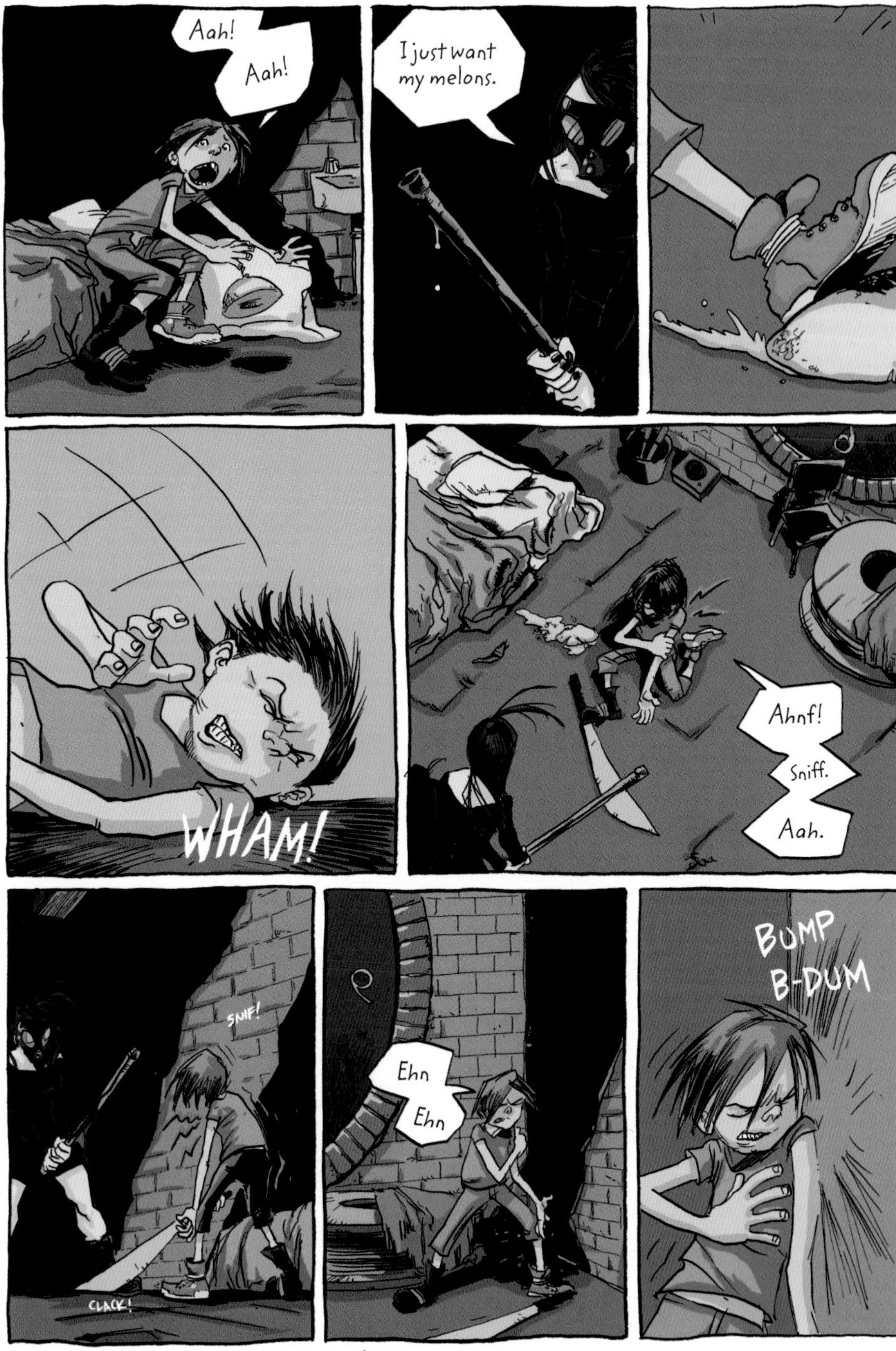
Aah!
Aah!
I just want my melons.
WHAM!
Ahnf!
Sniff.
Aah.
SNIF!
CLACK!
Ehn
Ehn
BUMP
B-DUM

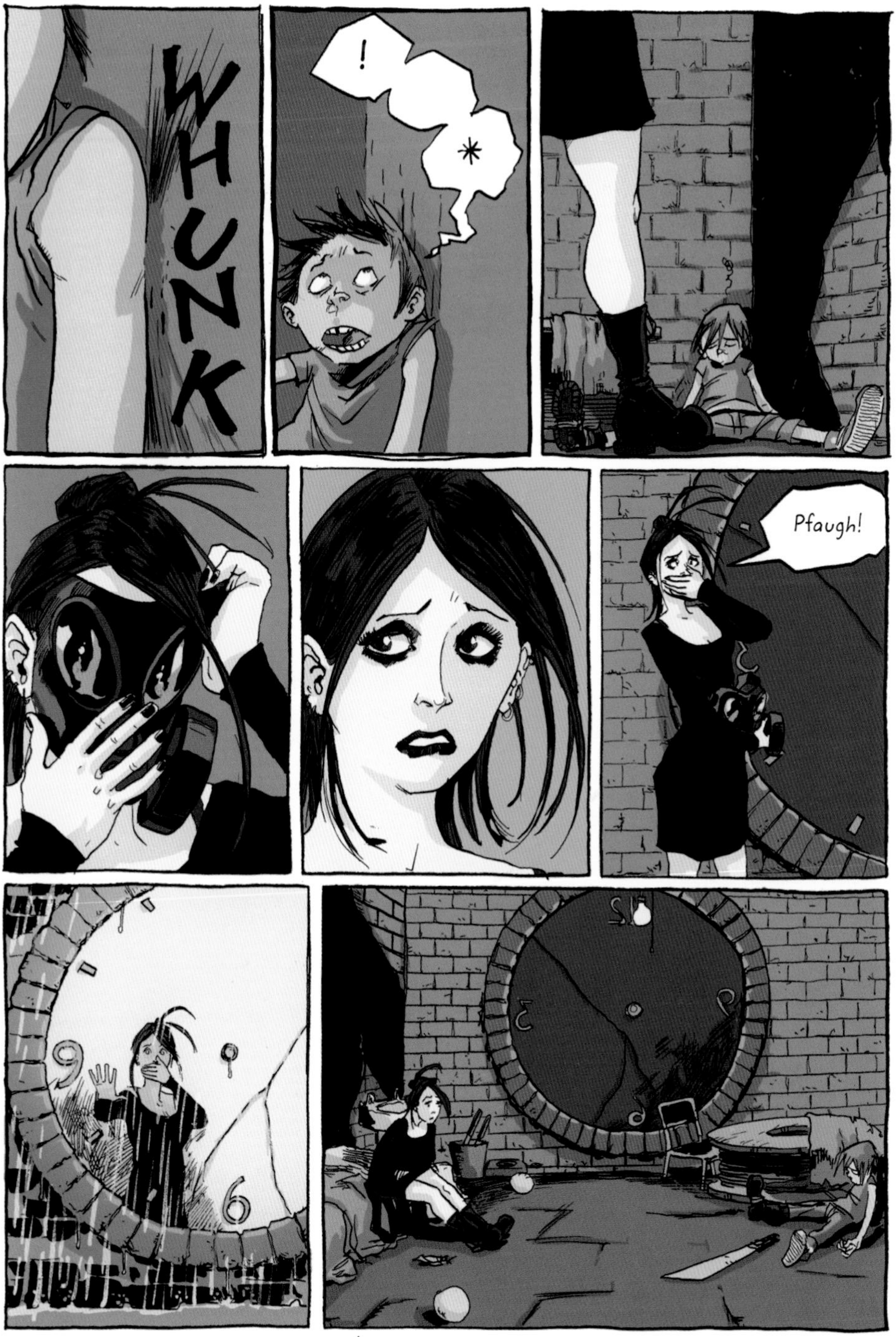
WHUNK
!
*
Pfaugh!

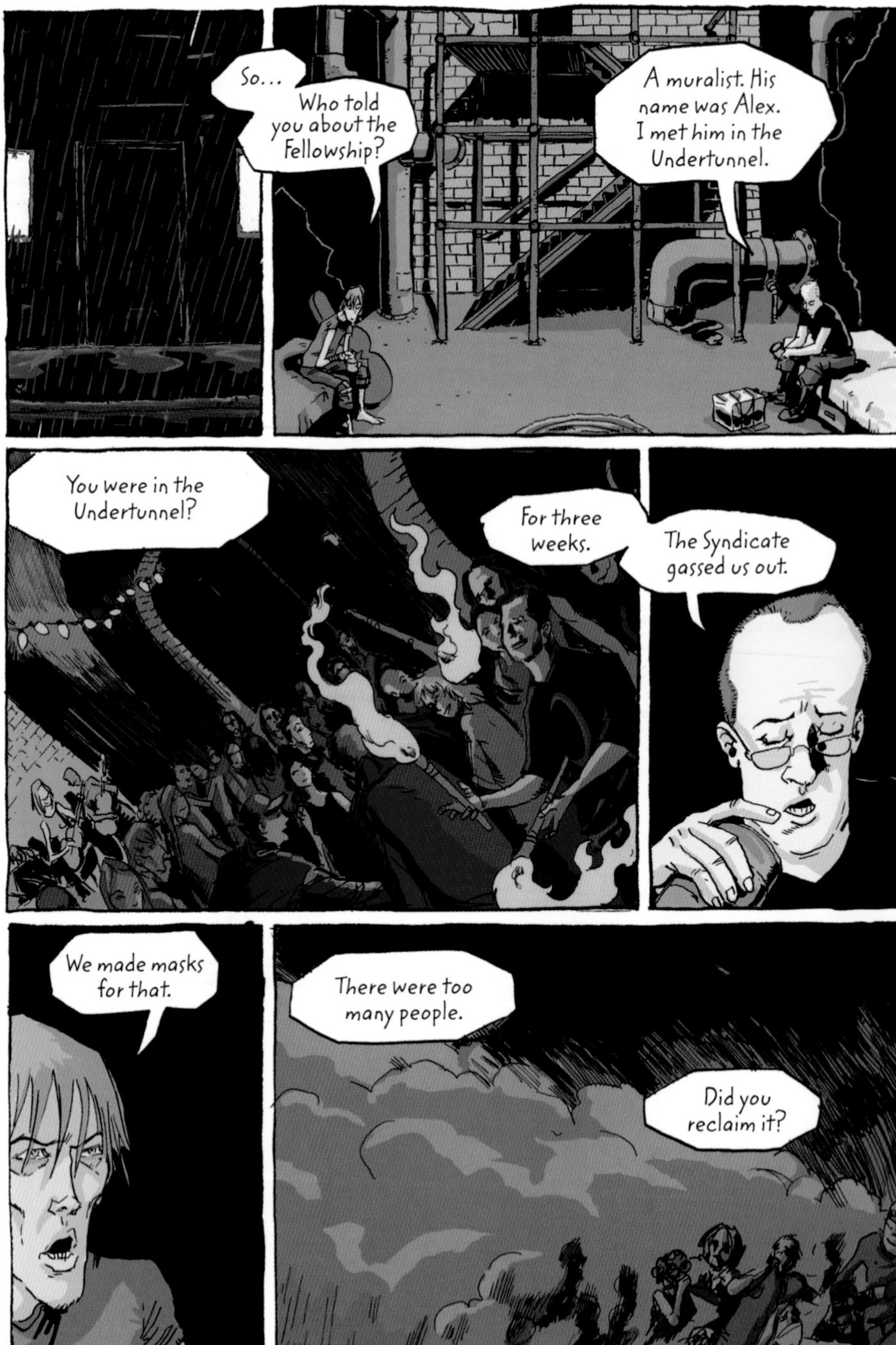
So…
Who told you about the Fellowship?
A muralist. His name was Alex. I met him in the Undertunnel.
You were in the Undertunnel?
For three weeks.
The Syndicate gassed us out.
We made masks for that.
There were too many people.
Did you reclaim it?

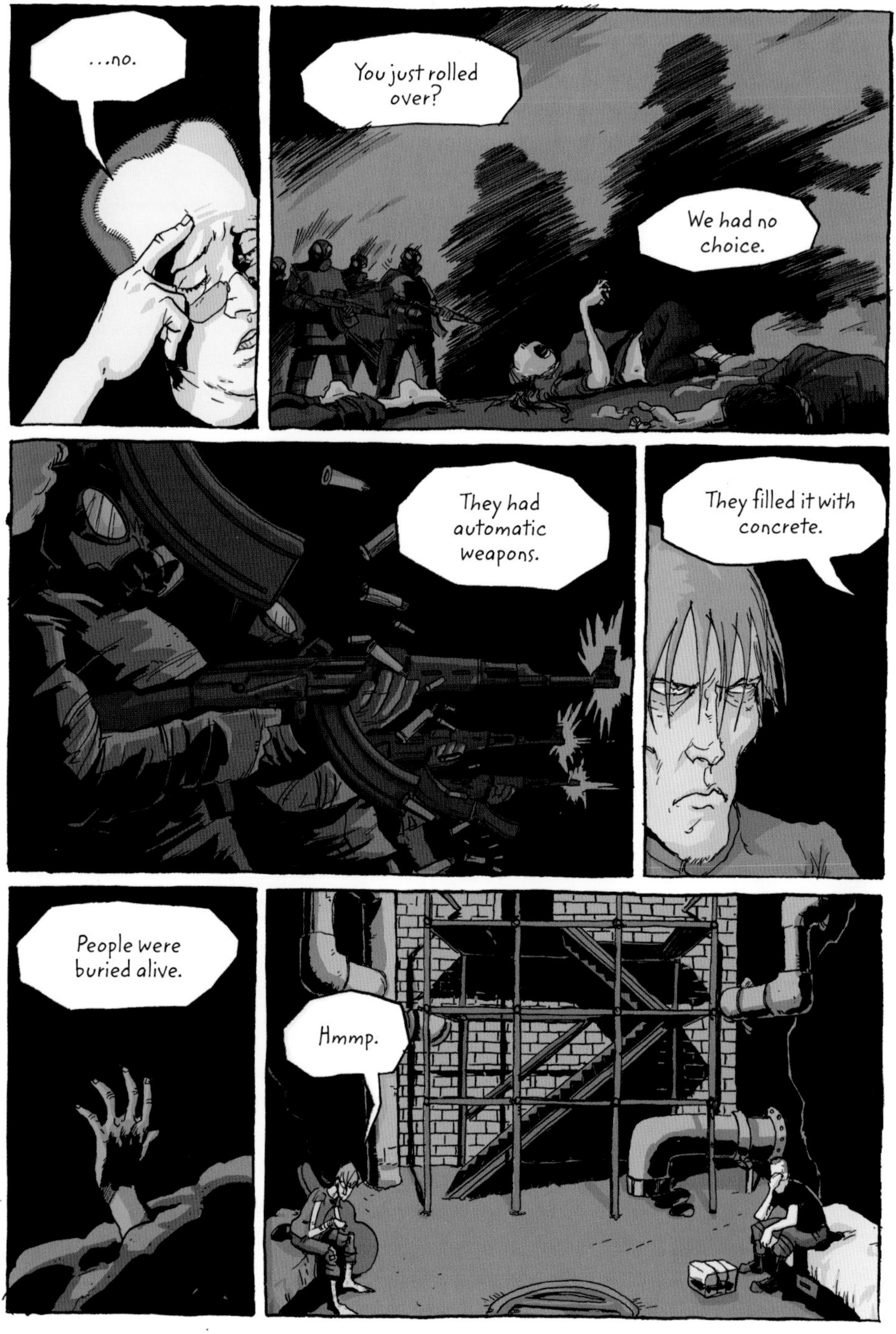
...no.
You just rolled over?
We had no choice.
They had automatic weapons.
They filled it with concrete.
People were buried alive.
Hmmp.

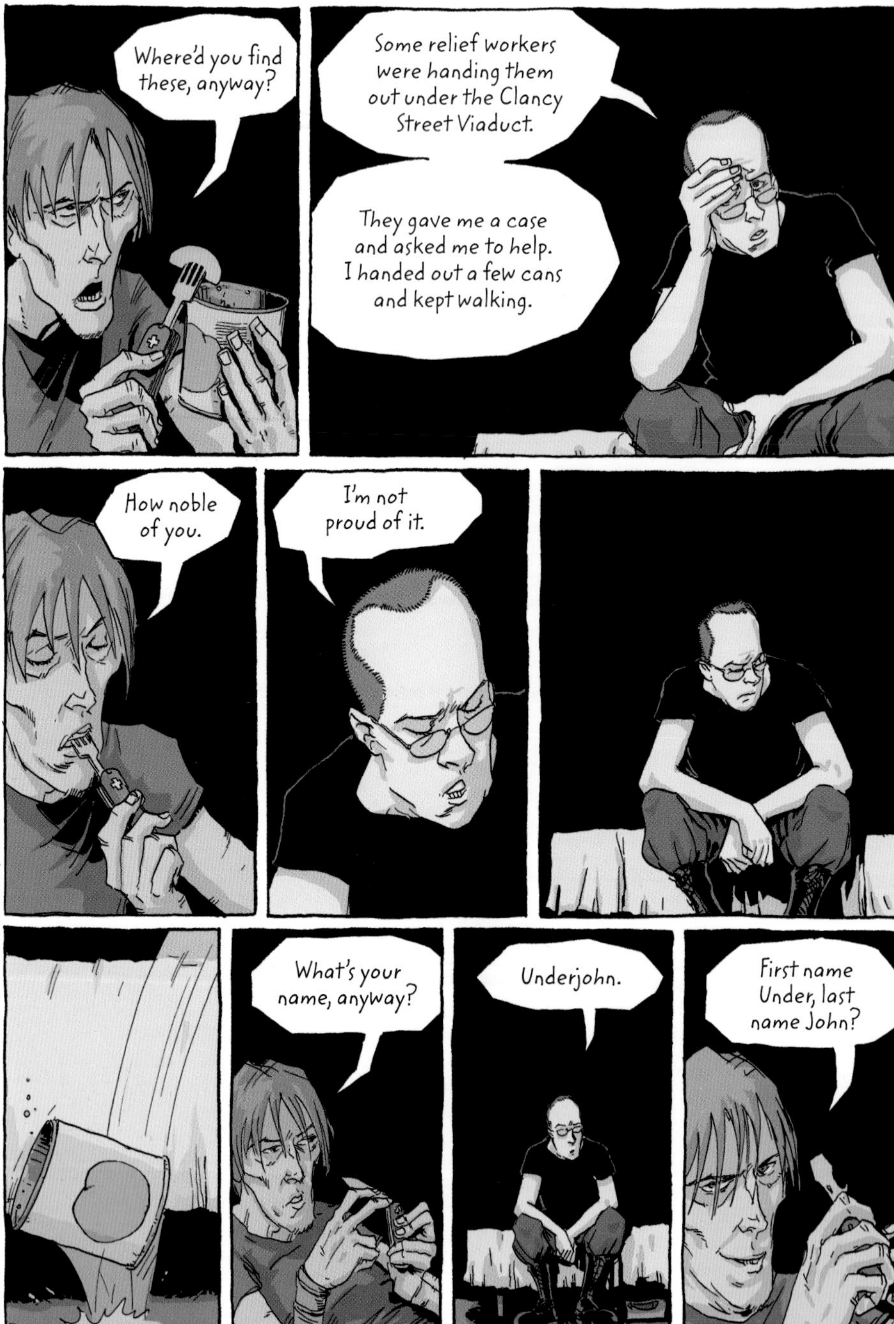
Where'd you find these, anyway?
Some relief workers were handing them out under the Clancy Street Viaduct.
They gave me a case and asked me to help. I handed out a few cans and kept walking.
How noble of you.
I'm not proud of it.
What's your name, anyway?
Underjohn.
First name Under, last name John?

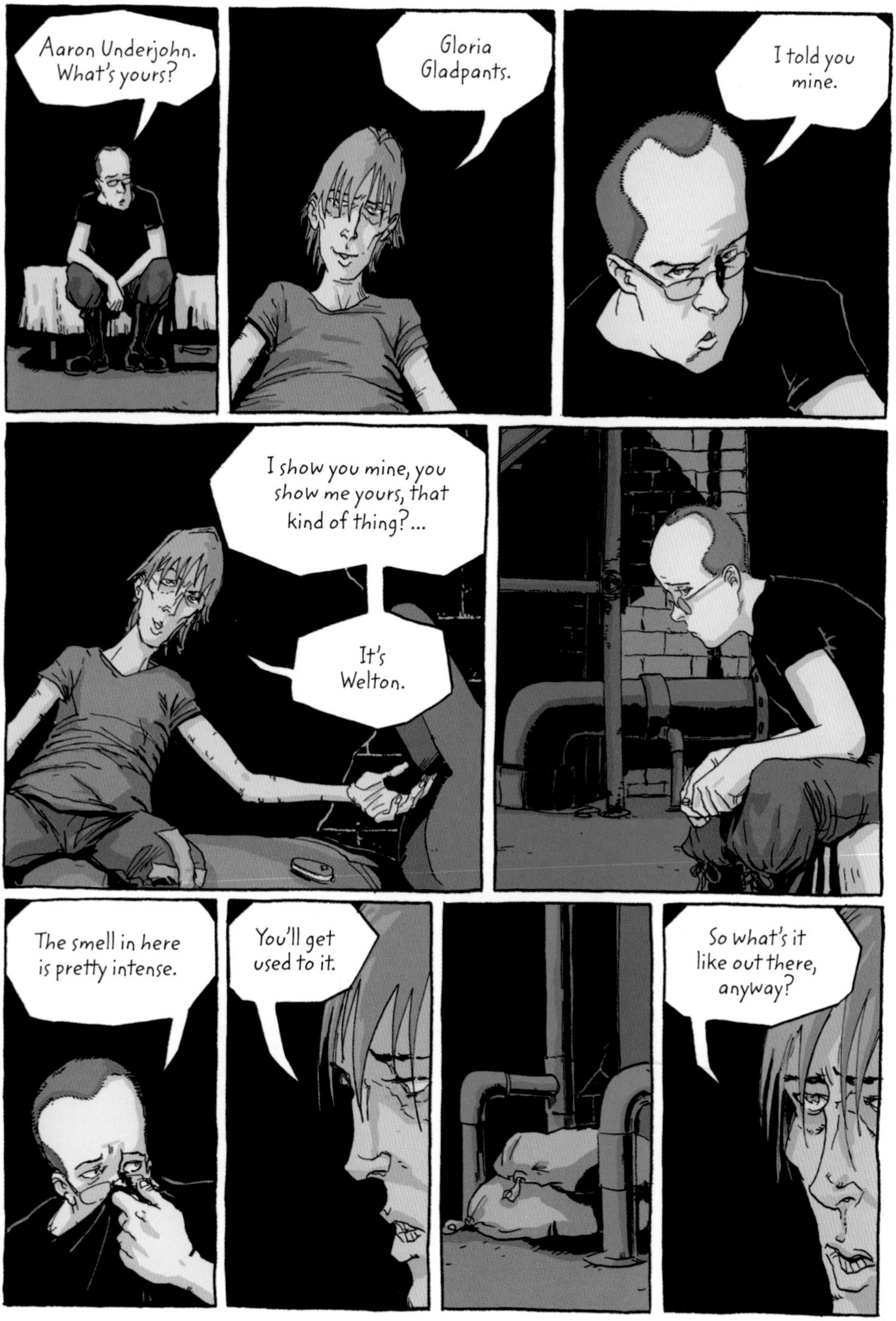
Aaron Underjohn. What's yours?
Gloria Gladpants.
I told you mine.
I show you mine, you show me yours, that kind of thing?...
It's Welton.
The smell in here is pretty intense.
You'll get used to it.
So what's it like out there, anyway?

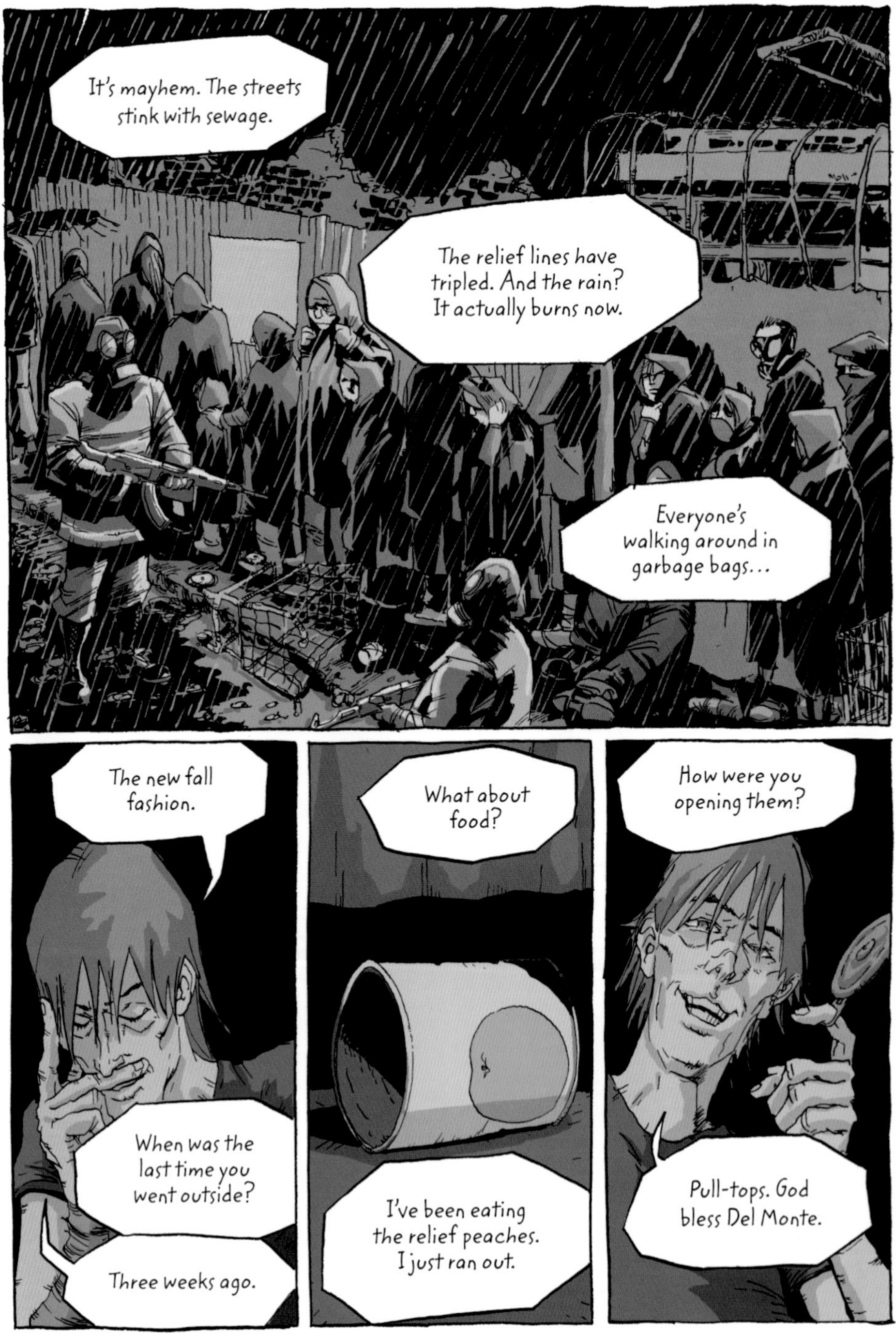
It's mayhem. The streets stink with sewage.
The relief lines have tripled. And the rain? It actually burns now.
Everyone's walking around in garbage bags...
The new fall fashion.
When was the last time you went outside?
Three weeks ago.
What about food?
I've been eating the relief peaches. I just ran out.
How were you opening them?
Pull-tops. God bless Del Monte.

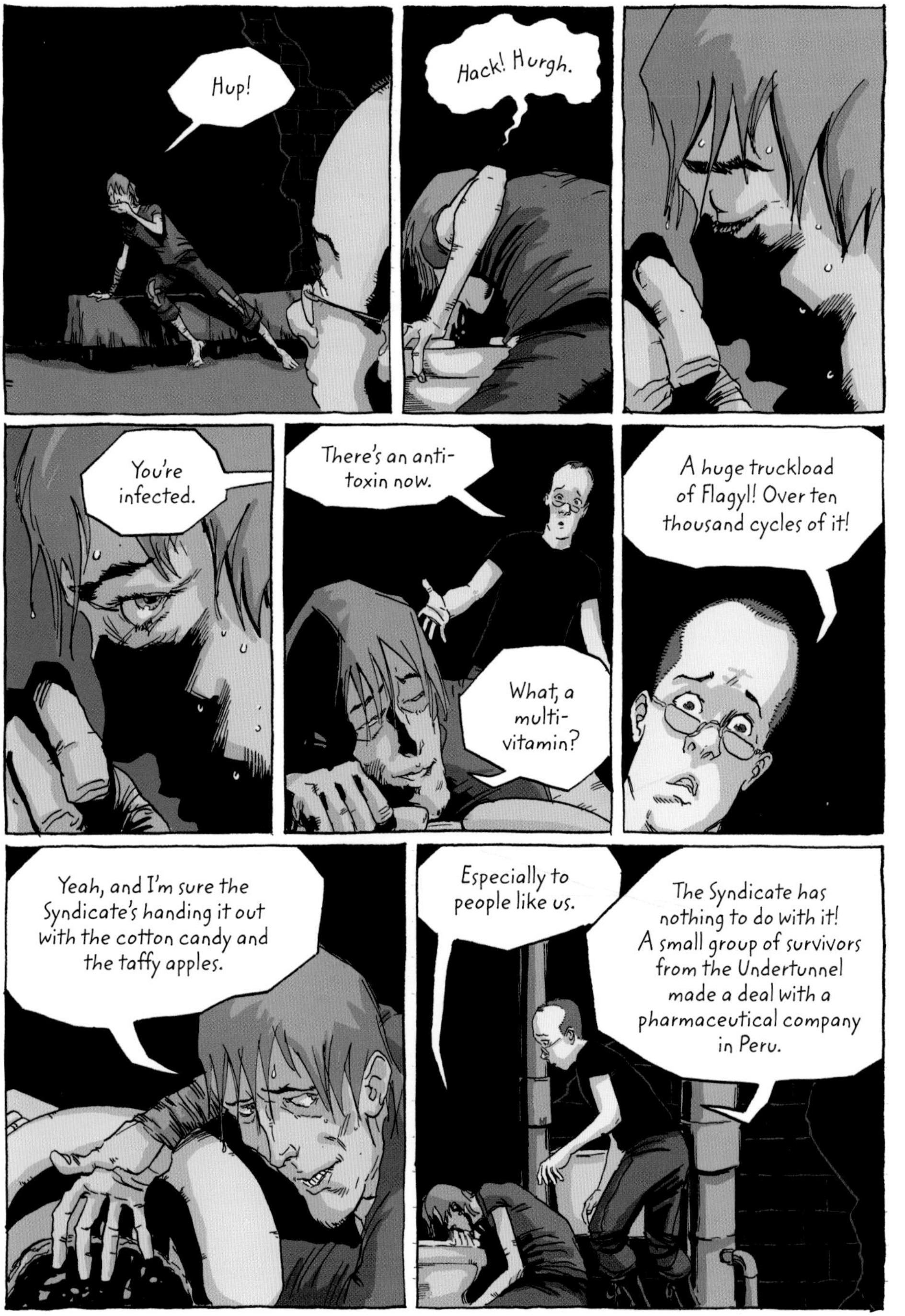
Hup!
Hack! Hurgh.
You're infected.
There's an anti-toxin now.
What, a multi-vitamin?
A huge truckload of Flagyl! Over ten thousand cycles of it!
Yeah, and I'm sure the Syndicate's handing it out with the cotton candy and the taffy apples.
Especially to people like us.
The Syndicate has nothing to do with it! A small group of survivors from the Undertunnel made a deal with a pharmaceutical company in Peru.

It just arrived yesterday.

Apparently they drove for a week straight.

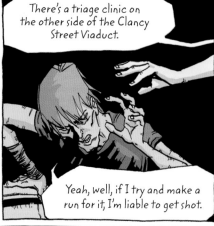

There's a triage clinic on the other side of the Clancy Street Viaduct.

Yeah, well, if I try and make a run for it, I'm liable to get shot.

Those Syndicate marshals in the Mylar suits—you know, the ones holding the AK-47s?

They're making it pretty tough to get anywhere right now.

There's always the subway tunnels.

Too fucking dangerous.

I'd say it's worth the risk. You could die.

How do you know about all of this antitoxin stuff, anyway?

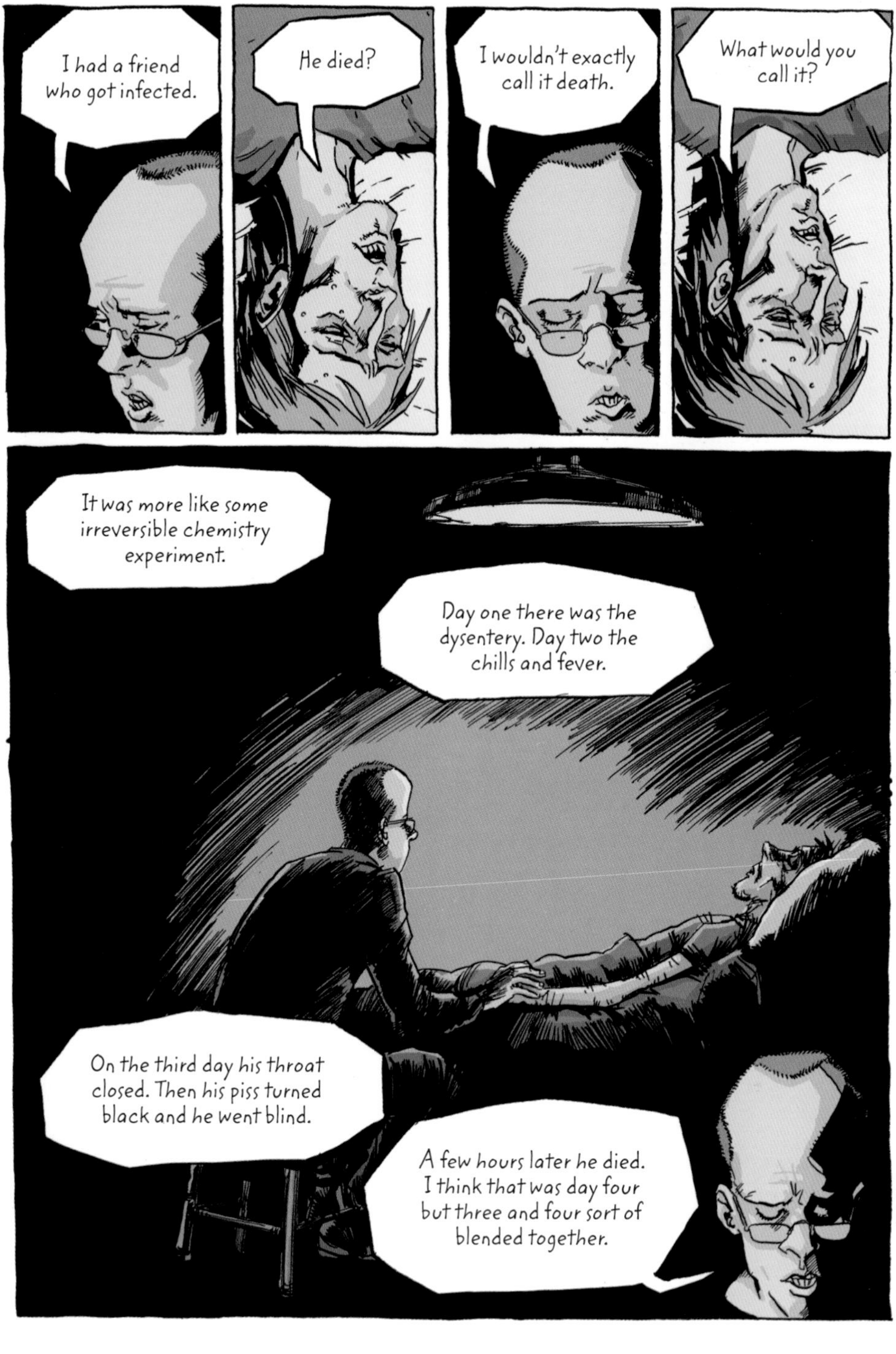
I had a friend who got infected.
He died?
I wouldn't exactly call it death.
What would you call it?
It was more like some irreversible chemistry experiment.
Day one there was the dysentery. Day two the chills and fever.
On the third day his throat closed. Then his piss turned black and he went blind.
A few hours later he died. I think that was day four but three and four sort of blended together.

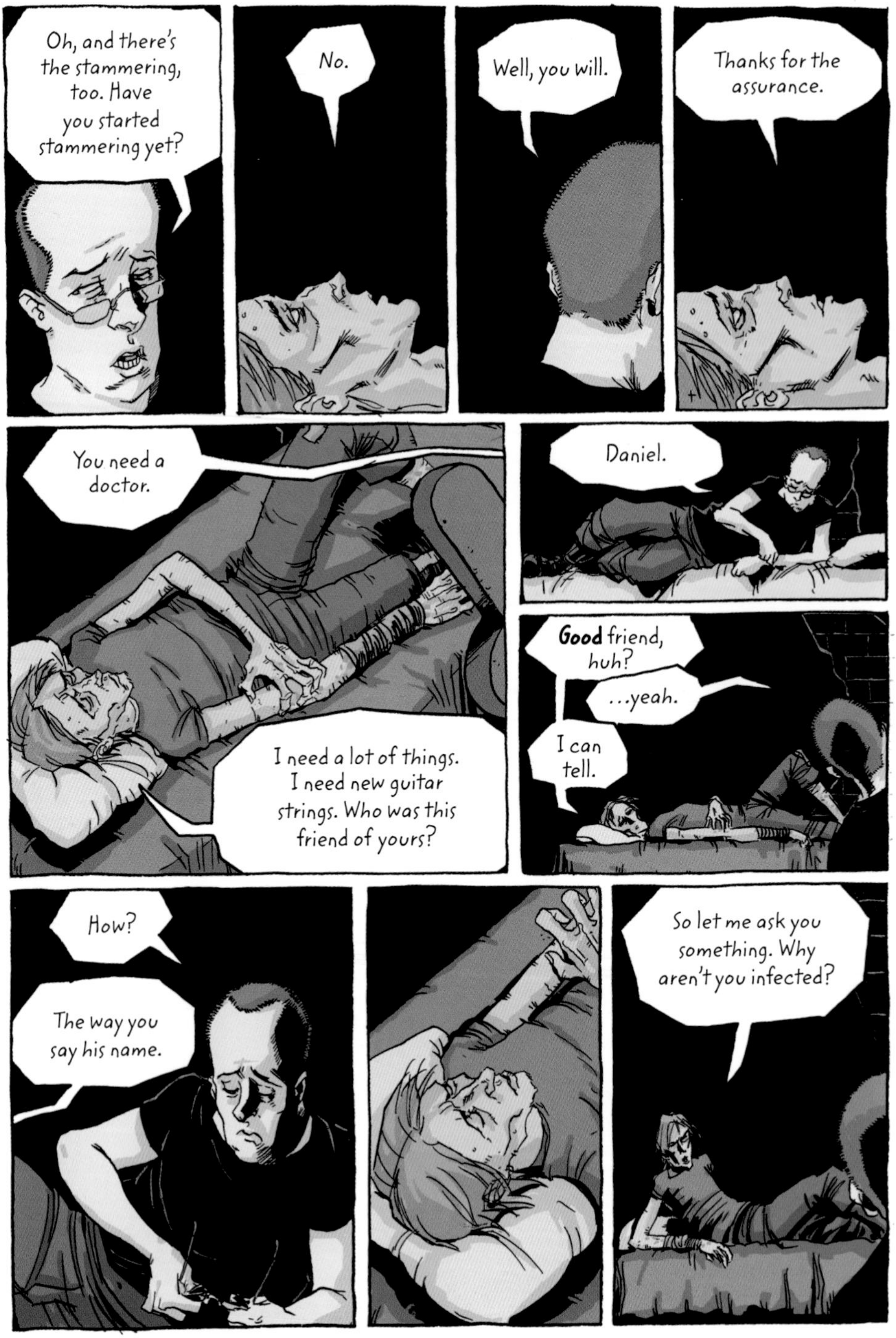
Oh, and there's the stammering, too. Have you started stammering yet?
No.
Well, you will.
Thanks for the assurance.
You need a doctor.
I need a lot of things. I need new guitar strings. Who was this friend of yours?
Daniel.
Good friend, huh?
...yeah.
I can tell.
How?
The way you say his name.
So let me ask you something. Why aren't you infected?

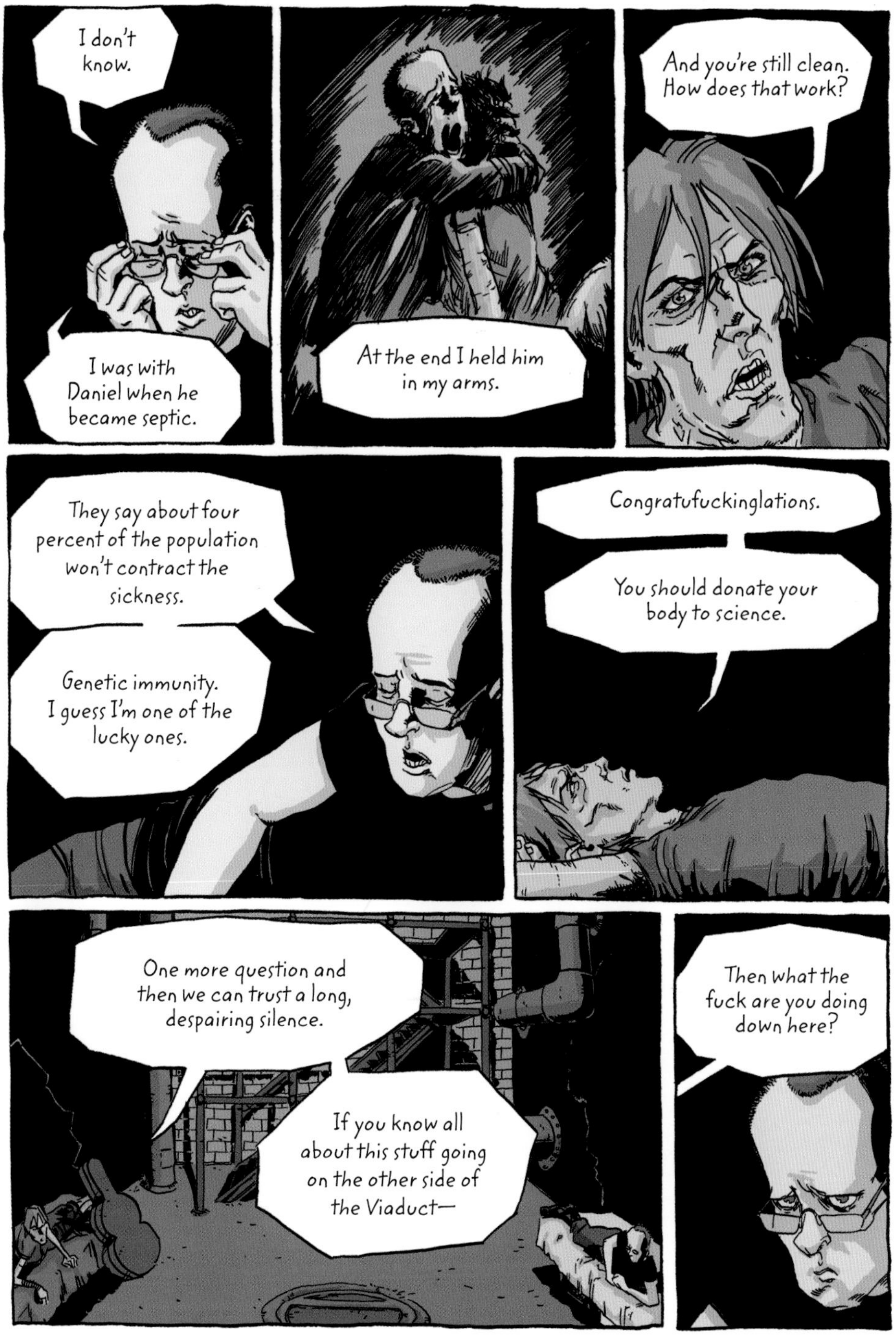
I don't know.
I was with Daniel when he became septic.
At the end I held him in my arms.
And you're still clean. How does that work?
They say about four percent of the population won't contract the sickness.
Genetic immunity. I guess I'm one of the lucky ones.
Congratufuckinglations.
You should donate your body to science.
One more question and then we can trust a long, despairing silence.
If you know all about this stuff going on the other side of the Viaduct—
Then what the fuck are you doing down here?

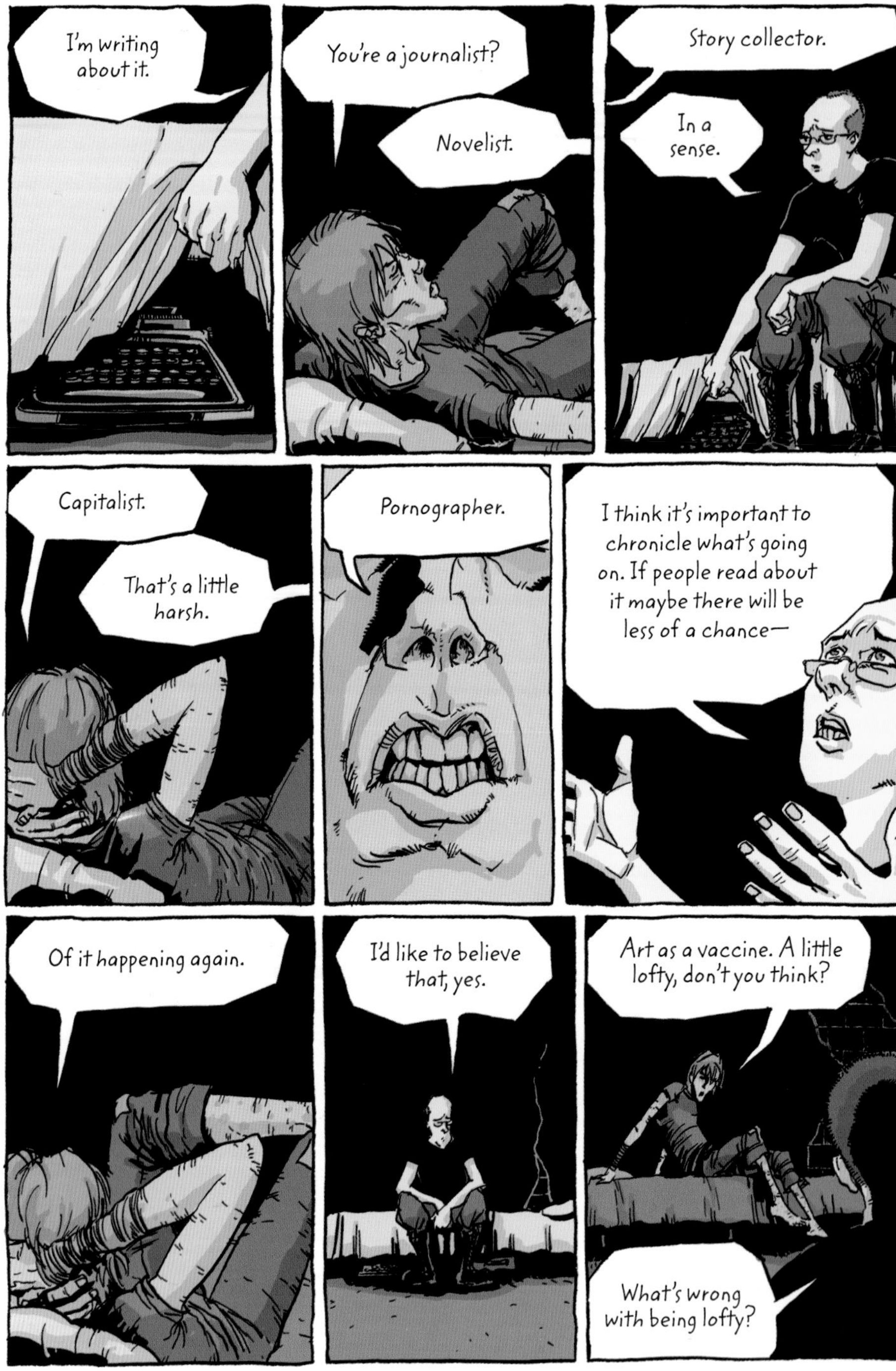
I'm writing about it.
You're a journalist?
Novelist.
Story collector.
In a sense.
Capitalist.
That's a little harsh.
Pornographer.
I think it's important to chronicle what's going on. If people read about it maybe there will be less of a chance—
Of it happening again.
I'd like to believe that, yes.
Art as a vaccine. A little lofty, don't you think?
What's wrong with being lofty?

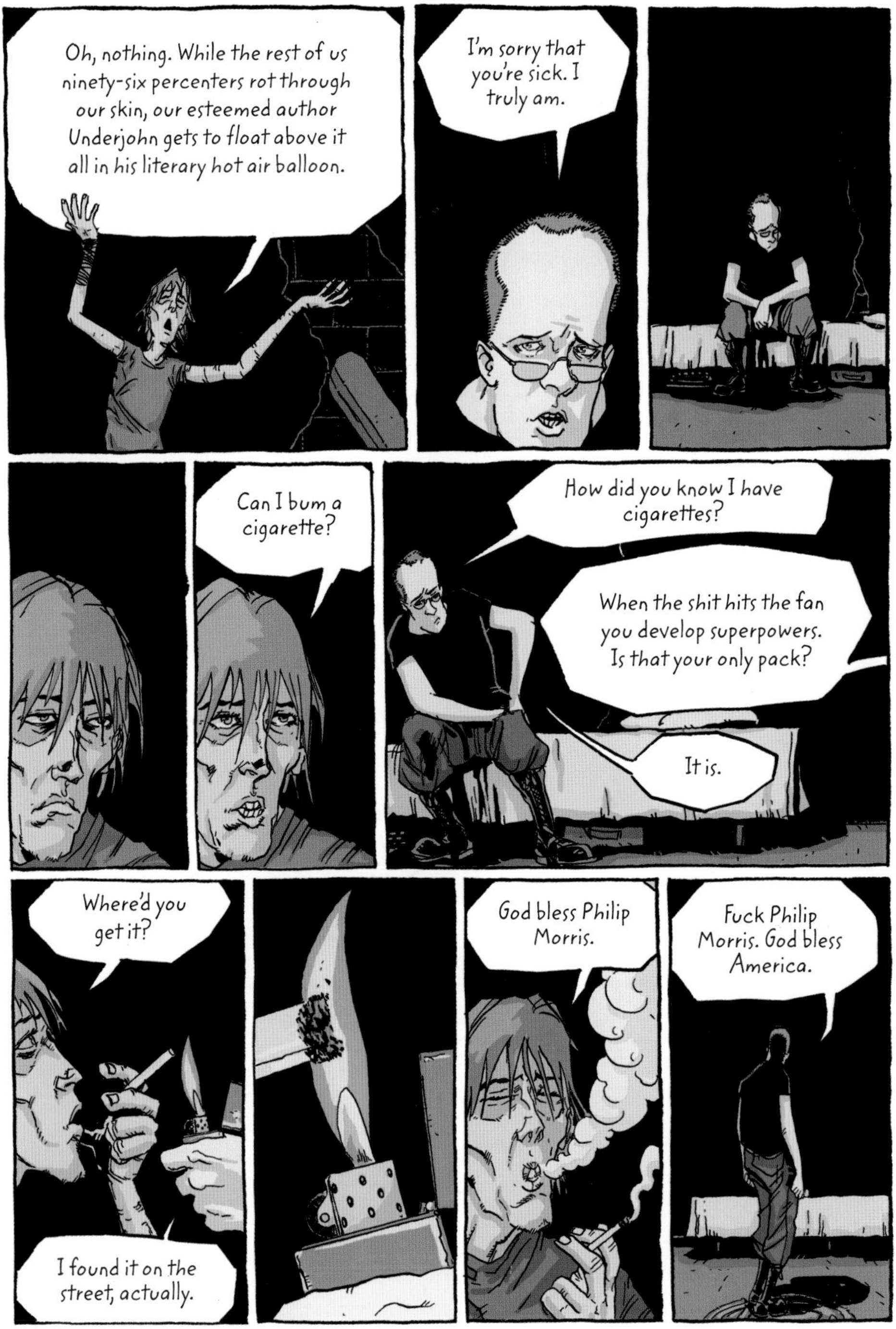
Oh, nothing. While the rest of us ninety-six percenters rot through our skin, our esteemed author Underjohn gets to float above it all in his literary hot air balloon.
I'm sorry that you're sick. I truly am.
Can I bum a cigarette?
How did you know I have cigarettes?
When the shit hits the fan you develop superpowers. Is that your only pack?
It is.
Where'd you get it?
I found it on the street, actually.
God bless Philip Morris.
Fuck Philip Morris. God bless America.

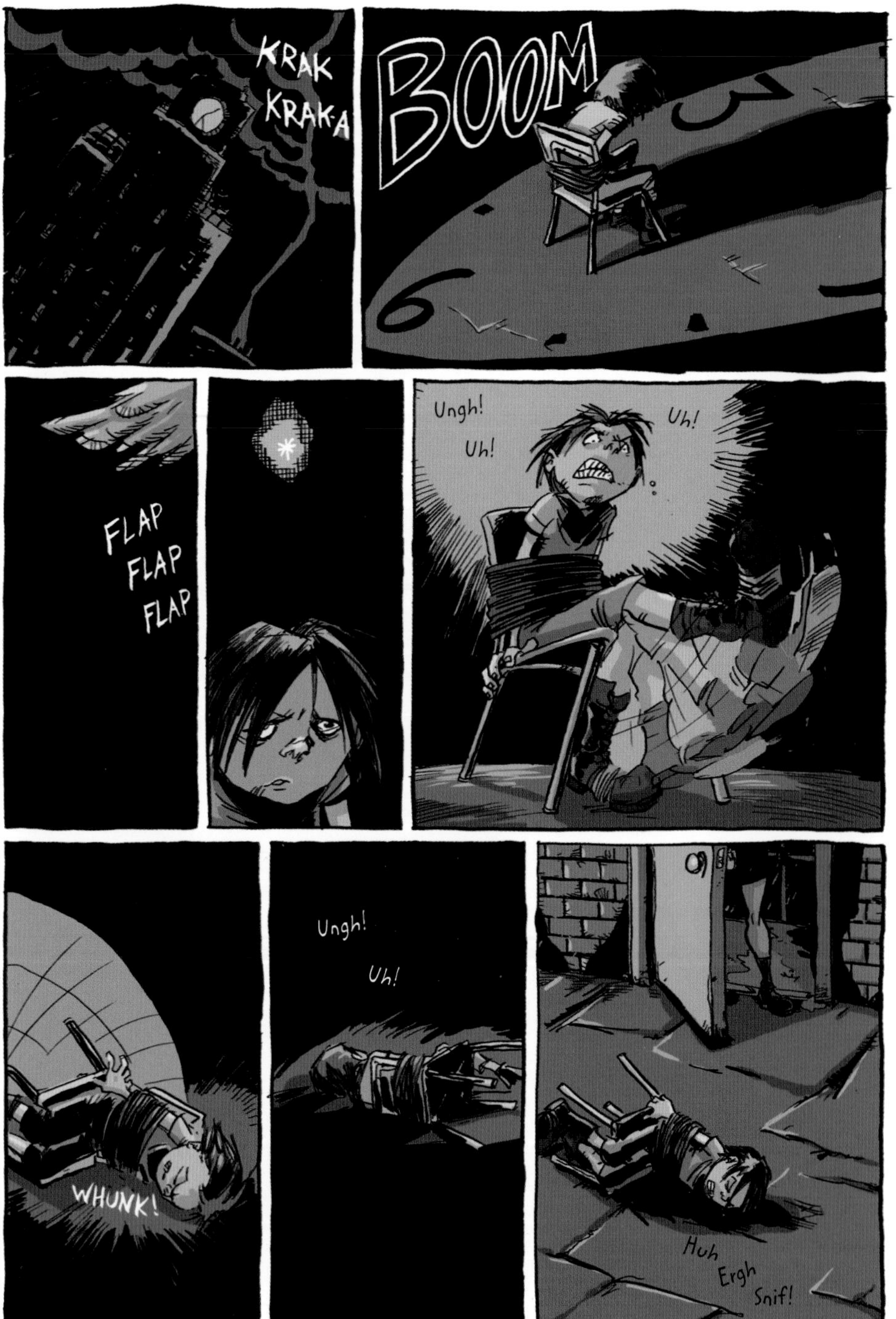
KRAK
KRAK-A
BOOM
FLAP
FLAP
FLAP
Ungh!
Uh!
Uh!
WHUNK!
Ungh!
Uh!
Huh
Ergh
Snif!

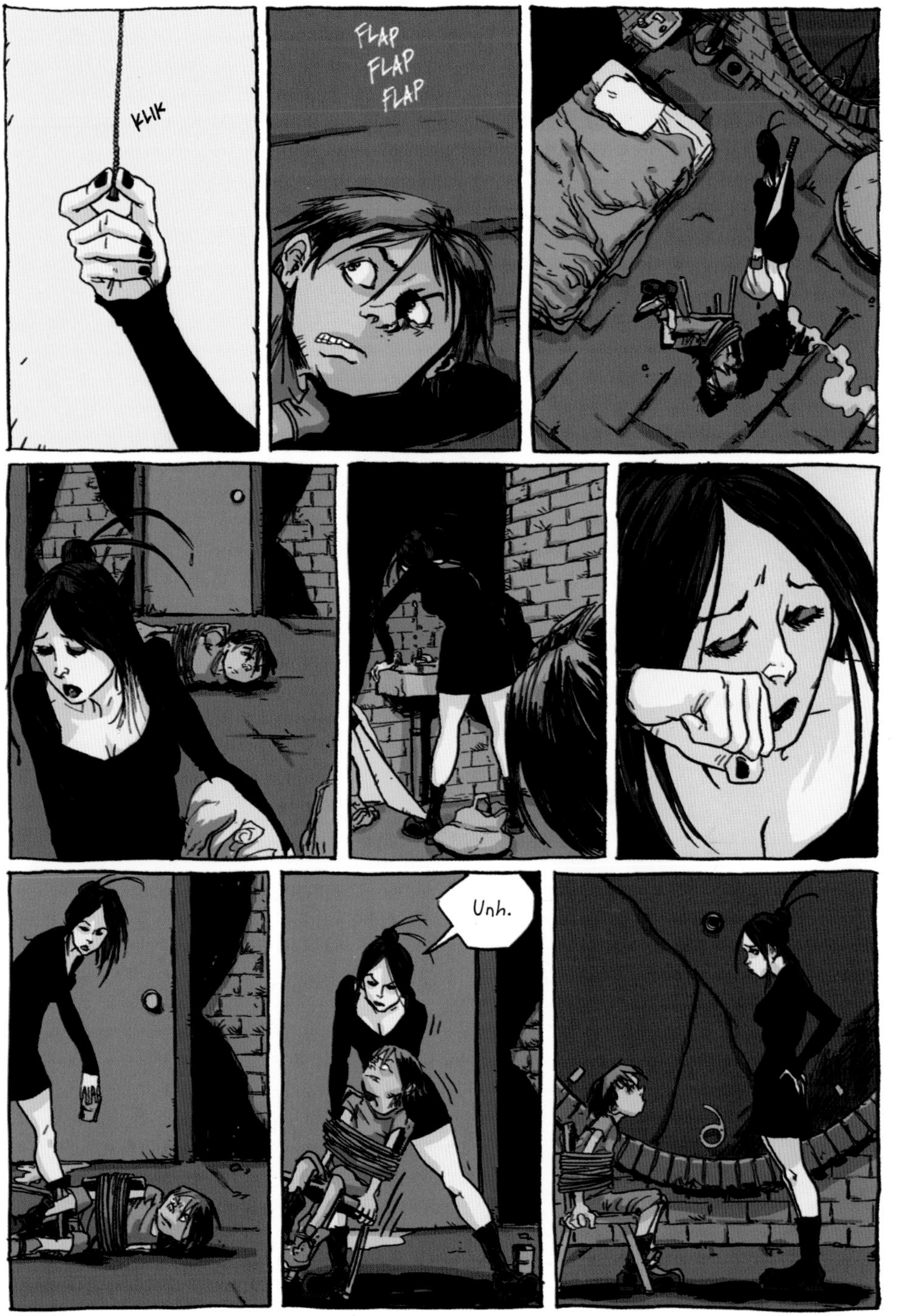
KLIK
FLAP
FLAP
FLAP
Unh.

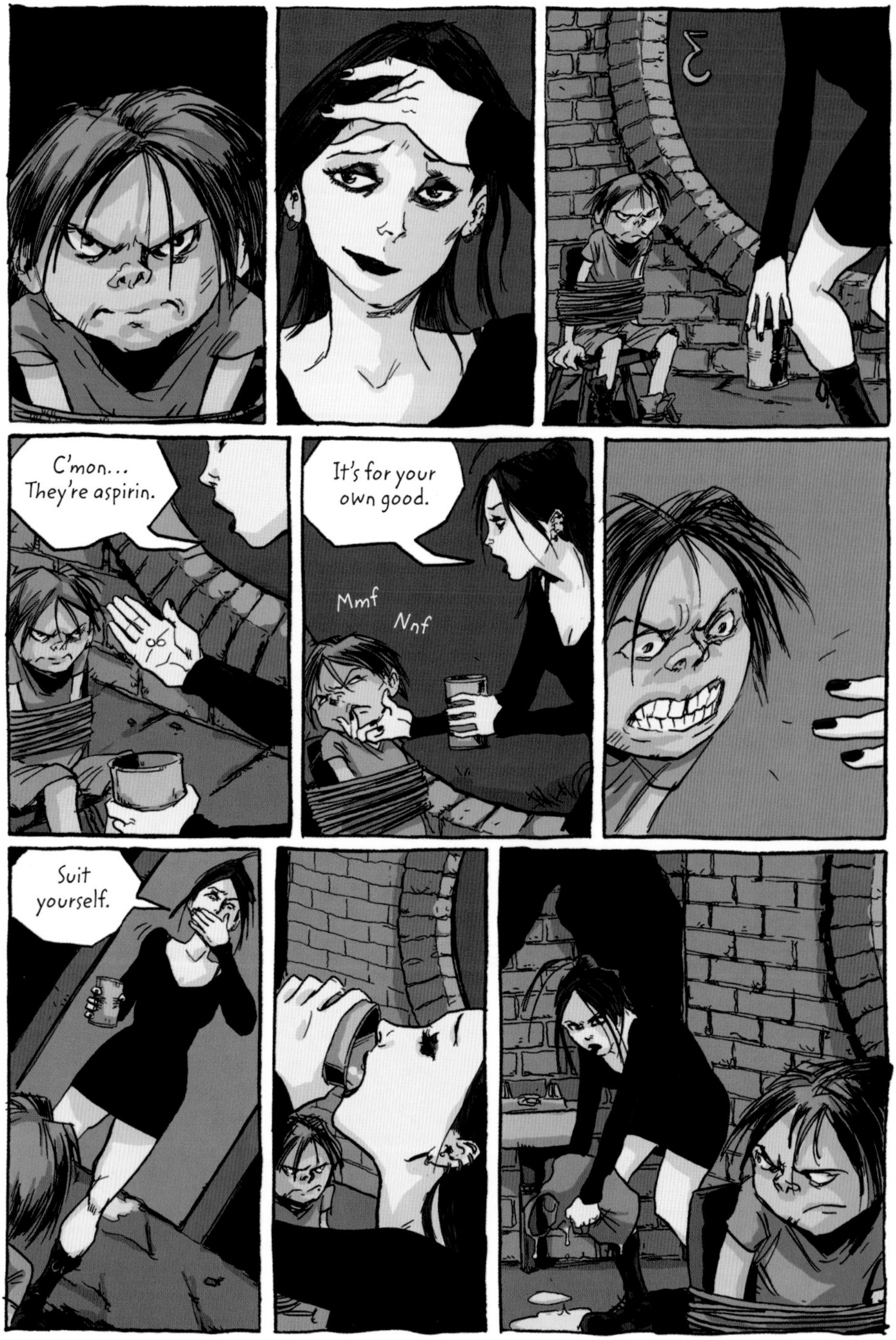

C'mon...
They're aspirin.
It's for your own good.
Mmf
Nnf
Suit yourself.

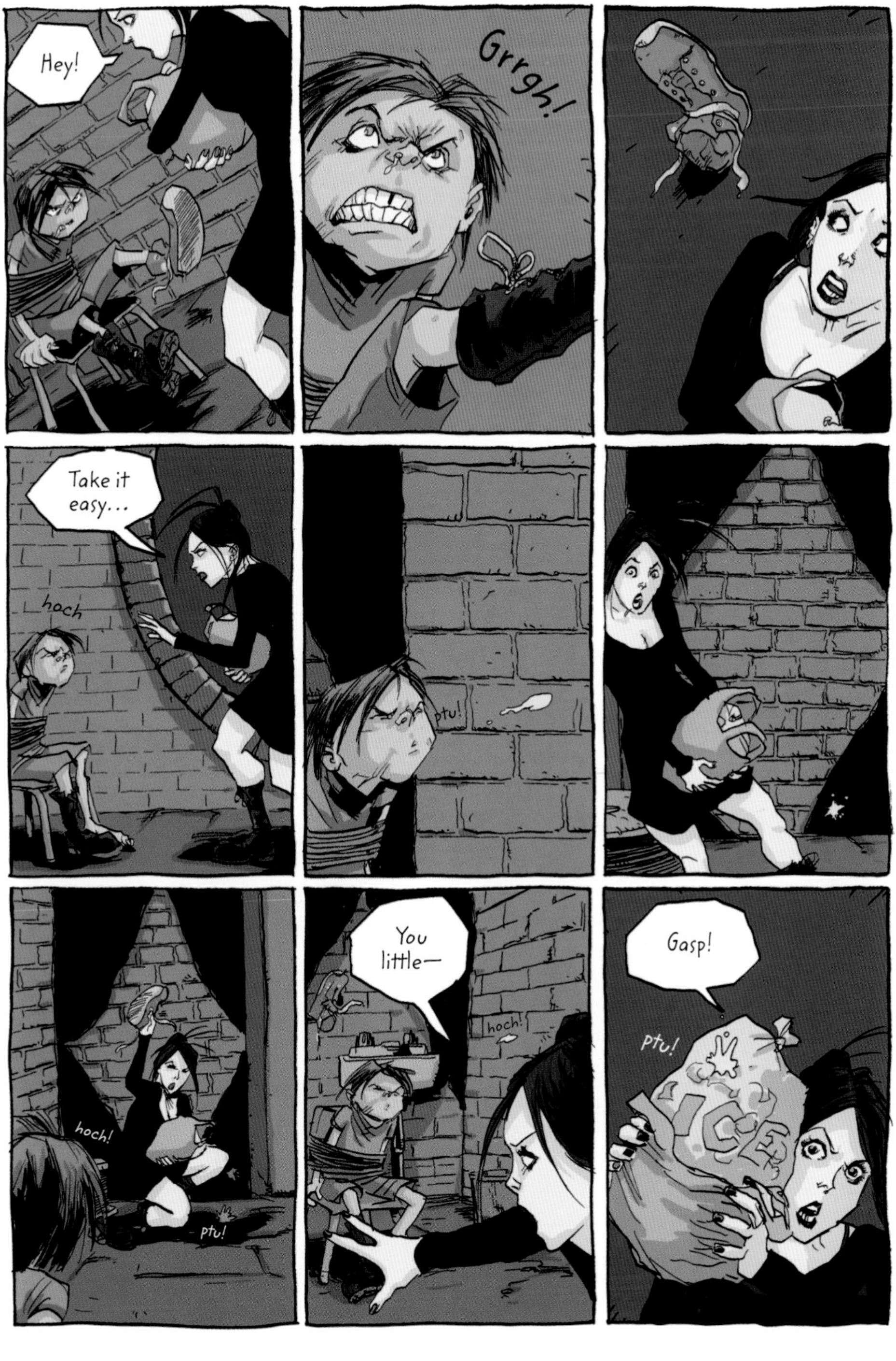

Hey!
Grrgh!
Take it easy...
hoch
ptu!
hoch!
ptu!
You little—
hoch!
Gasp!
ptu!
ICE

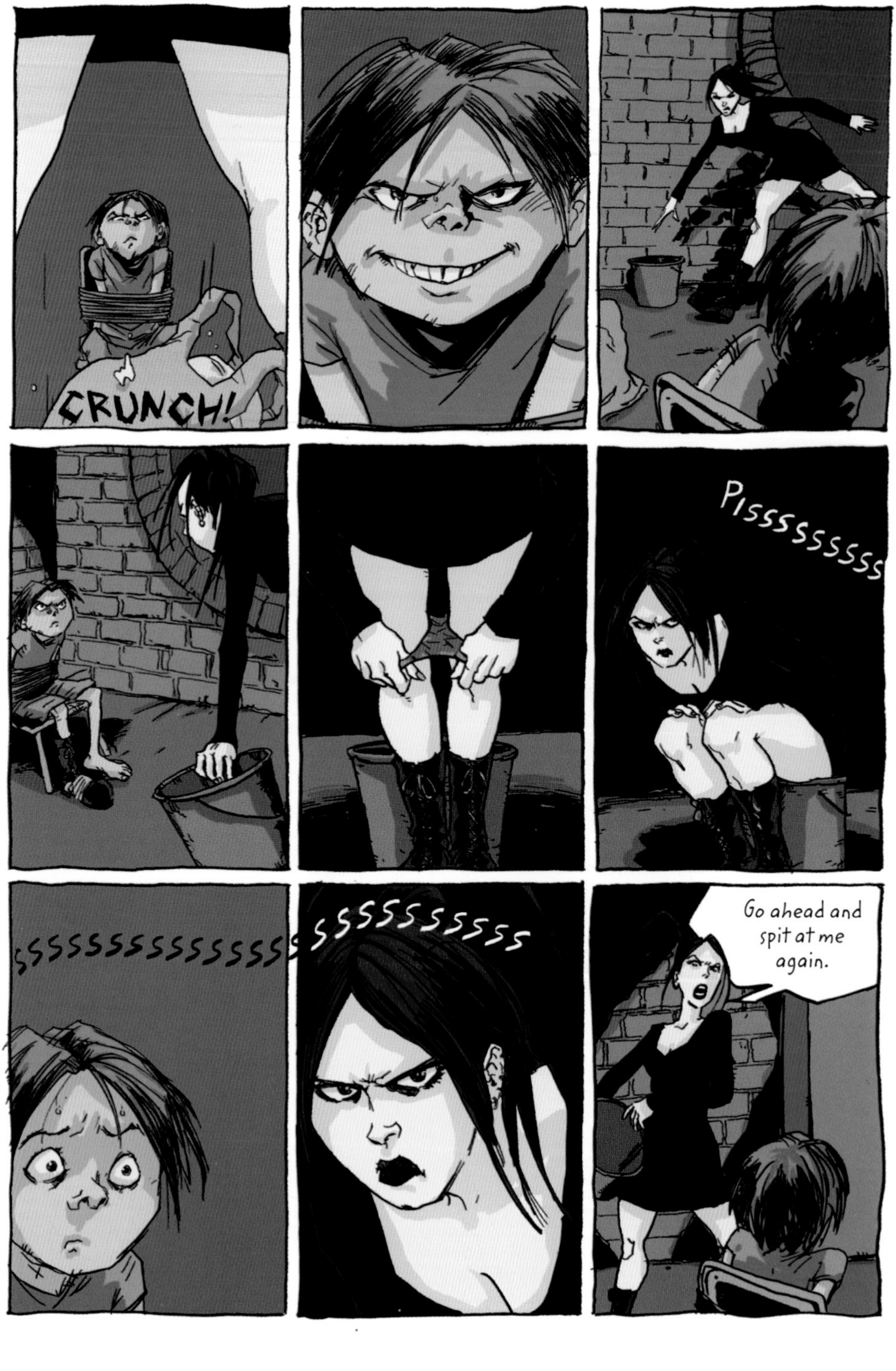
CRUNCH!
Pisssssssss
ssssssssssssssss
sssssssssss
Go ahead and spit at me again.

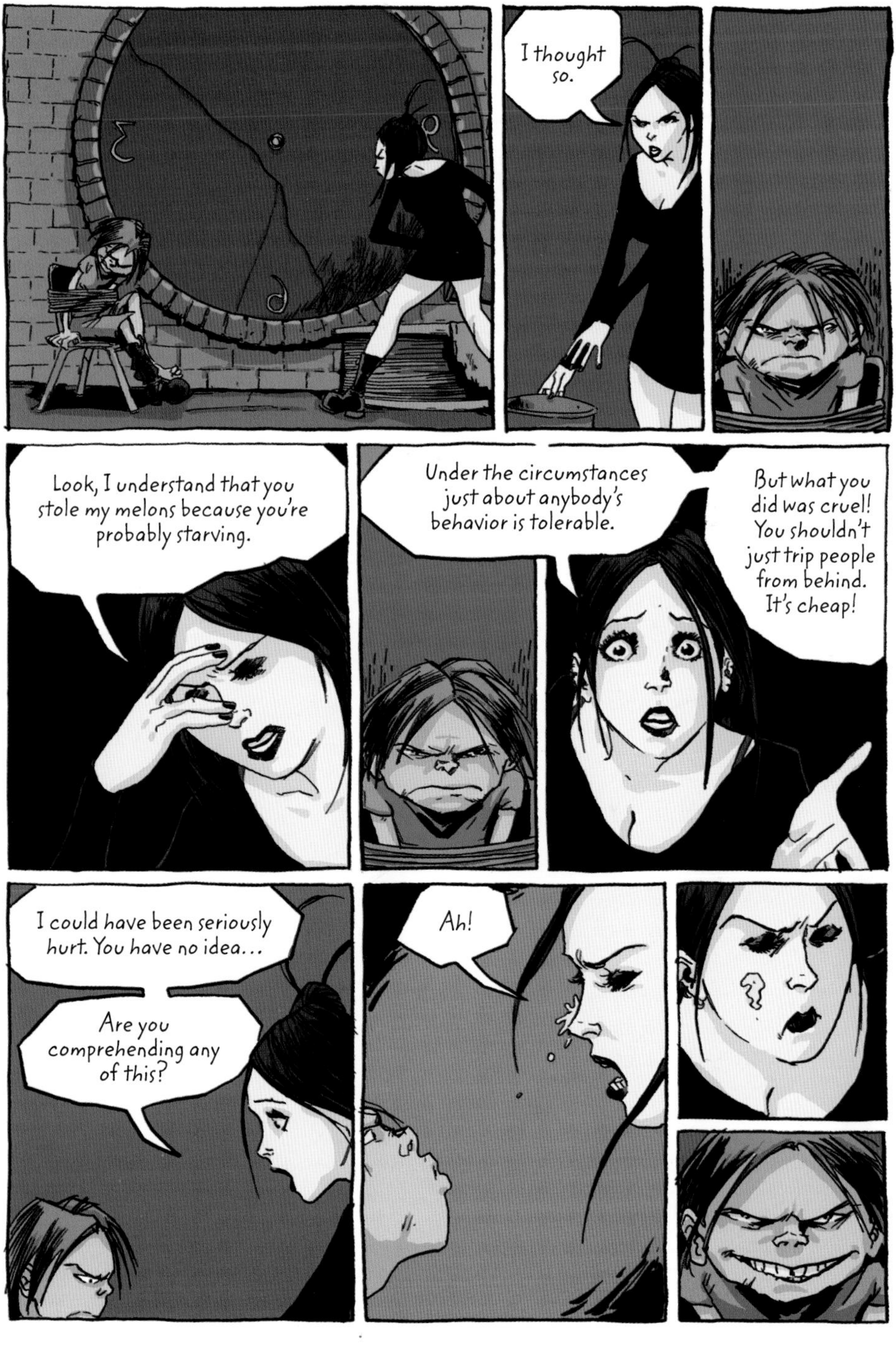
I thought so.
Look, I understand that you stole my melons because you're probably starving.
Under the circumstances just about anybody's behavior is tolerable.
But what you did was cruel! You shouldn't just trip people from behind. It's cheap!
I could have been seriously hurt. You have no idea...
Are you comprehending any of this?
Ah!

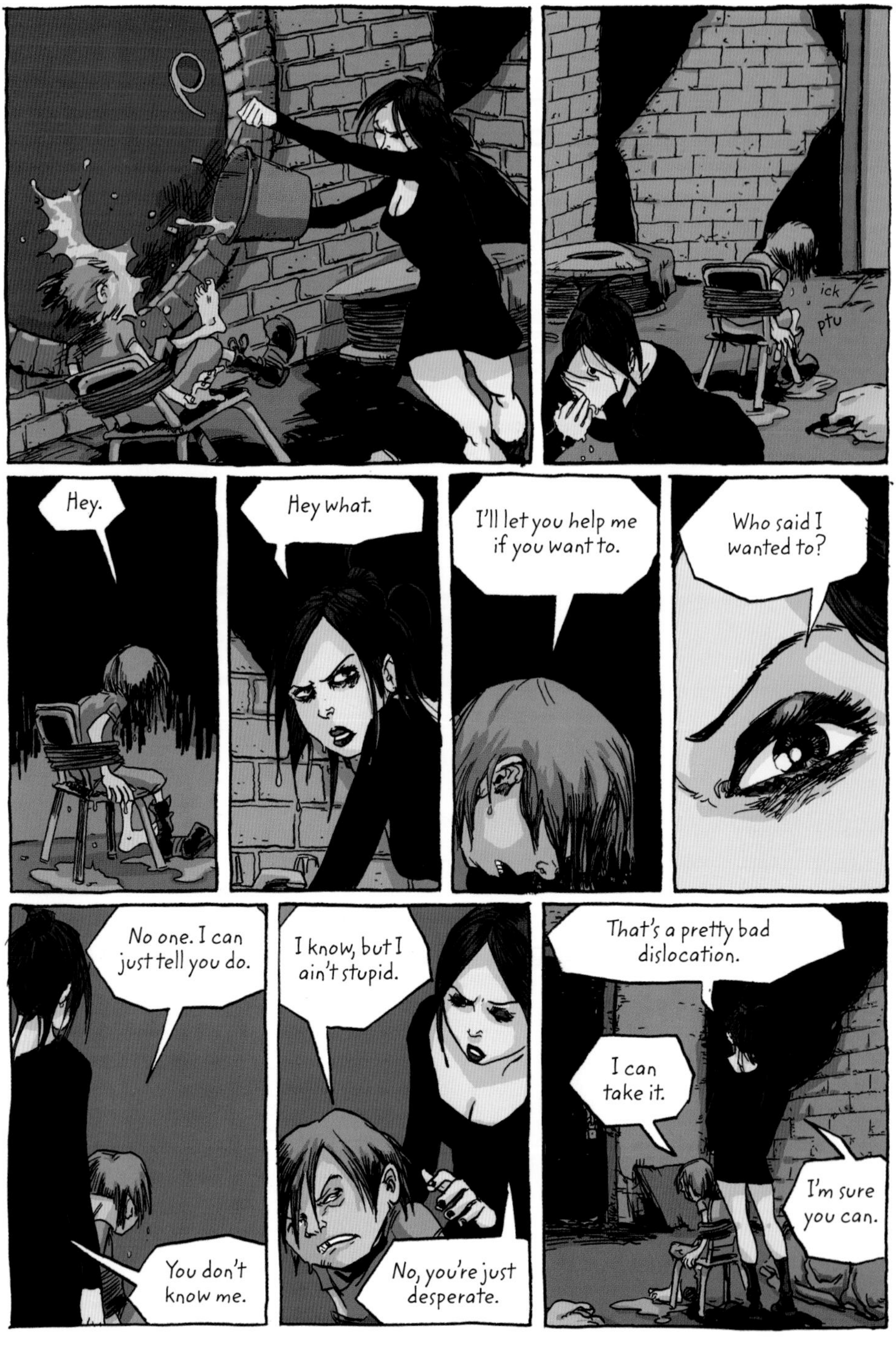
ick
ptu
Hey.
Hey what.
I'll let you help me if you want to.
Who said I wanted to?
No one. I can just tell you do.
You don't know me.
I know, but I ain't stupid.
No, you're just desperate.
That's a pretty bad dislocation.
I can take it.
I'm sure you can.

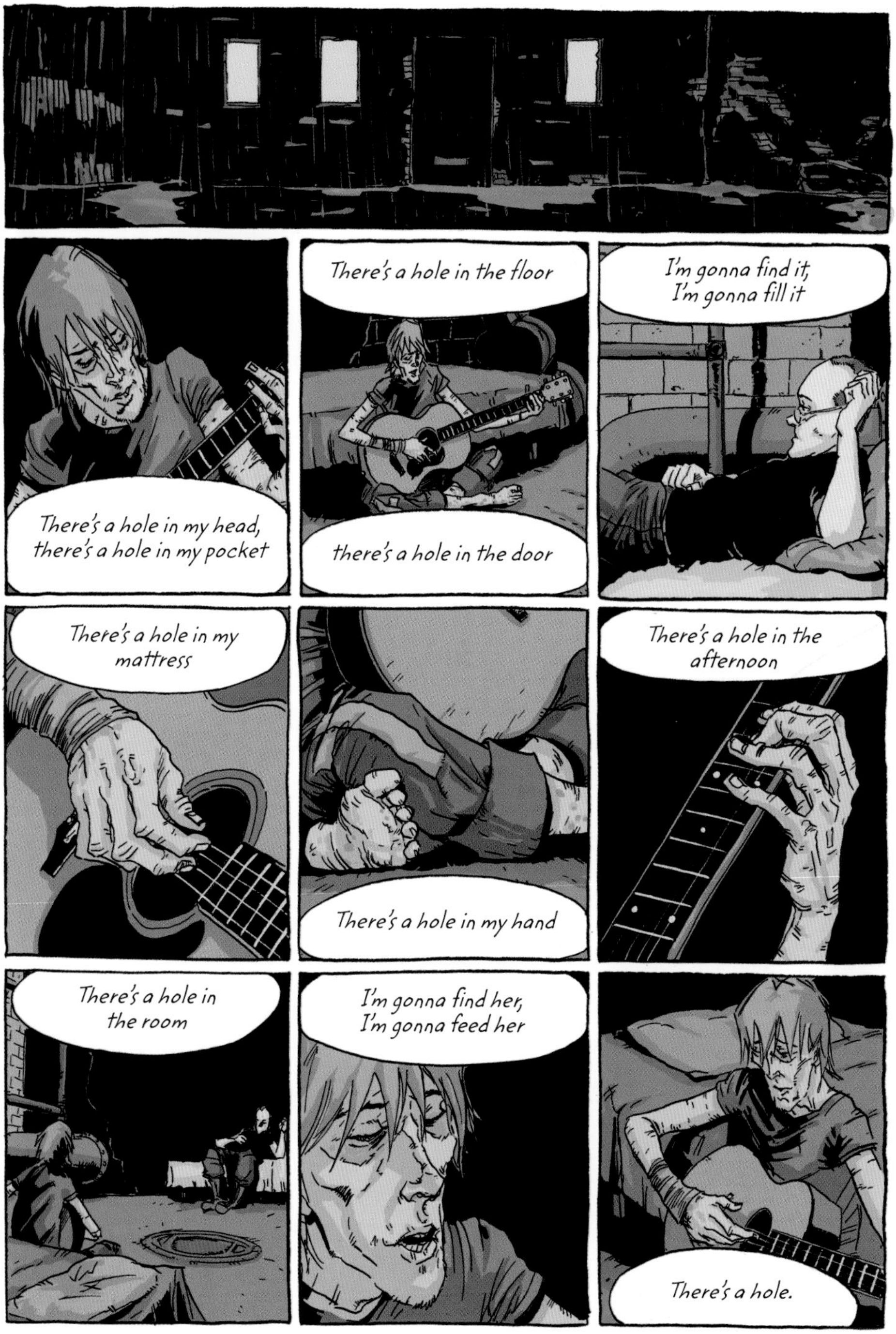
There's a hole in my head,
there's a hole in my pocket
There's a hole in the floor
there's a hole in the door
I'm gonna find it,
I'm gonna fill it
There's a hole in my
mattress
There's a hole in my hand
There's a hole in the
afternoon
There's a hole in
the room
I'm gonna find her,
I'm gonna feed her
There's a hole.

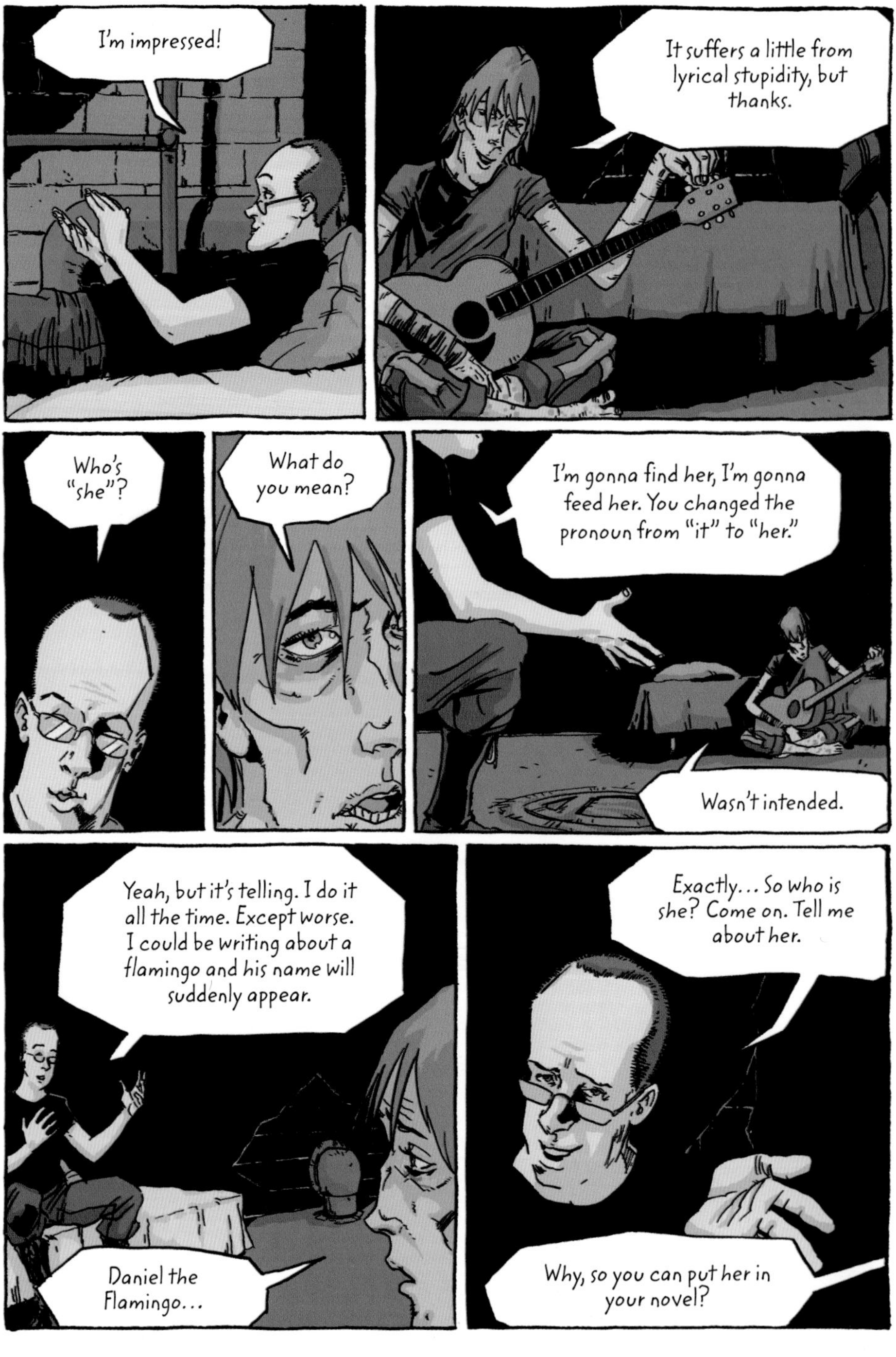
I'm impressed!
It suffers a little from lyrical stupidity, but thanks.
Who's "she"?
What do you mean?
I'm gonna find her, I'm gonna feed her. You changed the pronoun from "it" to "her."
Wasn't intended.
Yeah, but it's telling. I do it all the time. Except worse. I could be writing about a flamingo and his name will suddenly appear.
Daniel the Flamingo...
Exactly... So who is she? Come on. Tell me about her.
Why, so you can put her in your novel?

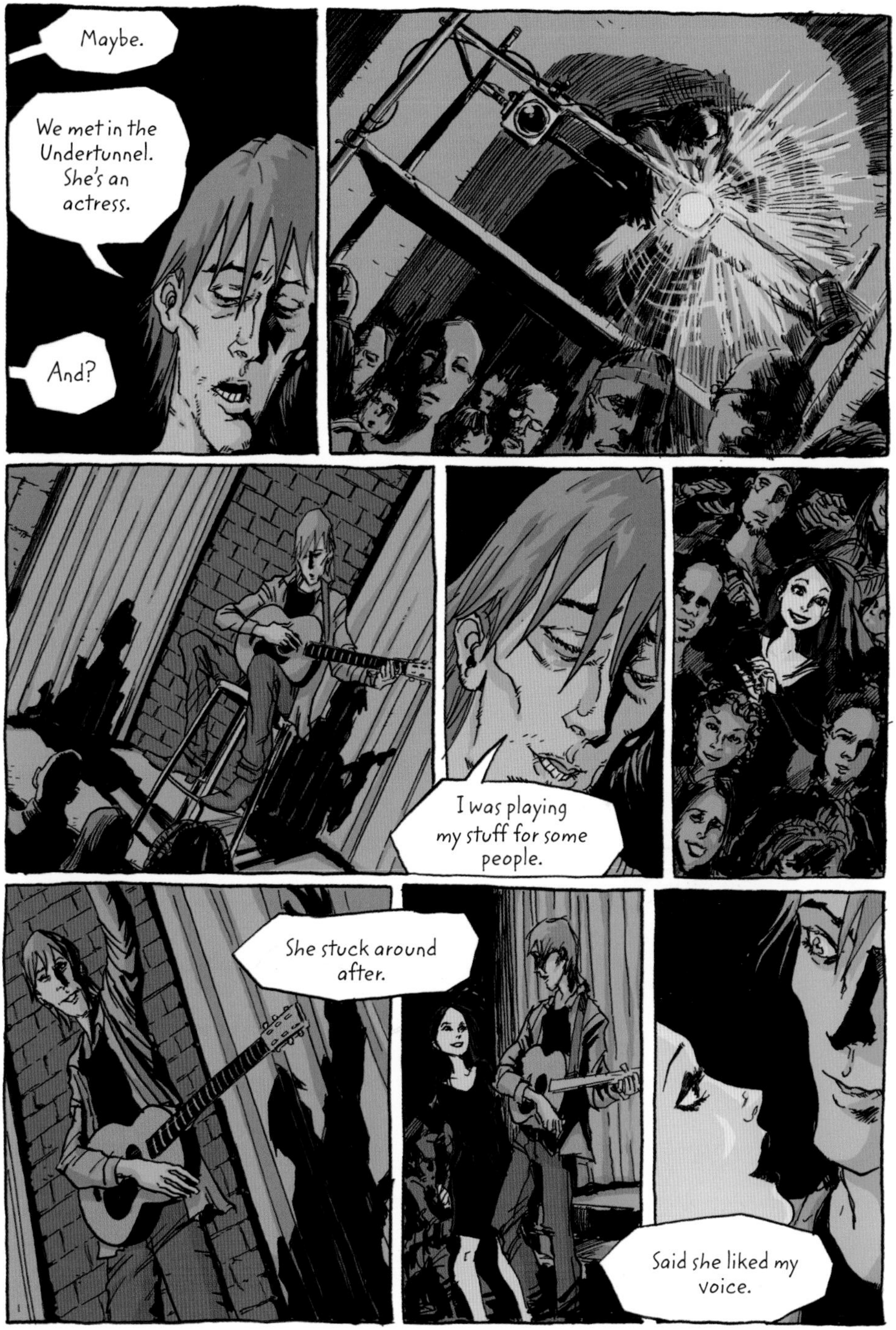
Maybe.
We met in the Undertunnel. She's an actress.
And?
I was playing my stuff for some people.
She stuck around after.
Said she liked my voice.

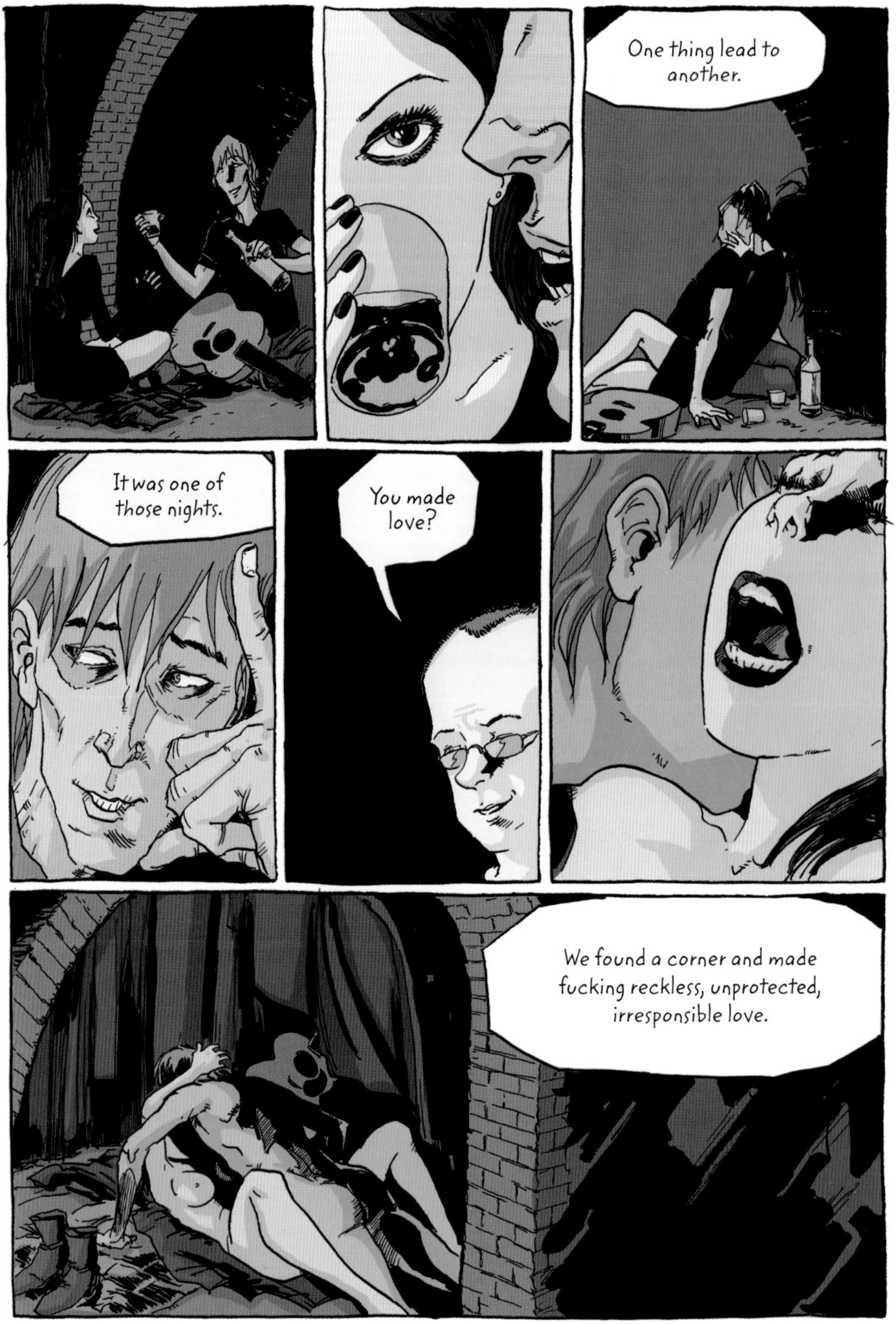
One thing lead to another.
It was one of those nights.
You made love?
We found a corner and made fucking reckless, unprotected, irresponsible love.

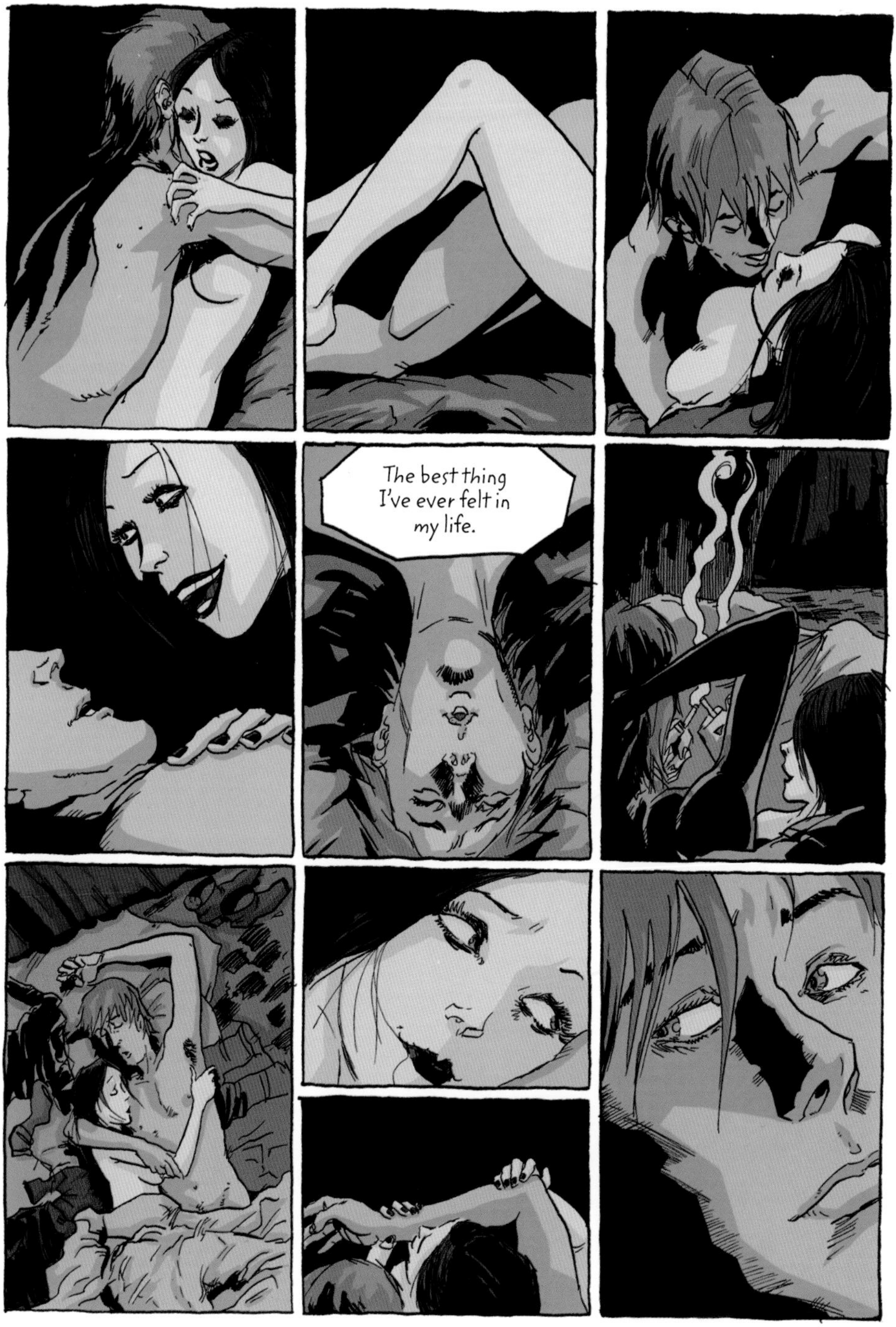
The best thing I've ever felt in my life.

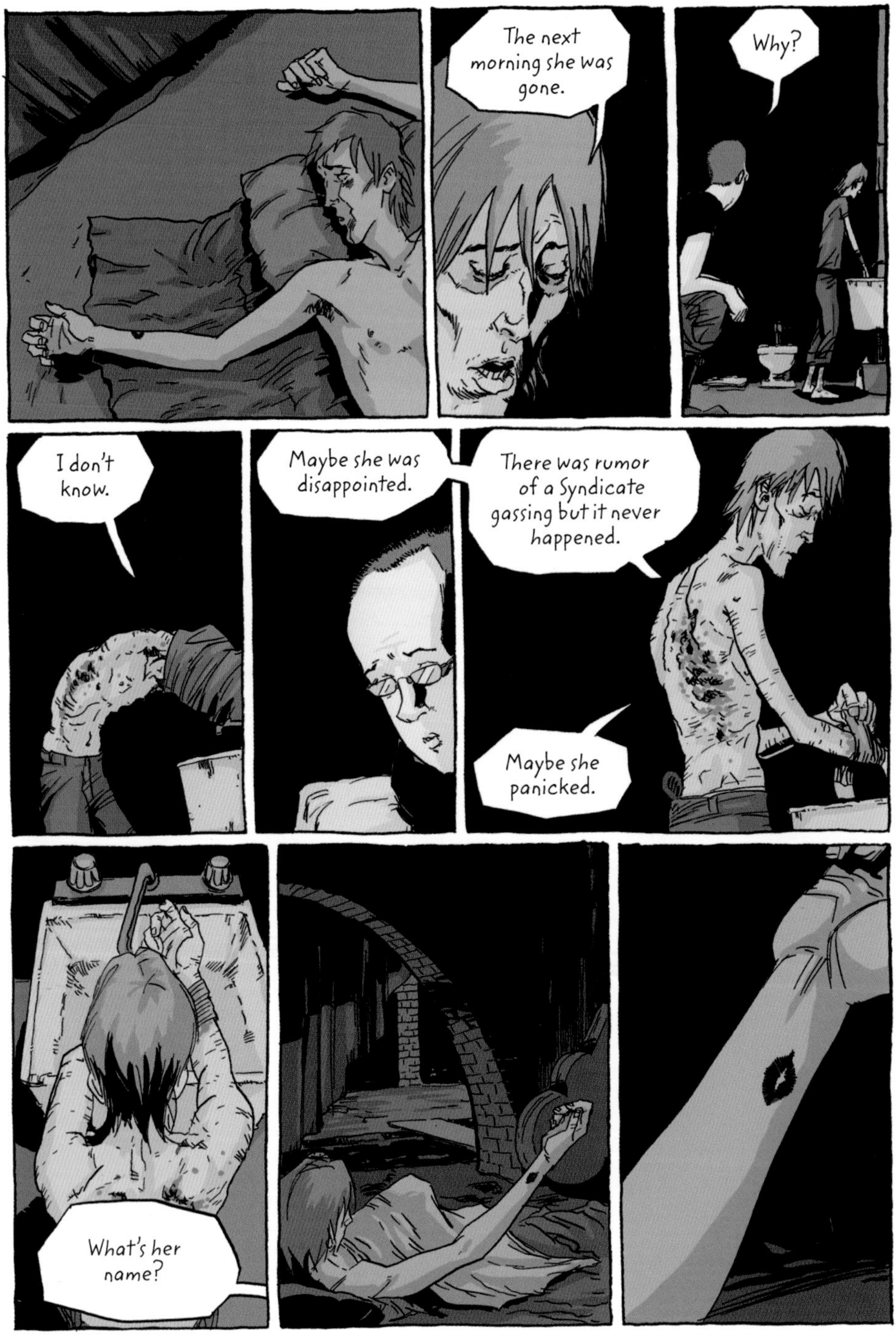
The next morning she was gone.
Why?
I don't know.
Maybe she was disappointed.
There was rumor of a Syndicate gassing but it never happened.
Maybe she panicked.
What's her name?

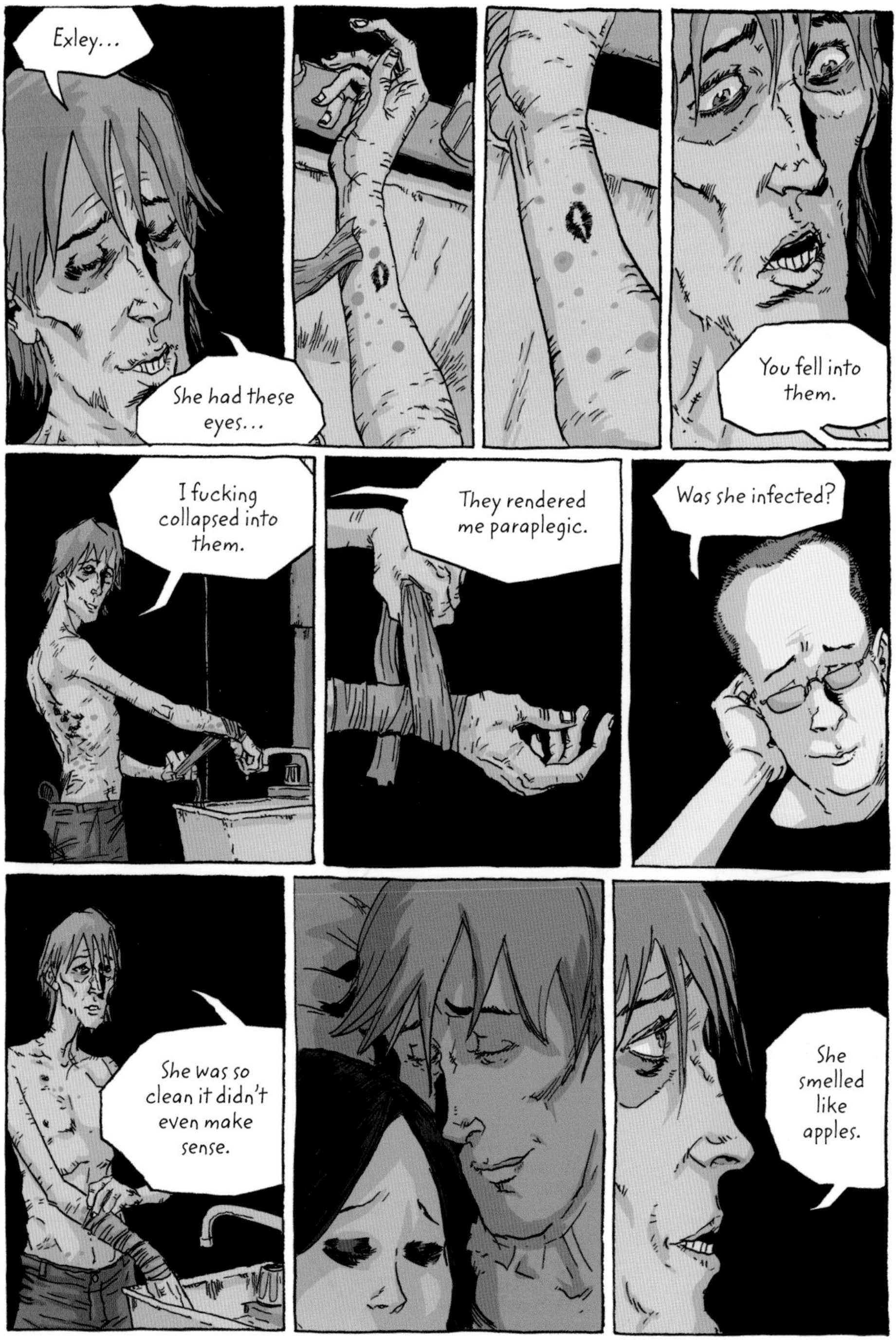

Exley...
She had these eyes...
You fell into them.
I fucking collapsed into them.
They rendered me paraplegic.
Was she infected?
She was so clean it didn't even make sense.
She smelled like apples.

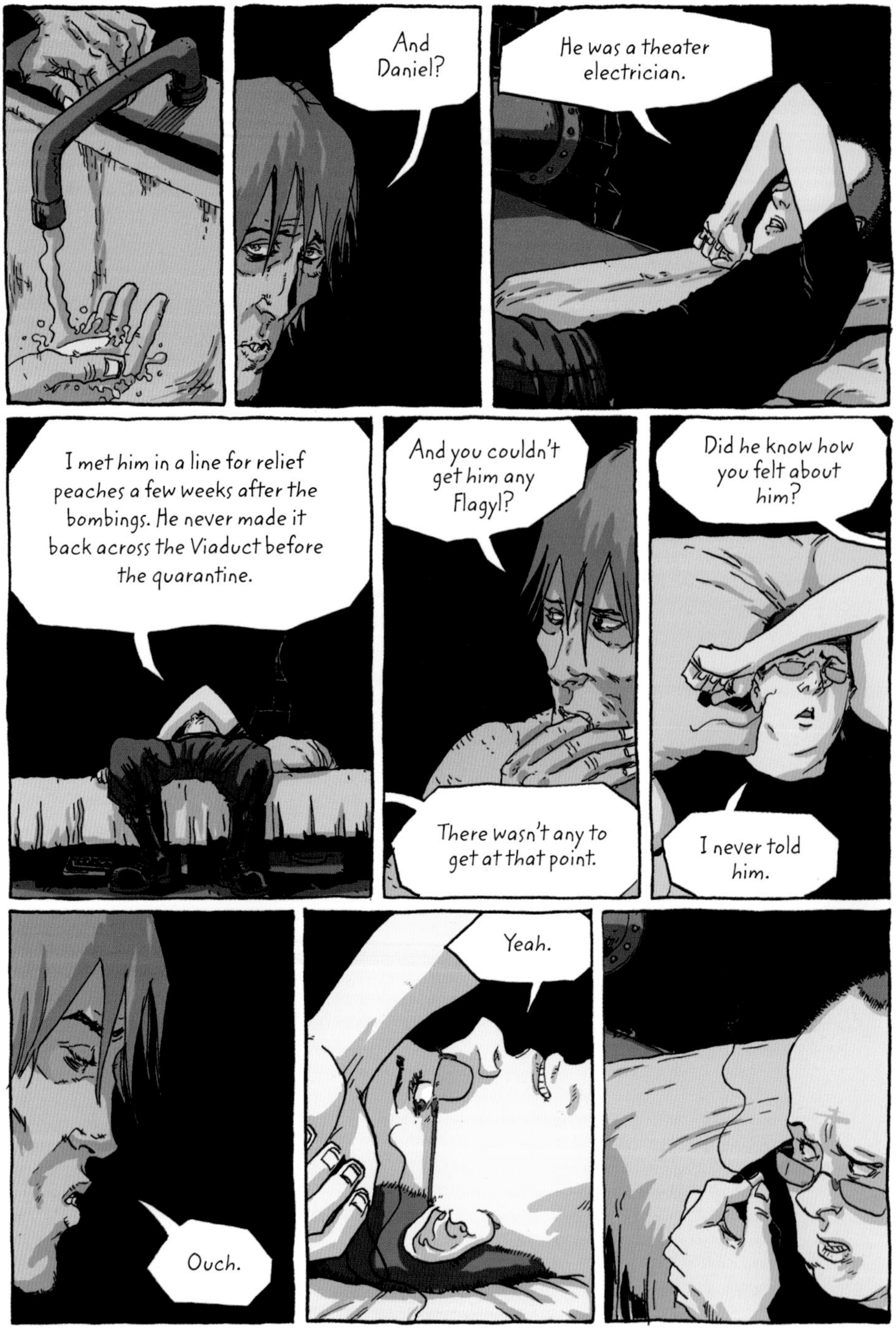
And Daniel?
He was a theater electrician.
I met him in a line for relief peaches a few weeks after the bombings. He never made it back across the Viaduct before the quarantine.
And you couldn't get him any Flagyl?
There wasn't any to get at that point.
Did he know how you felt about him?
I never told him.
Ouch.
Yeah.

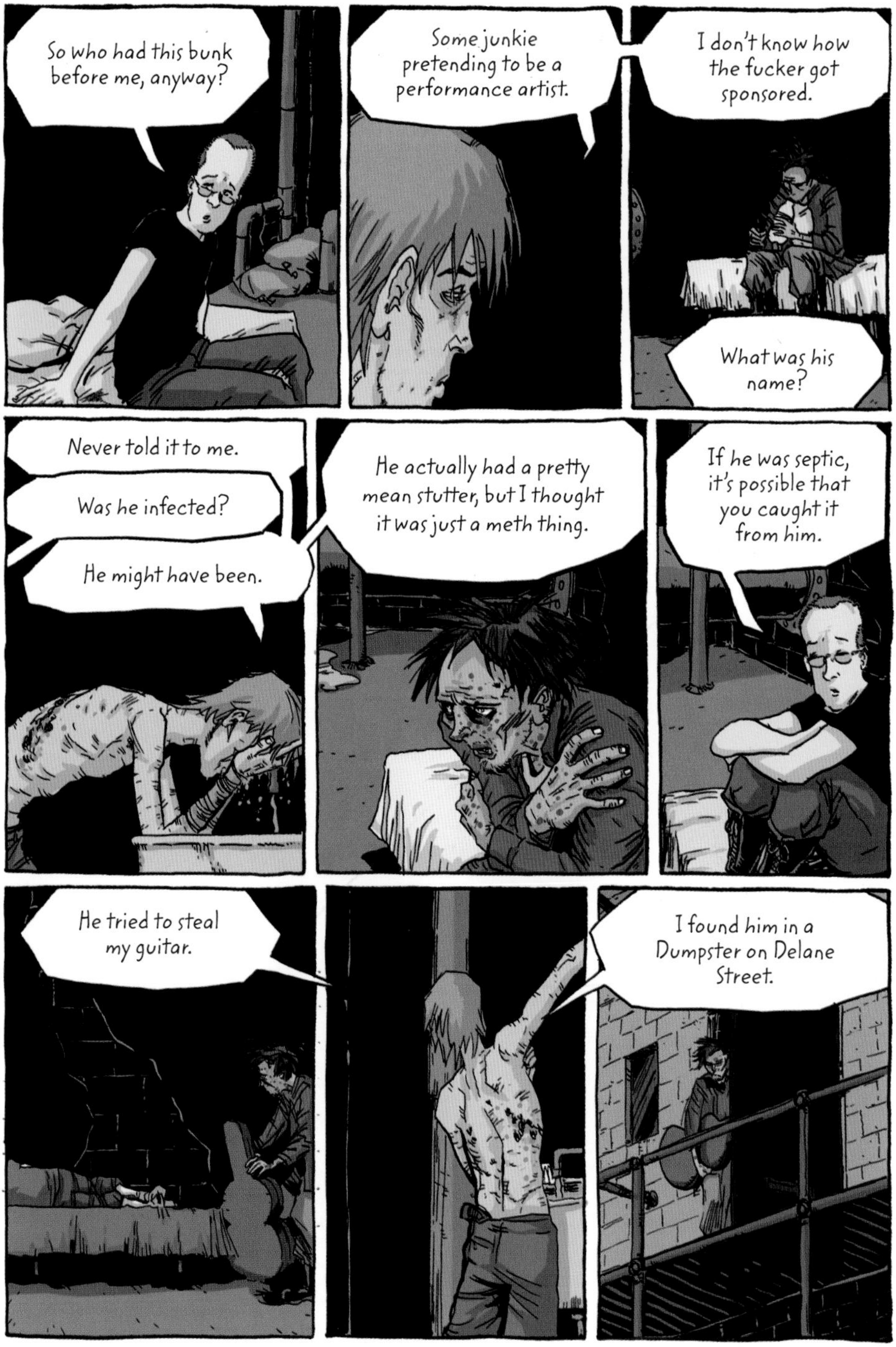
So who had this bunk before me, anyway?
Some junkie pretending to be a performance artist.
I don't know how the fucker got sponsored.
What was his name?
Never told it to me.
Was he infected?
He might have been.
He actually had a pretty mean stutter, but I thought it was just a meth thing.
If he was septic, it's possible that you caught it from him.
He tried to steal my guitar.
I found him in a Dumpster on Delane Street.

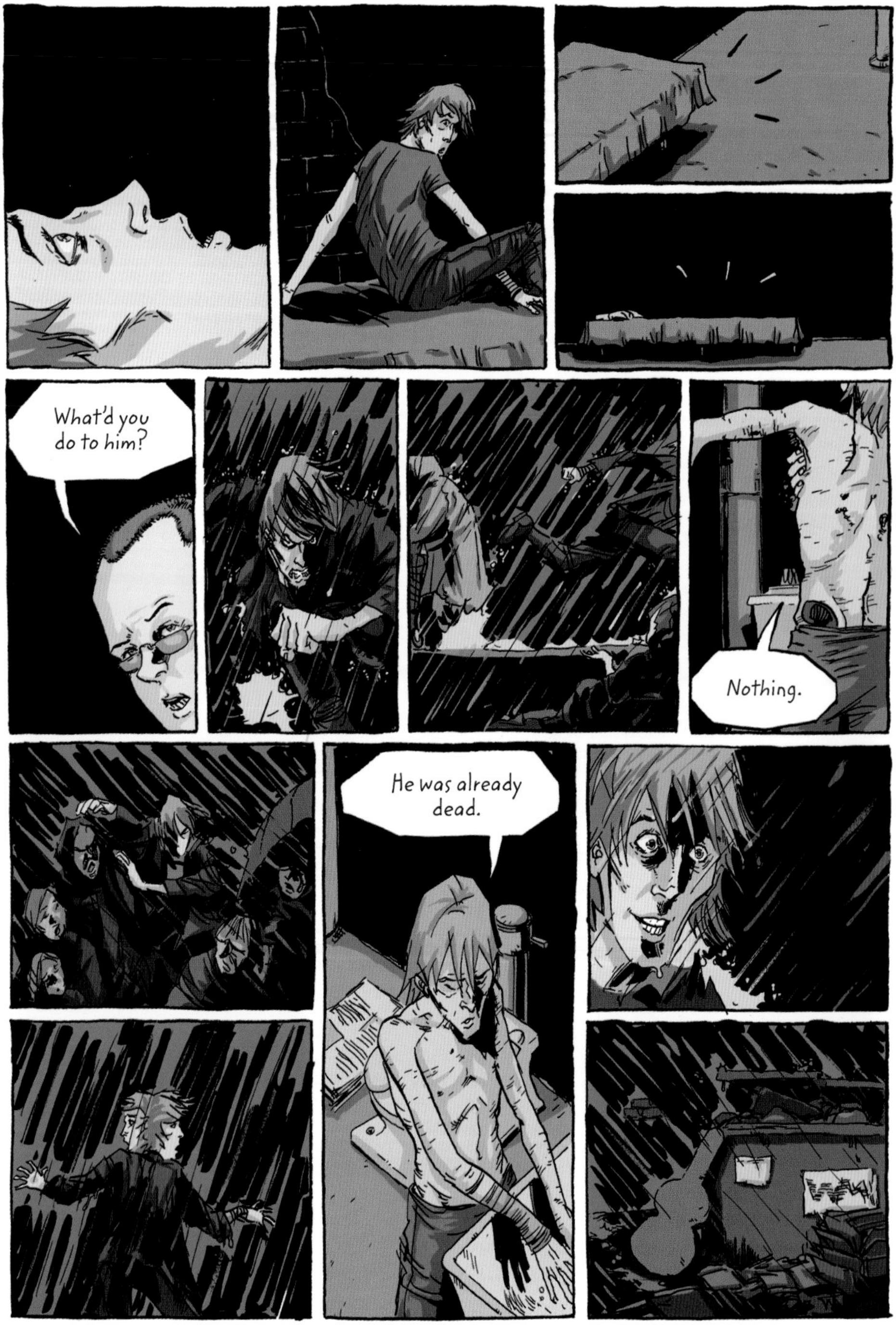
What'd you do to him?
Nothing.
He was already dead.

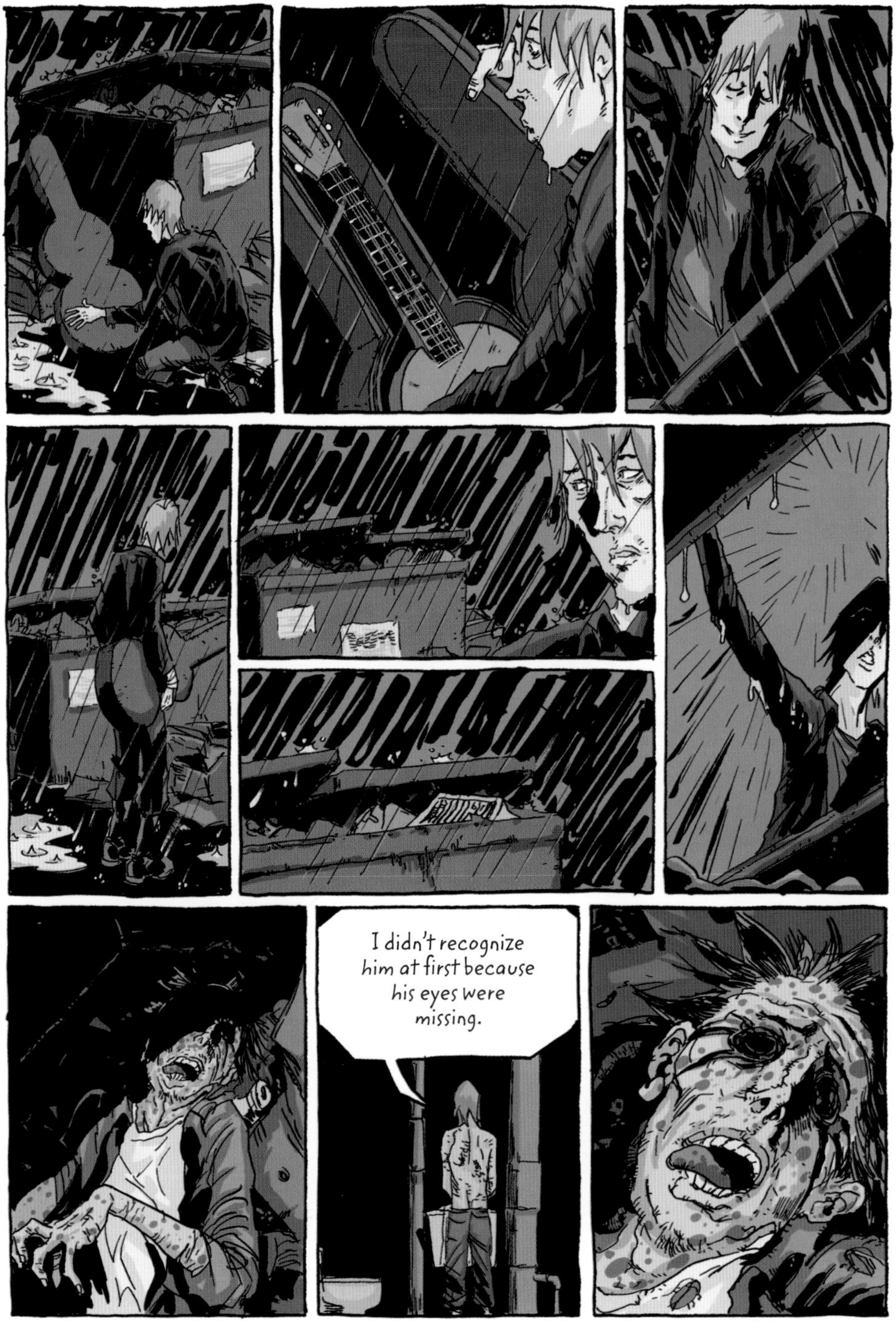
I didn't recognize him at first because his eyes were missing.

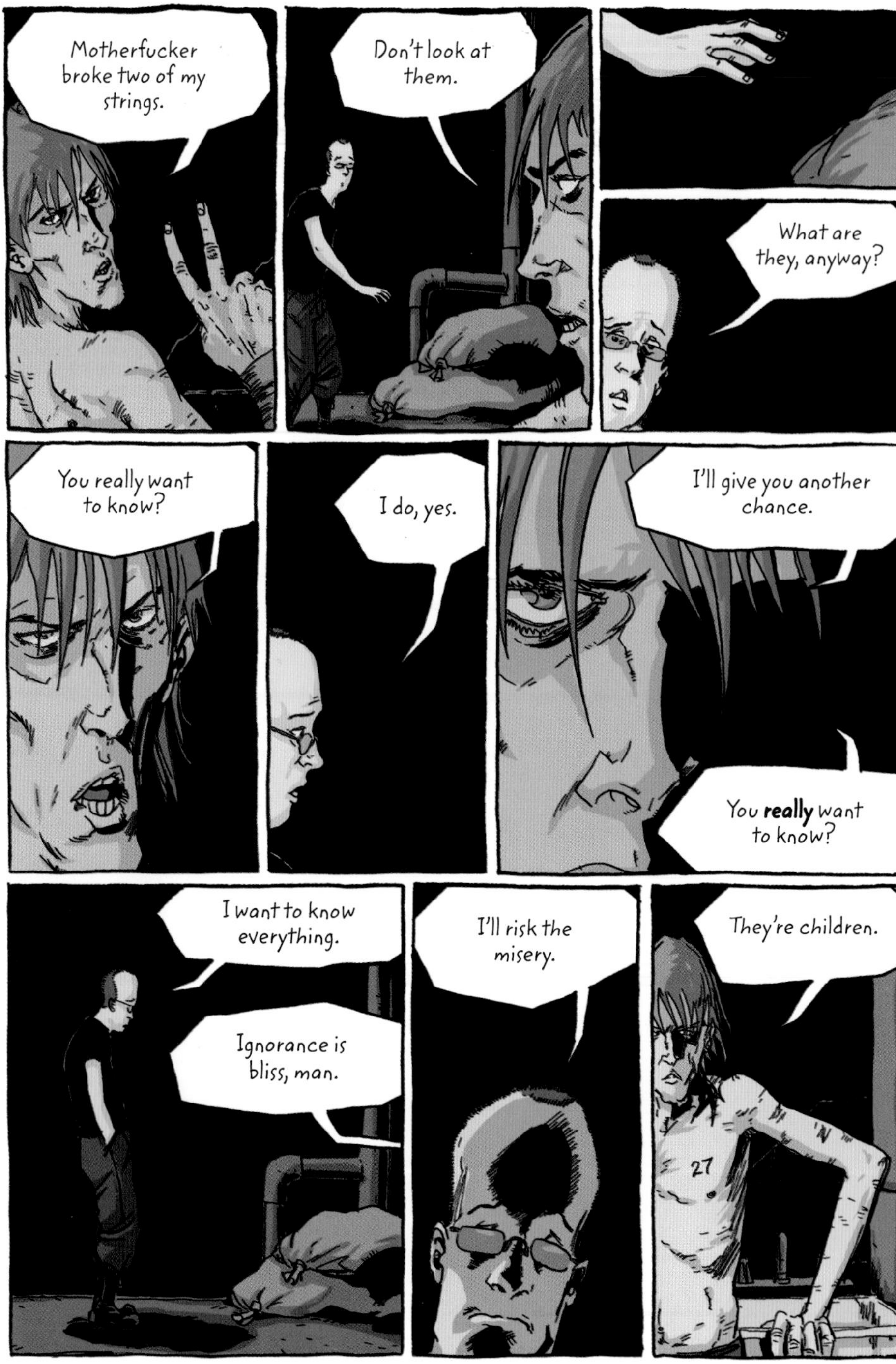
Motherfucker broke two of my strings.
Don't look at them.
What are they, anyway?
You really want to know?
I do, yes.
I'll give you another chance.
You **really** want to know?
I want to know everything.
Ignorance is bliss, man.
I'll risk the misery.
They're children.
27

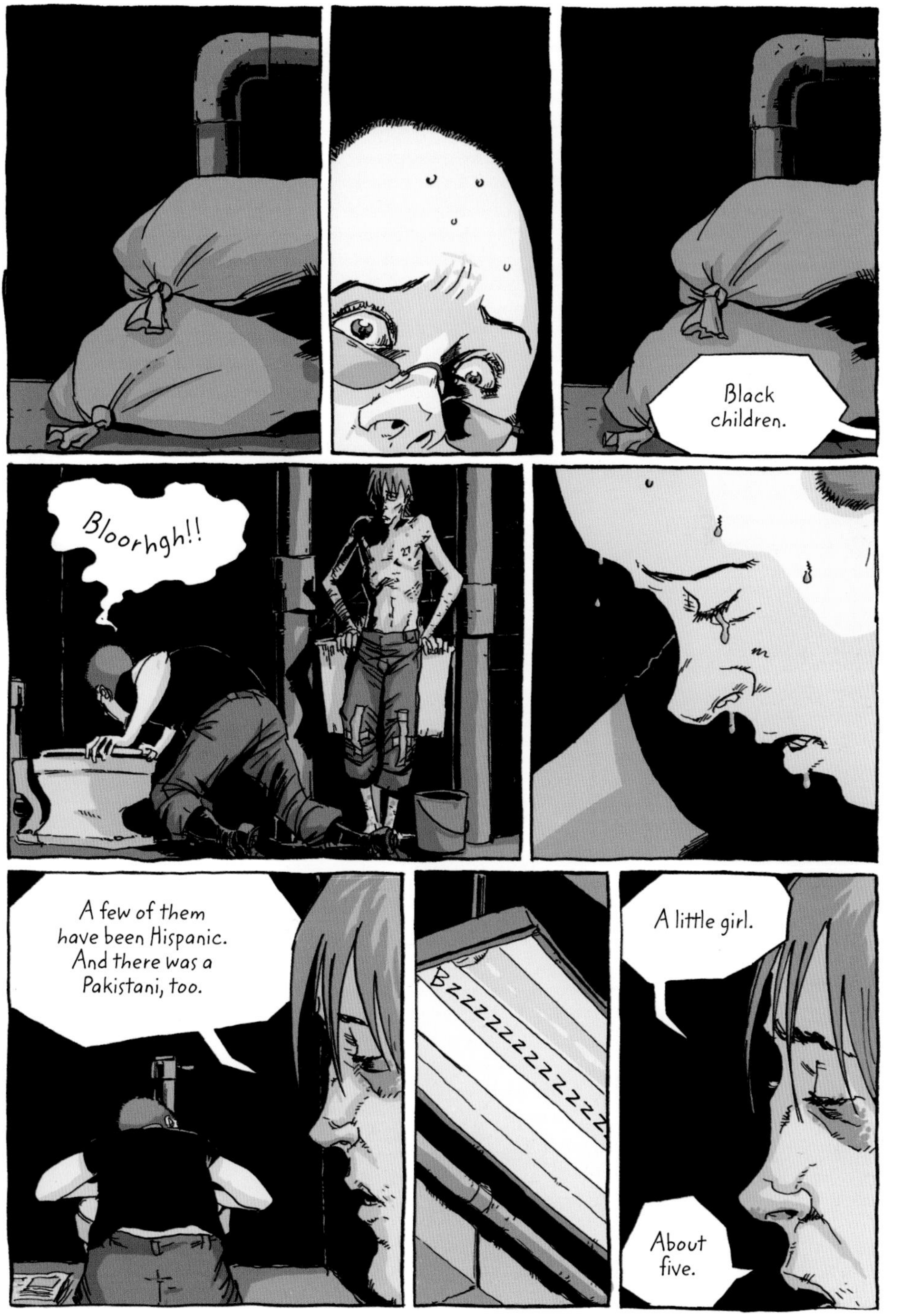

Black children.
Bloorhgh!!
A few of them have been Hispanic. And there was a Pakistani, too.
Bzzzzzzzzzzzzz
A little girl.
About five.

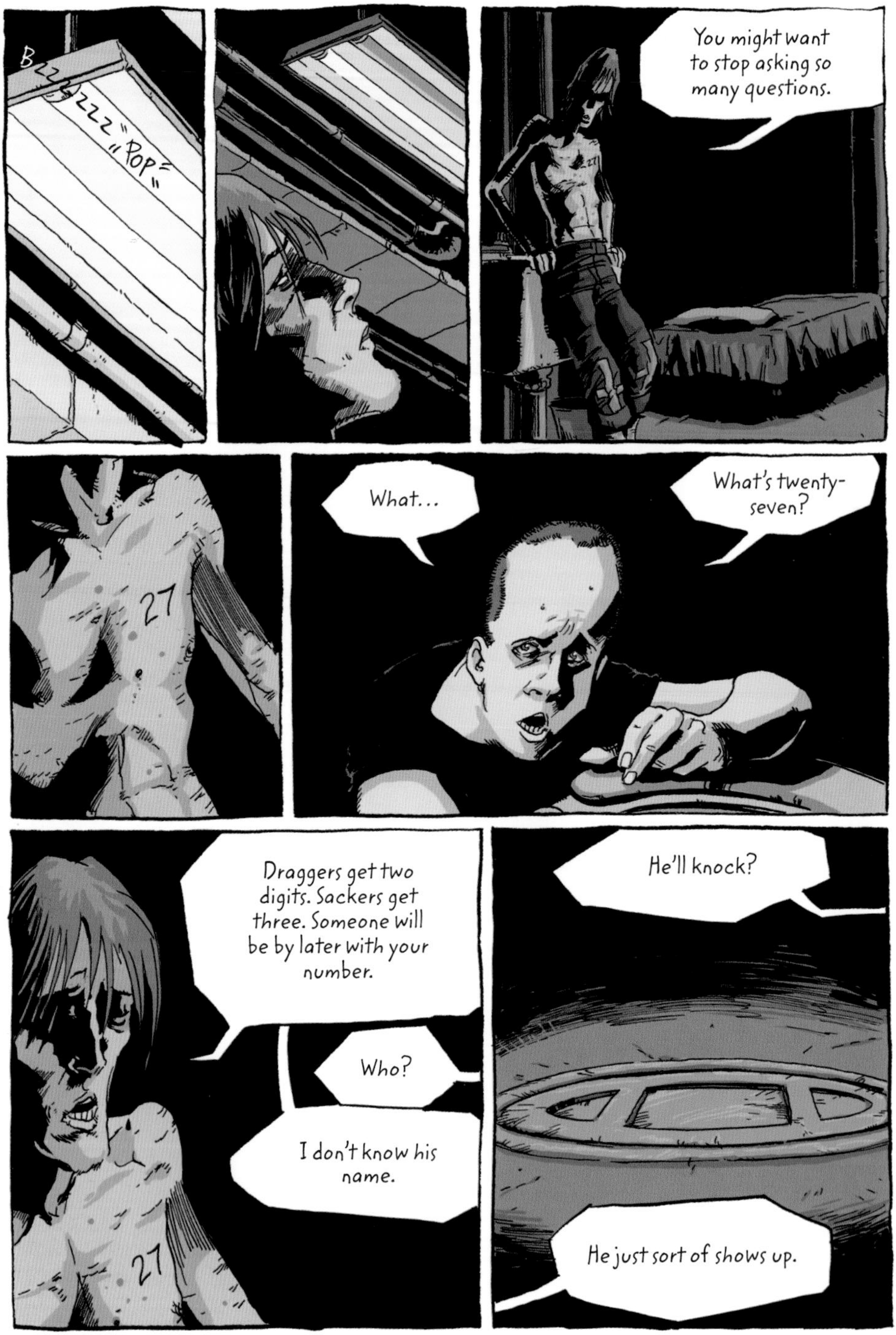
Bzzzzzzz "Pop"
You might want to stop asking so many questions.
27
What...
What's twenty-seven?
Draggers get two digits. Sackers get three. Someone will be by later with your number.
Who?
I don't know his name.
27
He'll knock?
He just sort of shows up.

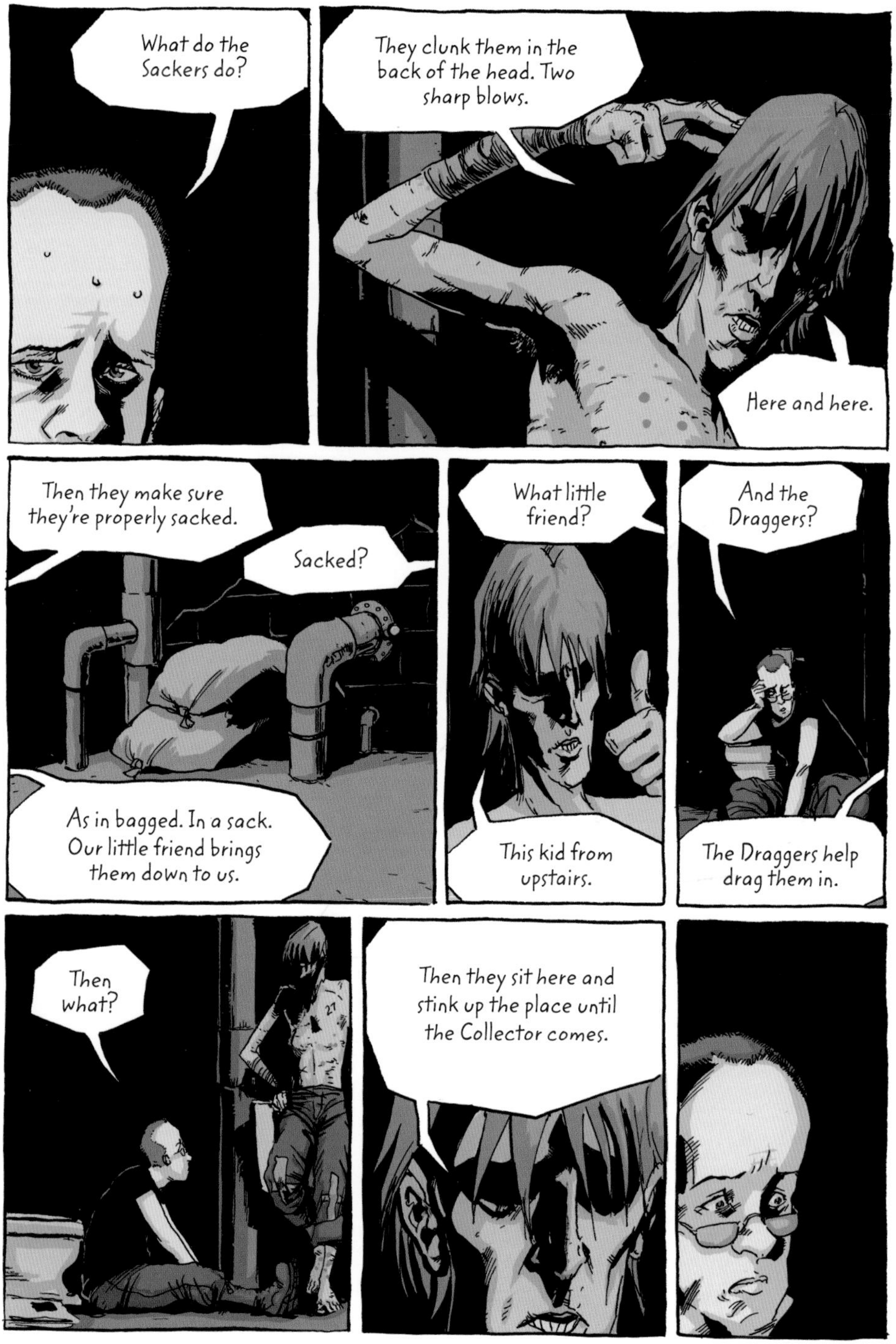
What do the Sackers do?
They clunk them in the back of the head. Two sharp blows.
Here and here.
Then they make sure they're properly sacked.
Sacked?
As in bagged. In a sack. Our little friend brings them down to us.
What little friend?
This kid from upstairs.
And the Draggers?
The Draggers help drag them in.
Then what?
Then they sit here and stink up the place until the Collector comes.

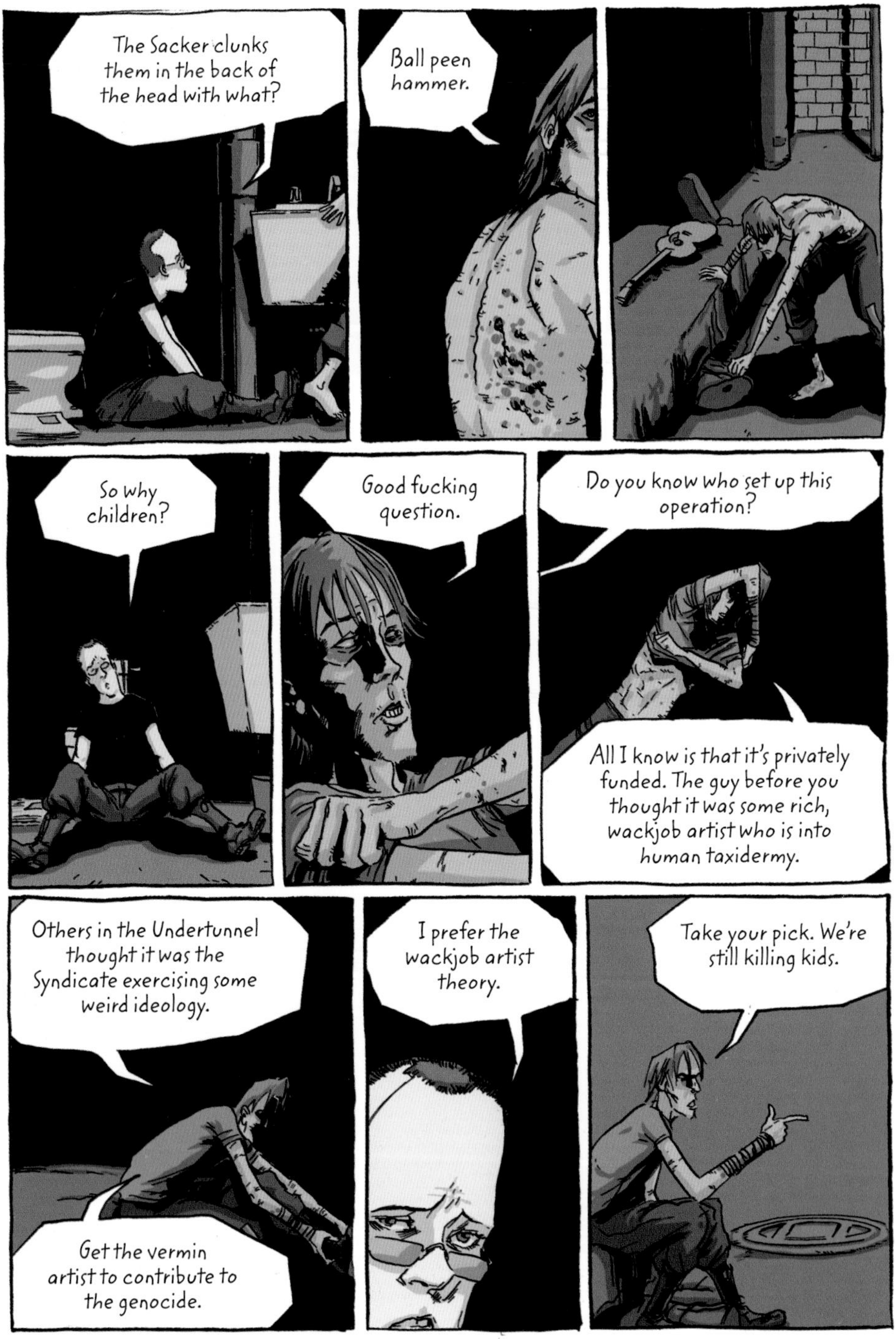
The Sacker clunks them in the back of the head with what?
Ball peen hammer.
So why children?
Good fucking question.
Do you know who set up this operation?
All I know is that it's privately funded. The guy before you thought it was some rich, wackjob artist who is into human taxidermy.
Others in the Undertunnel thought it was the Syndicate exercising some weird ideology.
Get the vermin artist to contribute to the genocide.
I prefer the wackjob artist theory.
Take your pick. We're still killing kids.

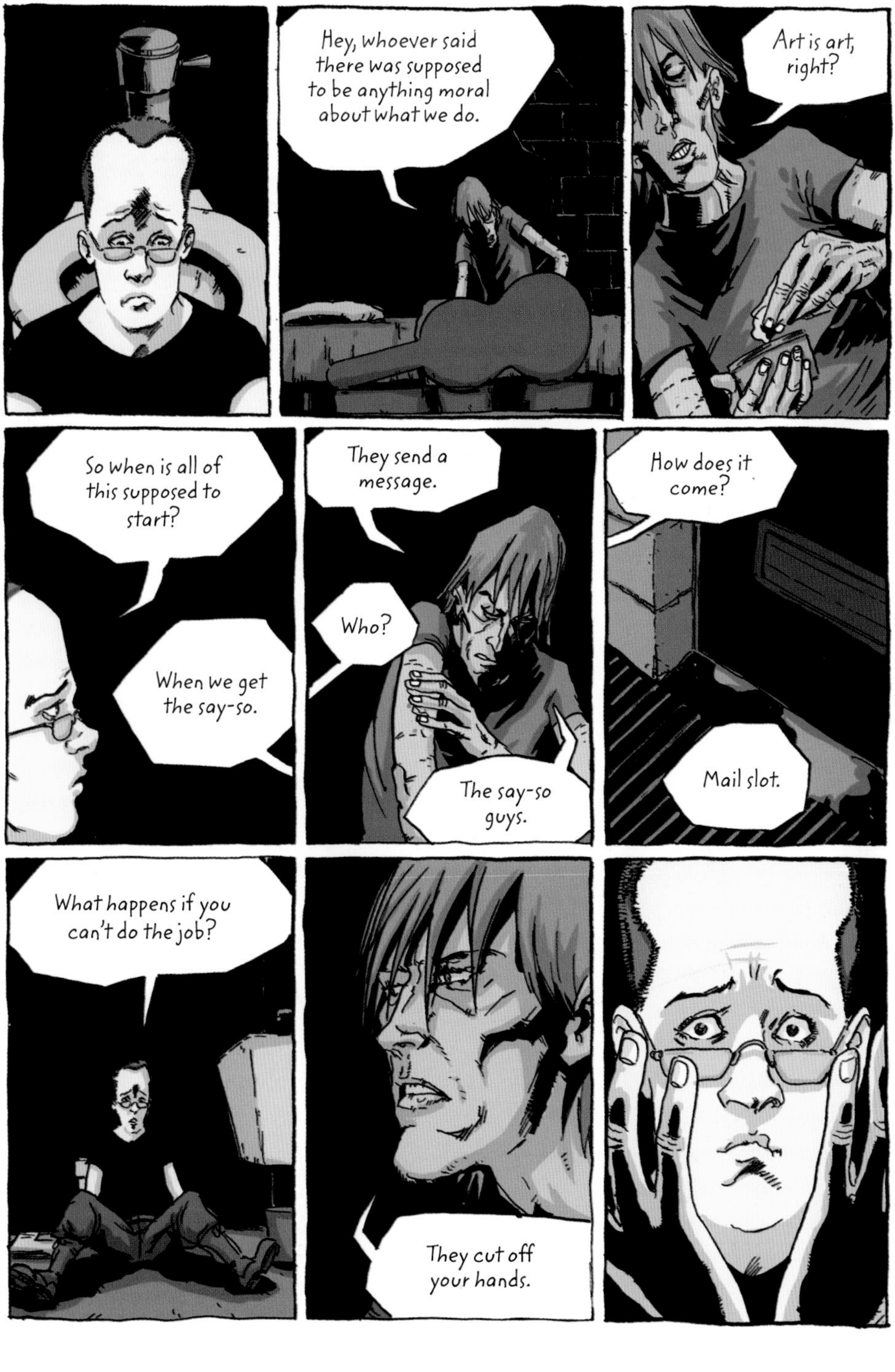
Hey, whoever said there was supposed to be anything moral about what we do.
Art is art, right?
So when is all of this supposed to start?
When we get the say-so.
They send a message.
Who?
The say-so guys.
How does it come?
Mail slot.
What happens if you can't do the job?
They cut off your hands.

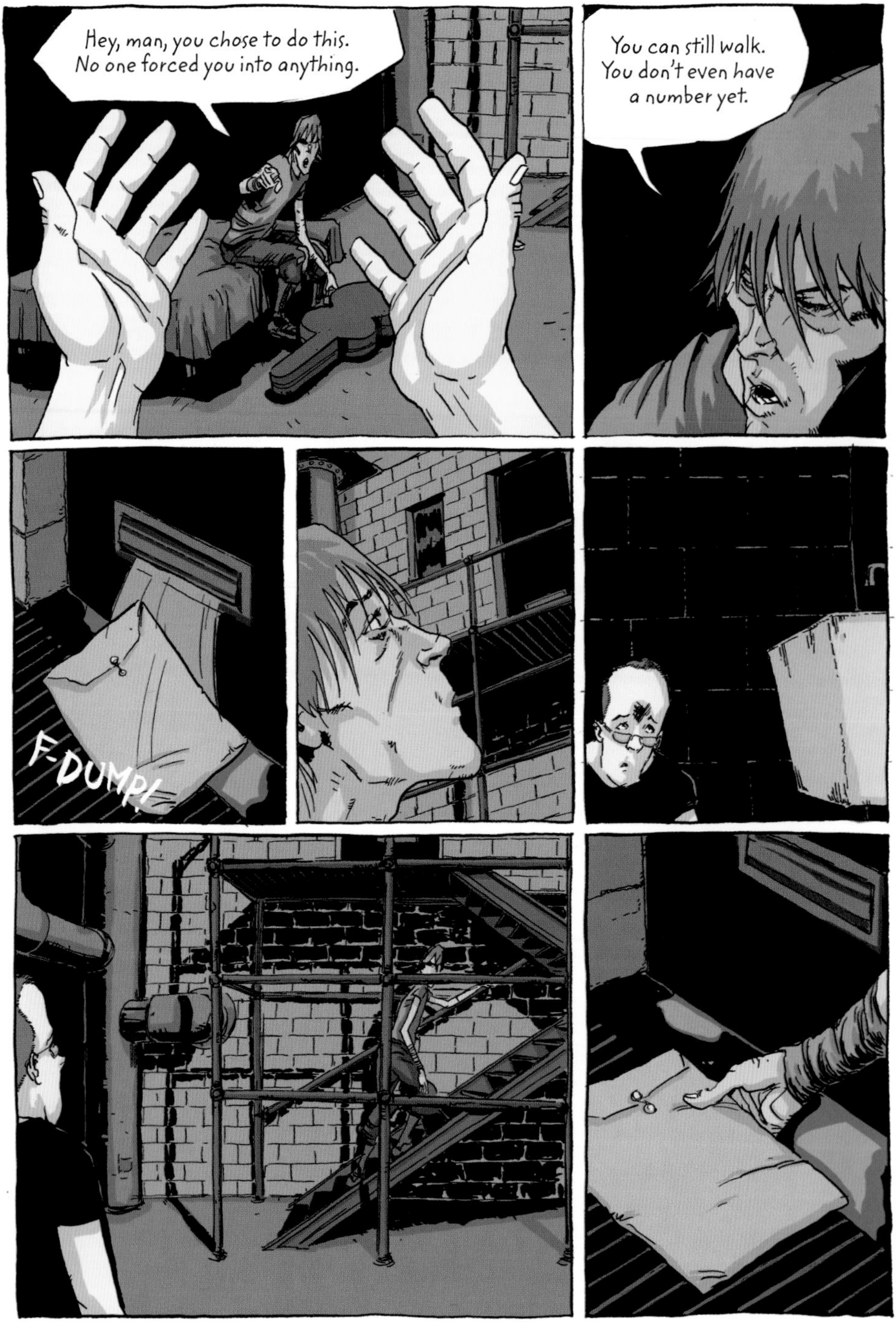
Hey, man, you chose to do this. No one forced you into anything.
You can still walk. You don't even have a number yet.
F-DUMP!

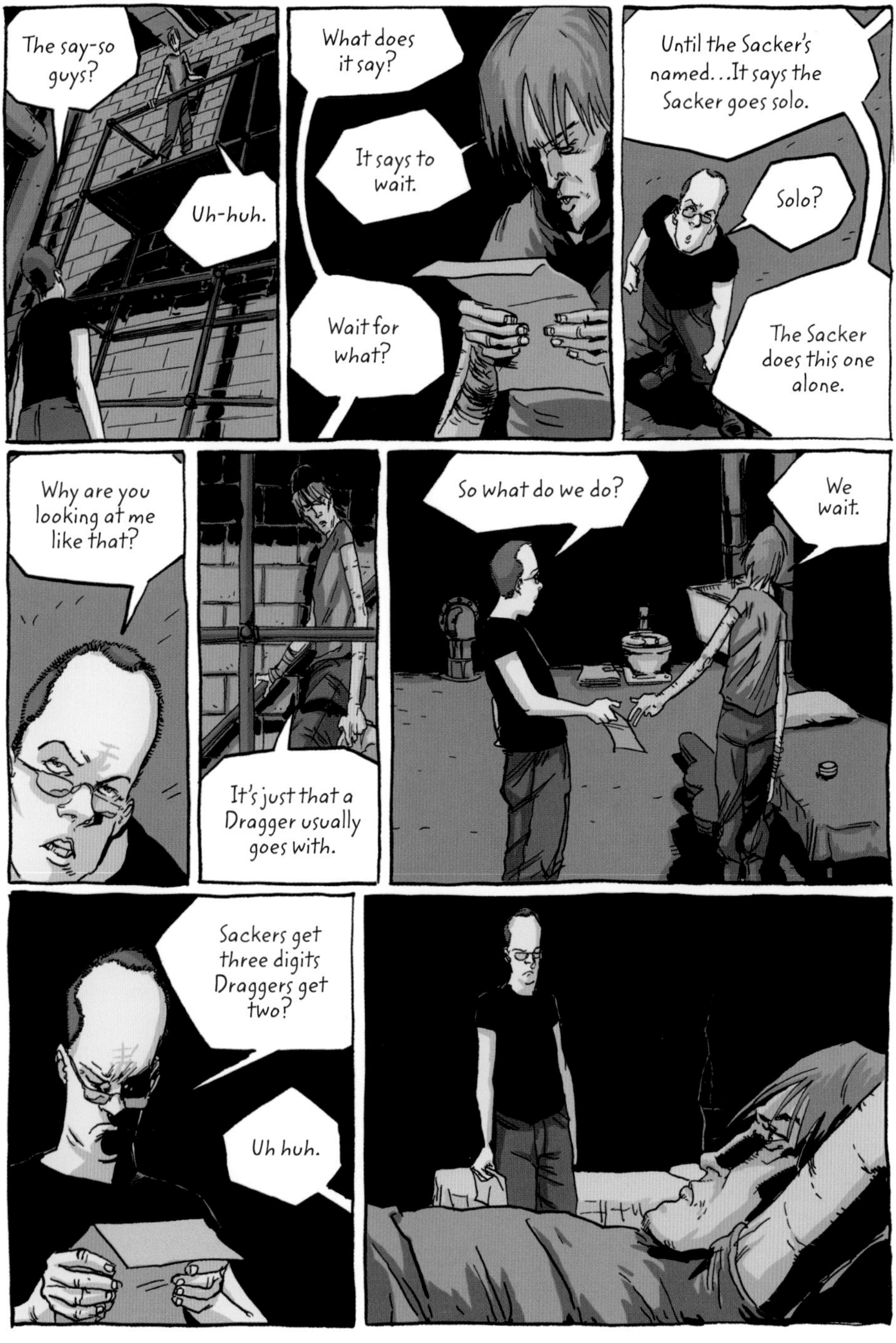
The say-so guys?
Uh-huh.
What does it say?
It says to wait.
Wait for what?
Until the Sacker's named...It says the Sacker goes solo.
Solo?
The Sacker does this one alone.
Why are you looking at me like that?
It's just that a Dragger usually goes with.
So what do we do?
We wait.
Sackers get three digits Draggers get two?
Uh huh.

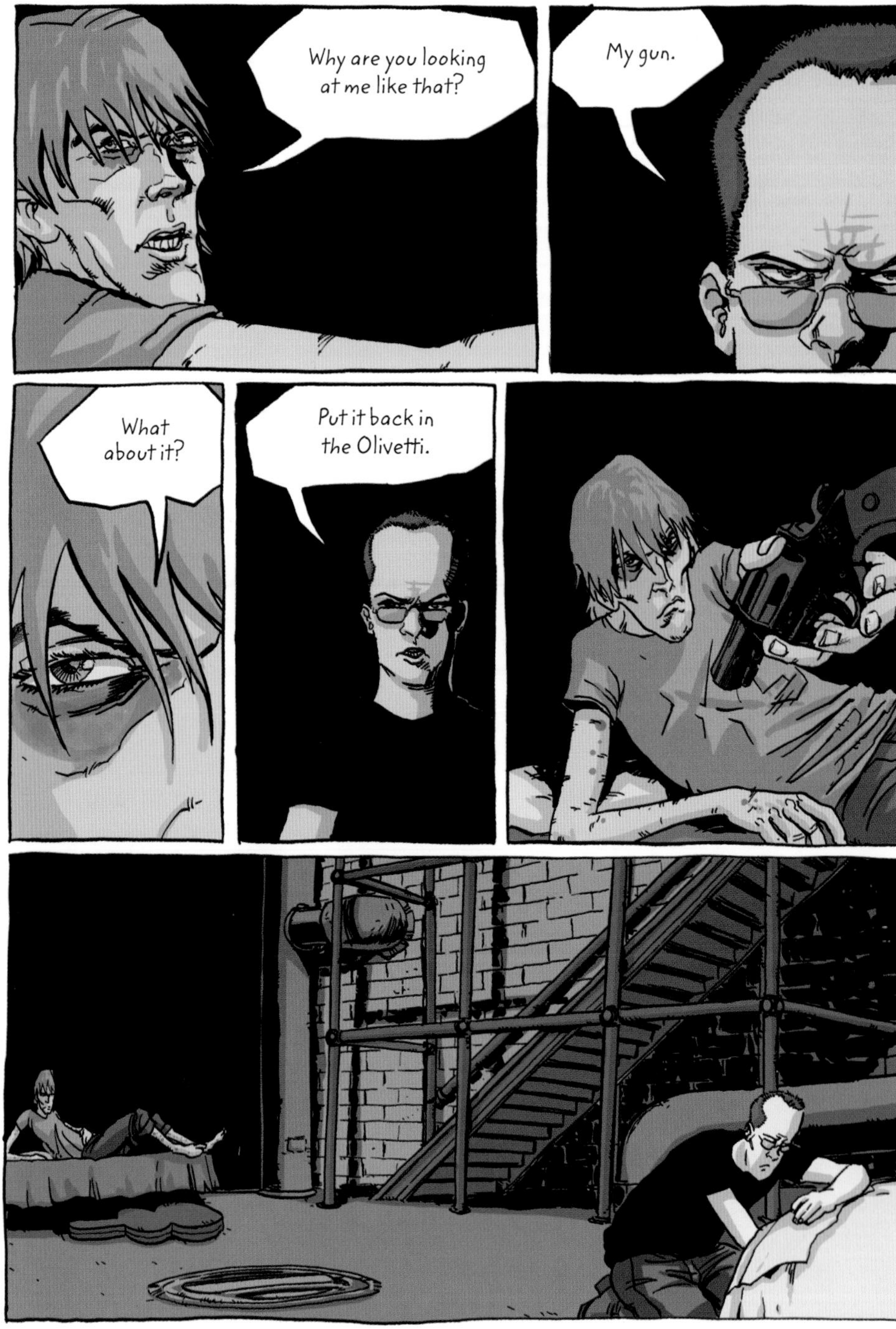
Why are you looking at me like that?
My gun.
What about it?
Put it back in the Olivetti.

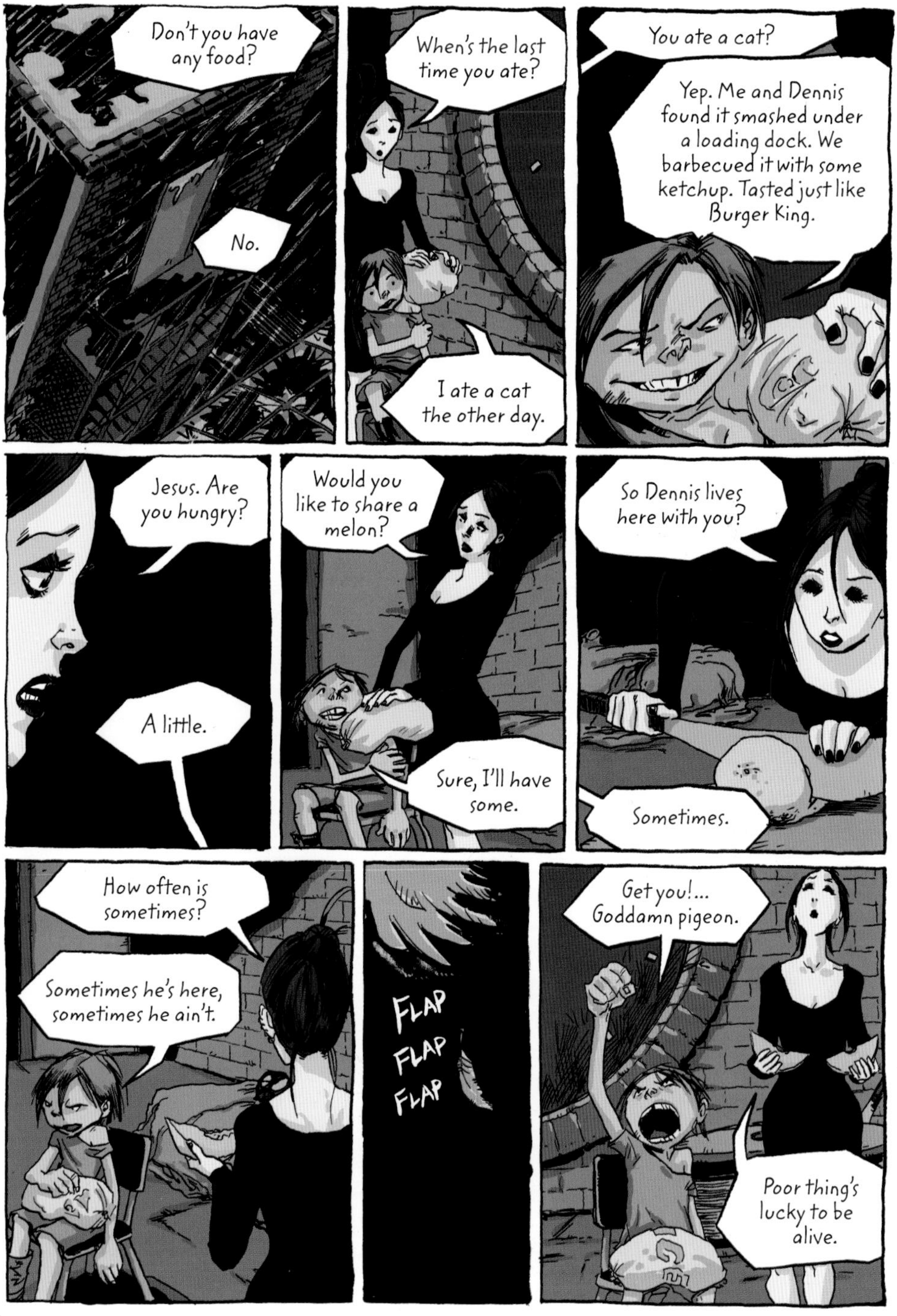
Don't you have any food?
No.
When's the last time you ate?
I ate a cat the other day.
You ate a cat?
Yep. Me and Dennis found it smashed under a loading dock. We barbecued it with some ketchup. Tasted just like Burger King.
Jesus. Are you hungry?
A little.
Would you like to share a melon?
Sure, I'll have some.
So Dennis lives here with you?
Sometimes.
How often is sometimes?
Sometimes he's here, sometimes he ain't.
FLAP
FLAP
FLAP
Get you!... Goddamn pigeon.
Poor thing's lucky to be alive.

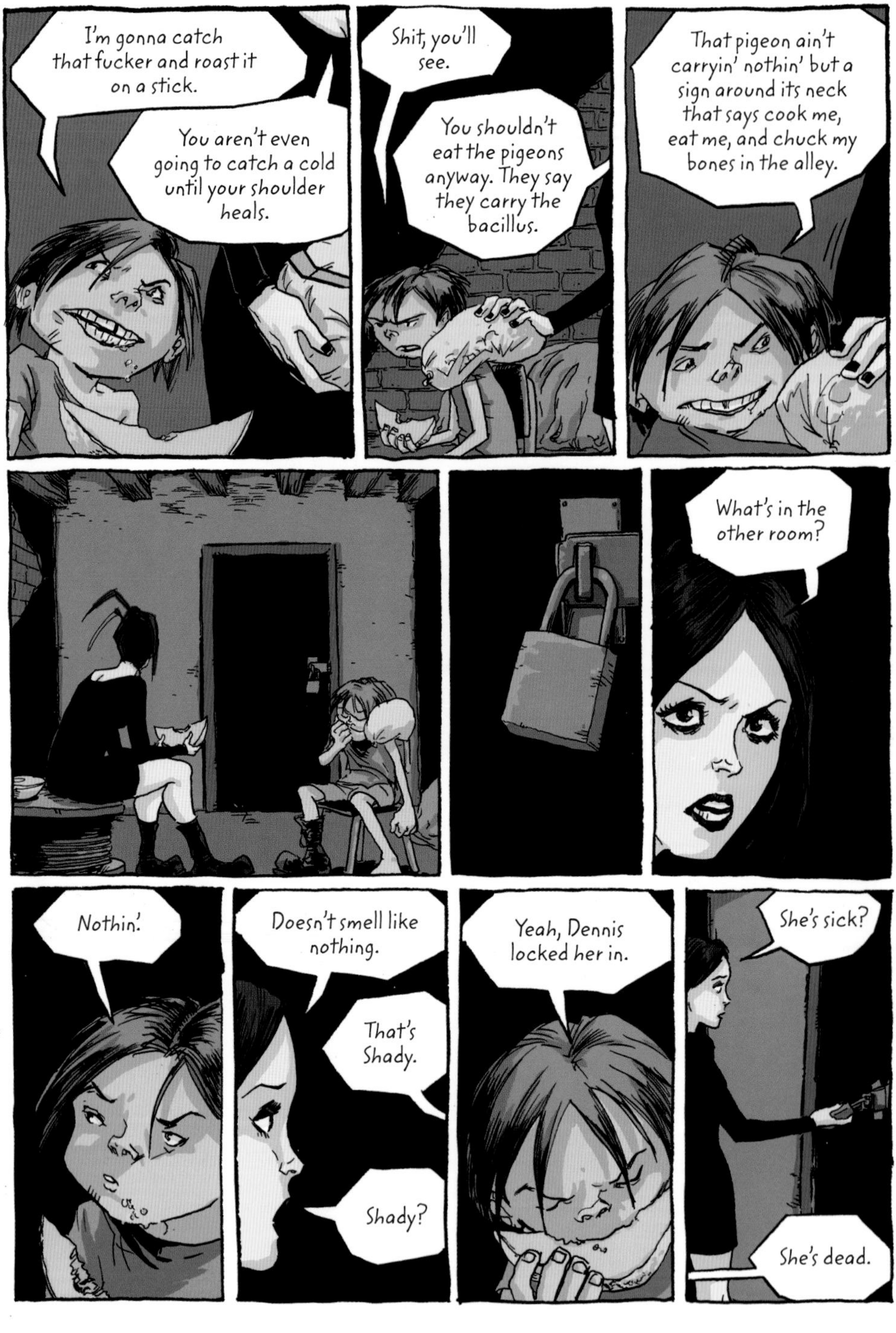
I'm gonna catch that fucker and roast it on a stick.
You aren't even going to catch a cold until your shoulder heals.
Shit, you'll see.
You shouldn't eat the pigeons anyway. They say they carry the bacillus.
That pigeon ain't carryin' nothin' but a sign around its neck that says cook me, eat me, and chuck my bones in the alley.
What's in the other room?
Nothin'.
Doesn't smell like nothing.
That's Shady.
Shady?
Yeah, Dennis locked her in.
She's sick?
She's dead.

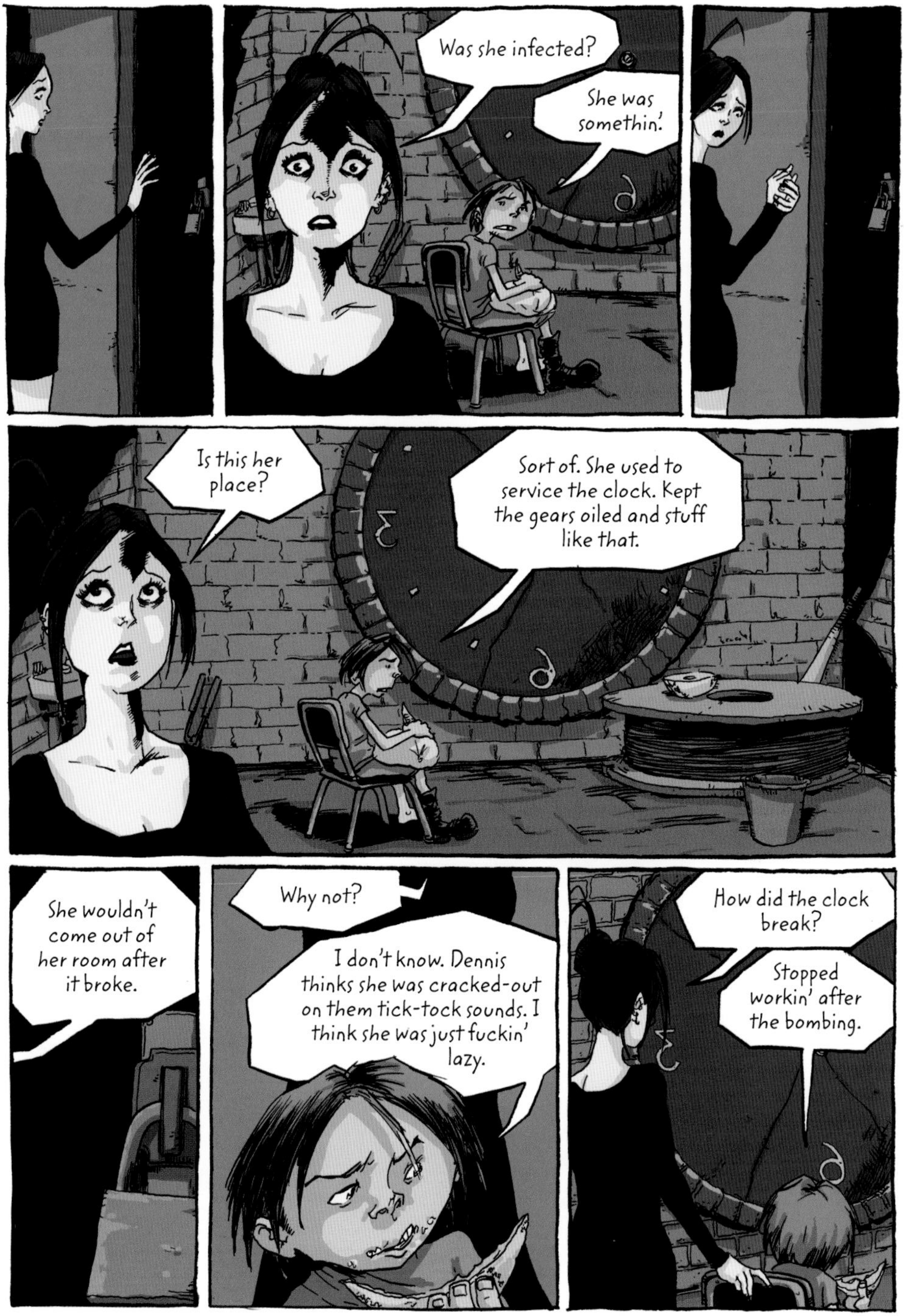
Was she infected?
She was somethin'.
Is this her place?
Sort of. She used to service the clock. Kept the gears oiled and stuff like that.
She wouldn't come out of her room after it broke.
Why not?
I don't know. Dennis thinks she was cracked-out on them tick-tock sounds. I think she was just fuckin' lazy.
How did the clock break?
Stopped workin' after the bombing.

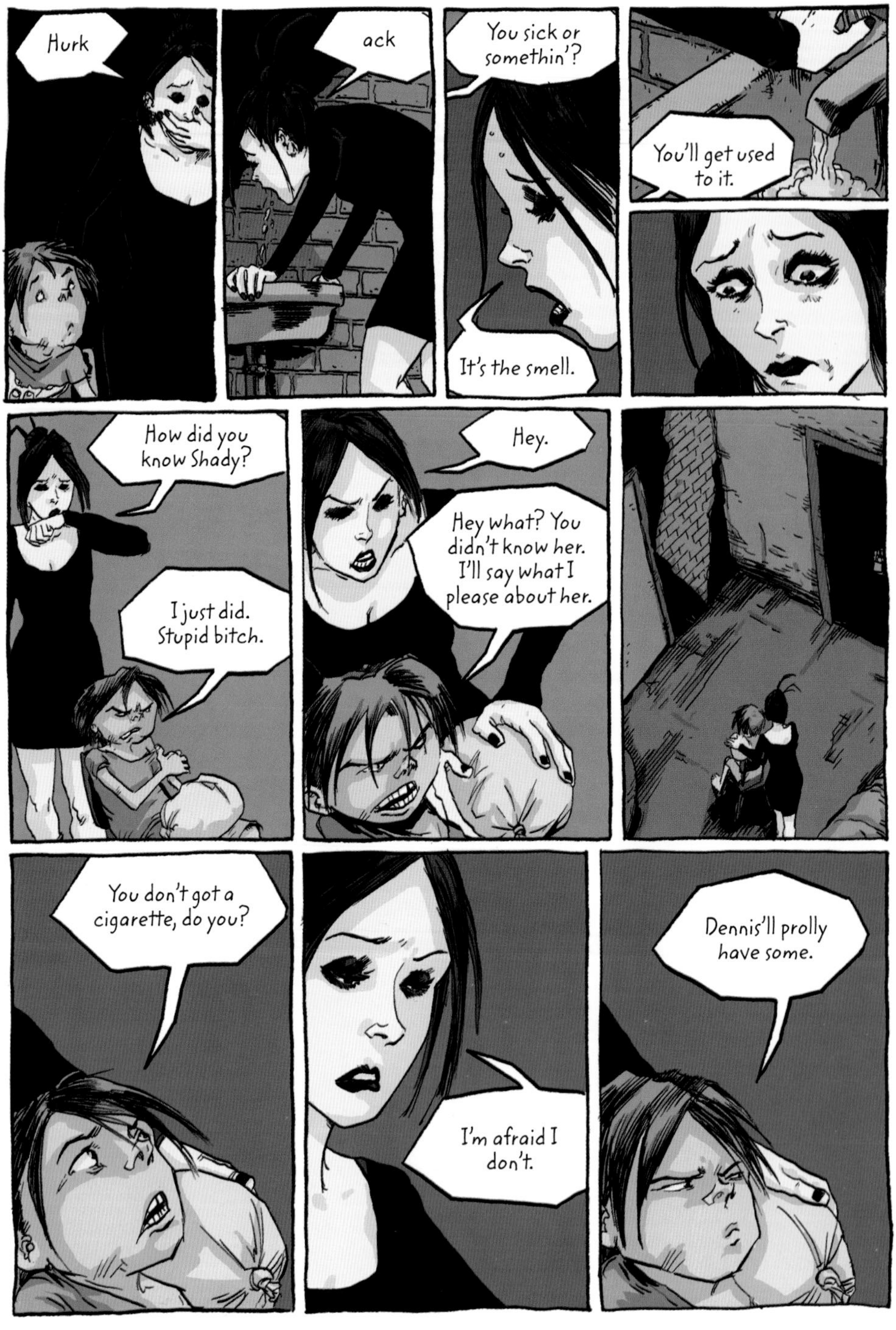
Hurk
ack
You sick or somethin'?
It's the smell.
You'll get used to it.
How did you know Shady?
I just did. Stupid bitch.
Hey.
Hey what? You didn't know her. I'll say what I please about her.
You don't got a cigarette, do you?
I'm afraid I don't.
Dennis'll prolly have some.

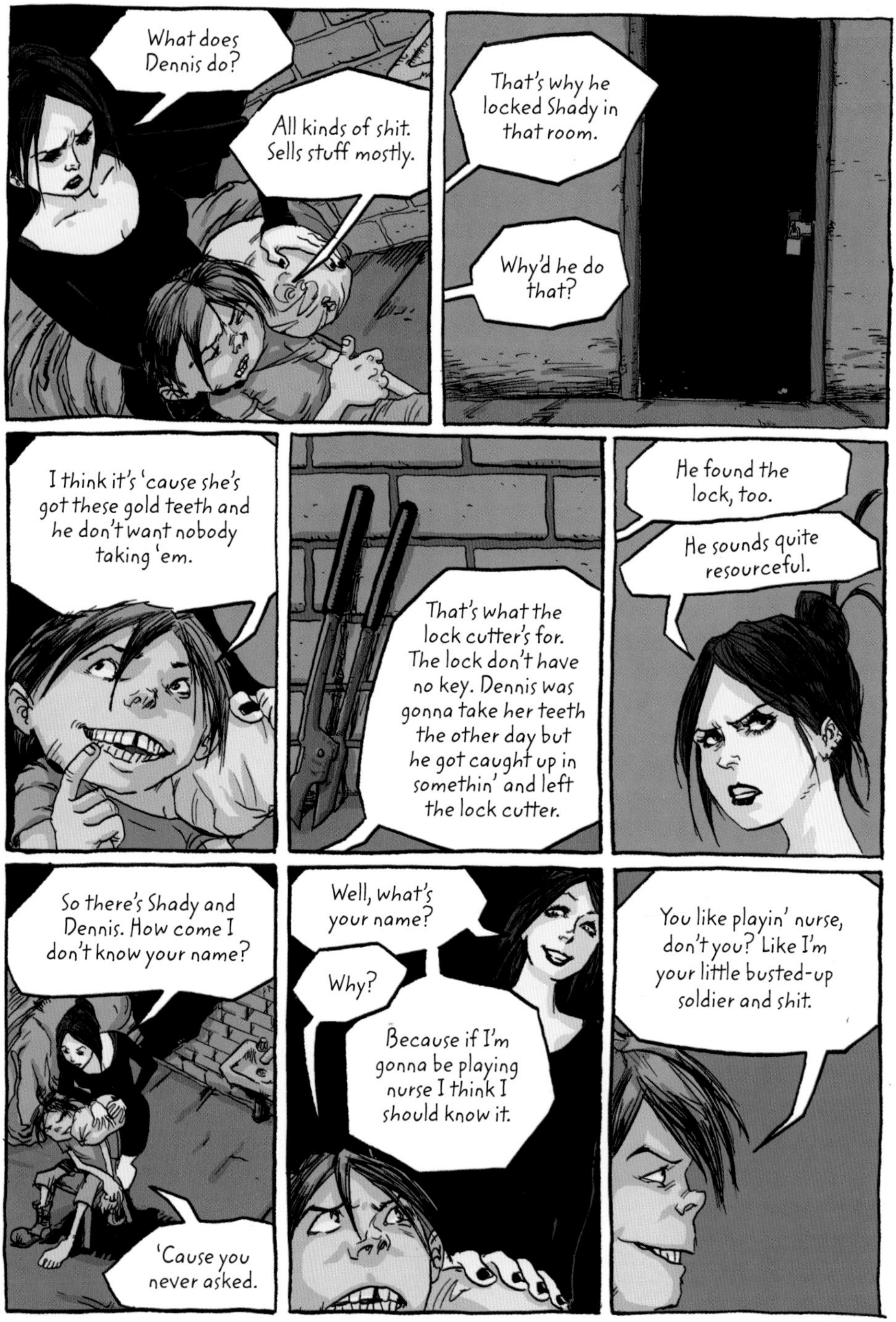

What does Dennis do?
All kinds of shit. Sells stuff mostly.
That's why he locked Shady in that room.
Why'd he do that?
I think it's 'cause she's got these gold teeth and he don't want nobody taking 'em.
That's what the lock cutter's for. The lock don't have no key. Dennis was gonna take her teeth the other day but he got caught up in somethin' and left the lock cutter.
He found the lock, too.
He sounds quite resourceful.
So there's Shady and Dennis. How come I don't know your name?
'Cause you never asked.
Well, what's your name?
Why?
Because if I'm gonna be playing nurse I think I should know it.
You like playin' nurse, don't you? Like I'm your little busted-up soldier and shit.

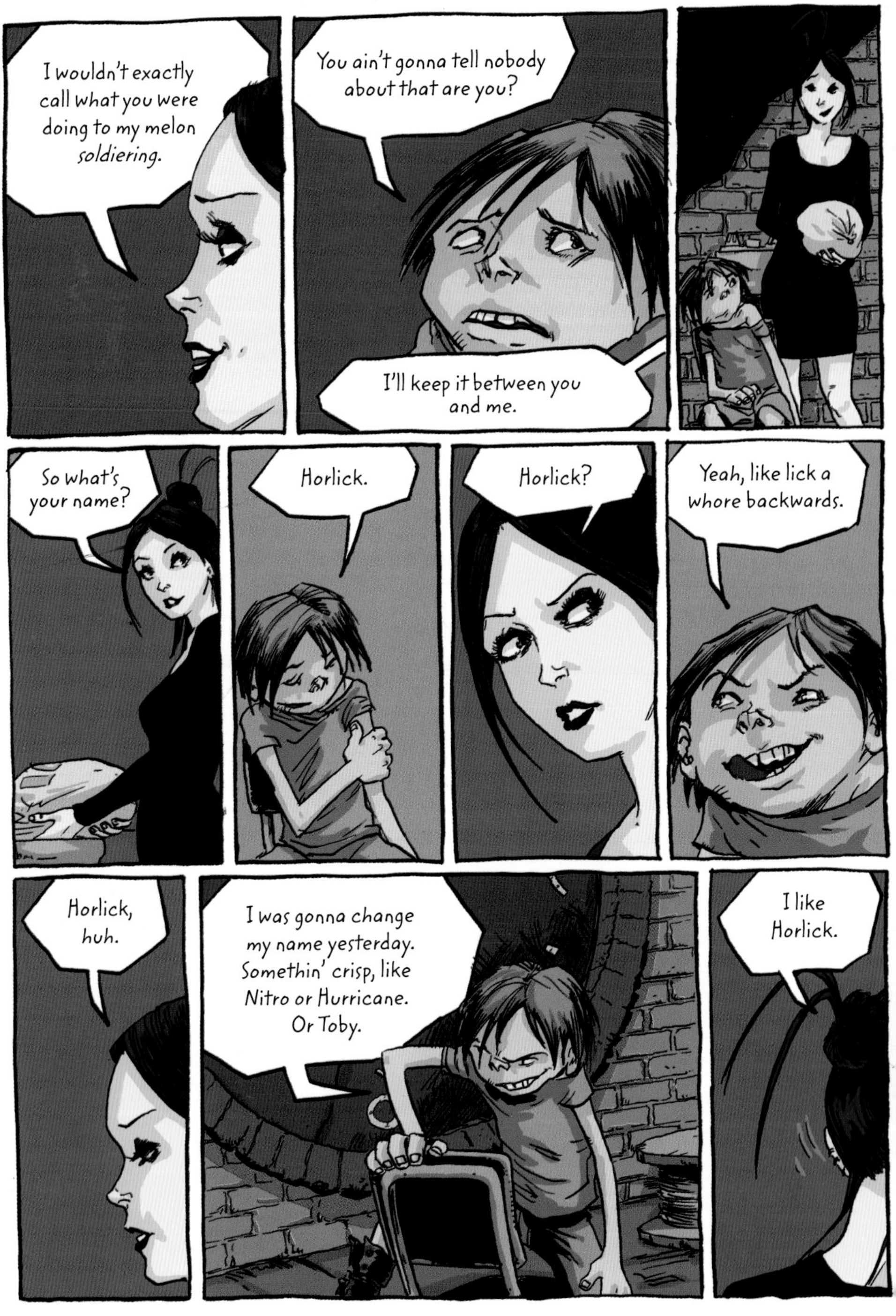
I wouldn't exactly call what you were doing to my melon soldiering.
You ain't gonna tell nobody about that are you?
I'll keep it between you and me.
So what's your name?
Horlick.
Horlick?
Yeah, like lick a whore backwards.
Horlick, huh.
I was gonna change my name yesterday. Somethin' crisp, like Nitro or Hurricane. Or Toby.
I like Horlick.

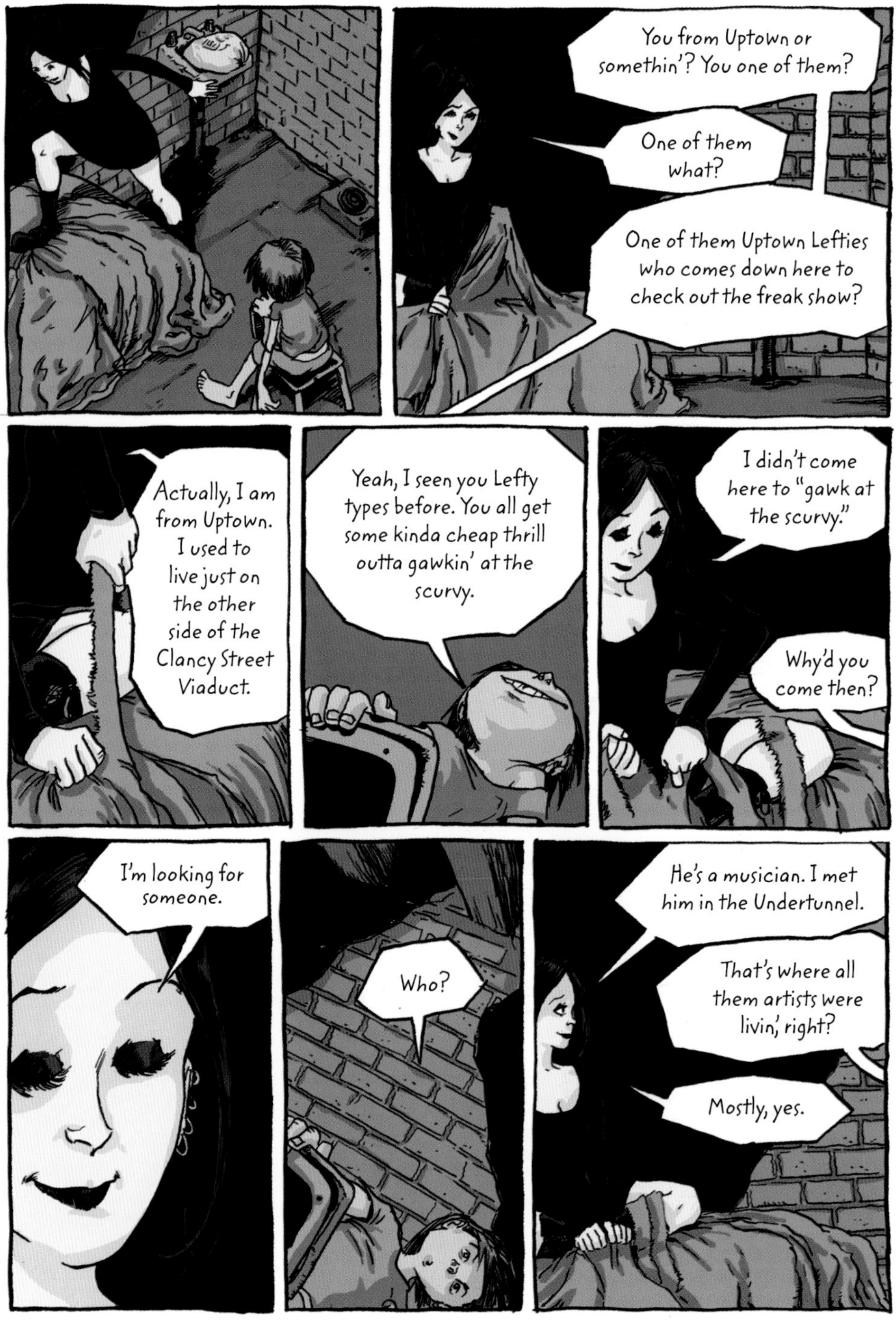
You from Uptown or somethin'? You one of them?
One of them what?
One of them Uptown Lefties who comes down here to check out the freak show?
Actually, I am from Uptown. I used to live just on the other side of the Clancy Street Viaduct.
Yeah, I seen you Lefty types before. You all get some kinda cheap thrill outta gawkin' at the scurvy.
I didn't come here to "gawk at the scurvy."
Why'd you come then?
I'm looking for someone.
Who?
He's a musician. I met him in the Undertunnel.
That's where all them artists were livin,' right?
Mostly, yes.

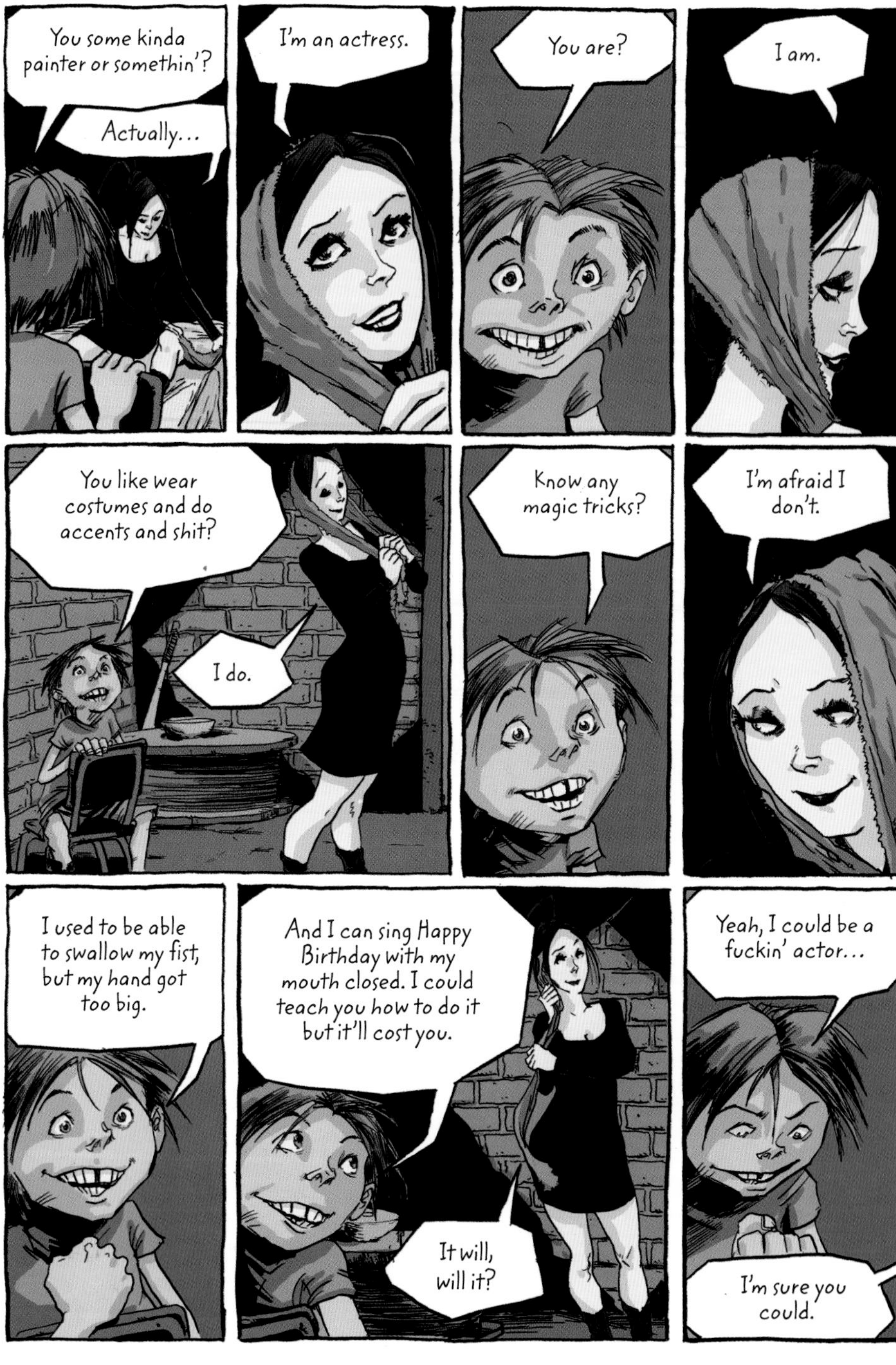
You some kinda painter or somethin'?
Actually...
I'm an actress.
You are?
I am.
You like wear costumes and do accents and shit?
I do.
Know any magic tricks?
I'm afraid I don't.
I used to be able to swallow my fist, but my hand got too big.
And I can sing Happy Birthday with my mouth closed. I could teach you how to do it but it'll cost you.
It will, will it?
Yeah, I could be a fuckin' actor...
I'm sure you could.

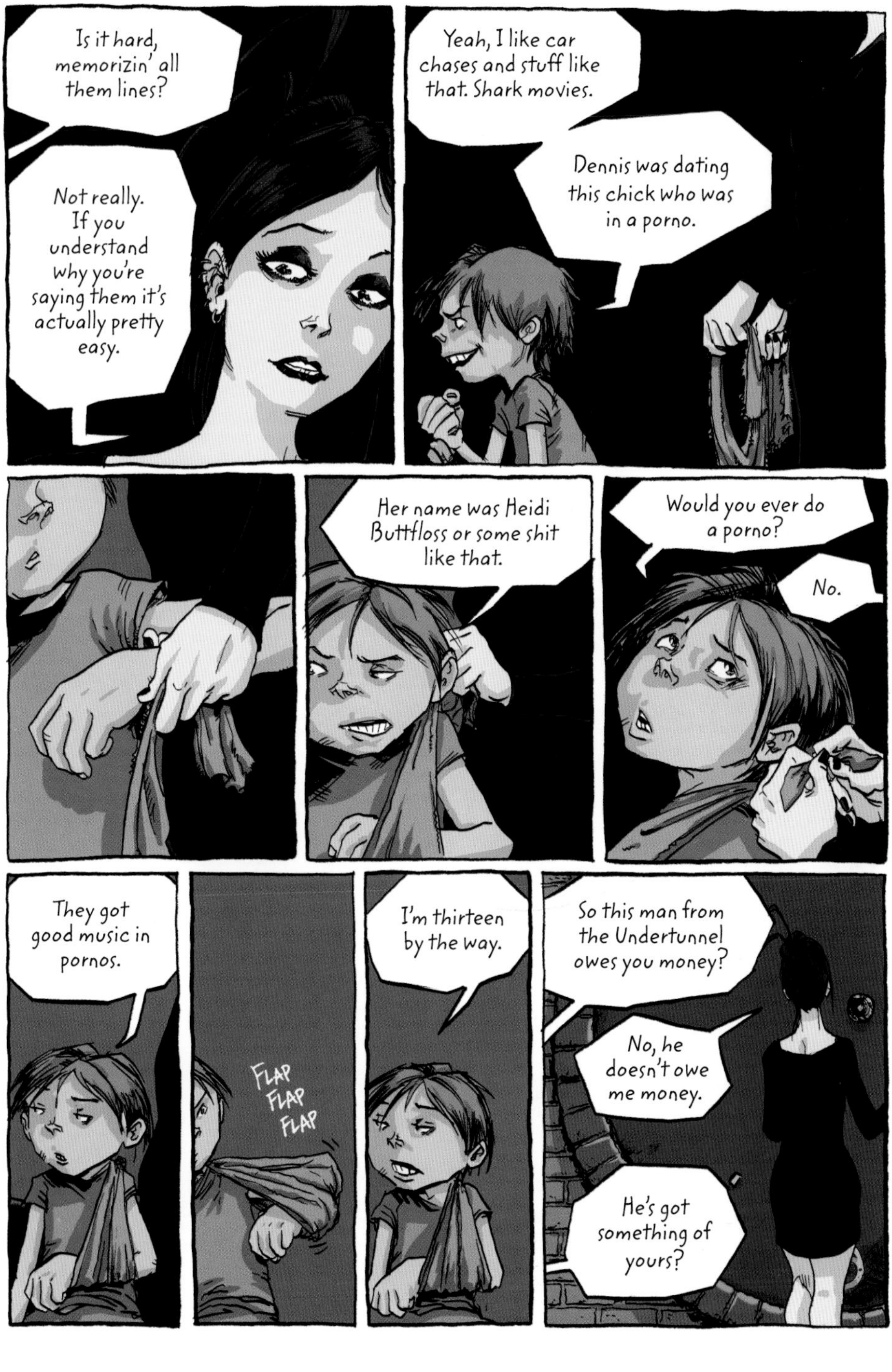
Is it hard, memorizin' all them lines?
Not really. If you understand why you're saying them it's actually pretty easy.
Yeah, I like car chases and stuff like that. Shark movies.
Dennis was dating this chick who was in a porno.
Her name was Heidi Buttfloss or some shit like that.
Would you ever do a porno?
No.
They got good music in pornos.
FLAP FLAP FLAP
I'm thirteen by the way.
So this man from the Undertunnel owes you money?
No, he doesn't owe me money.
He's got something of yours?

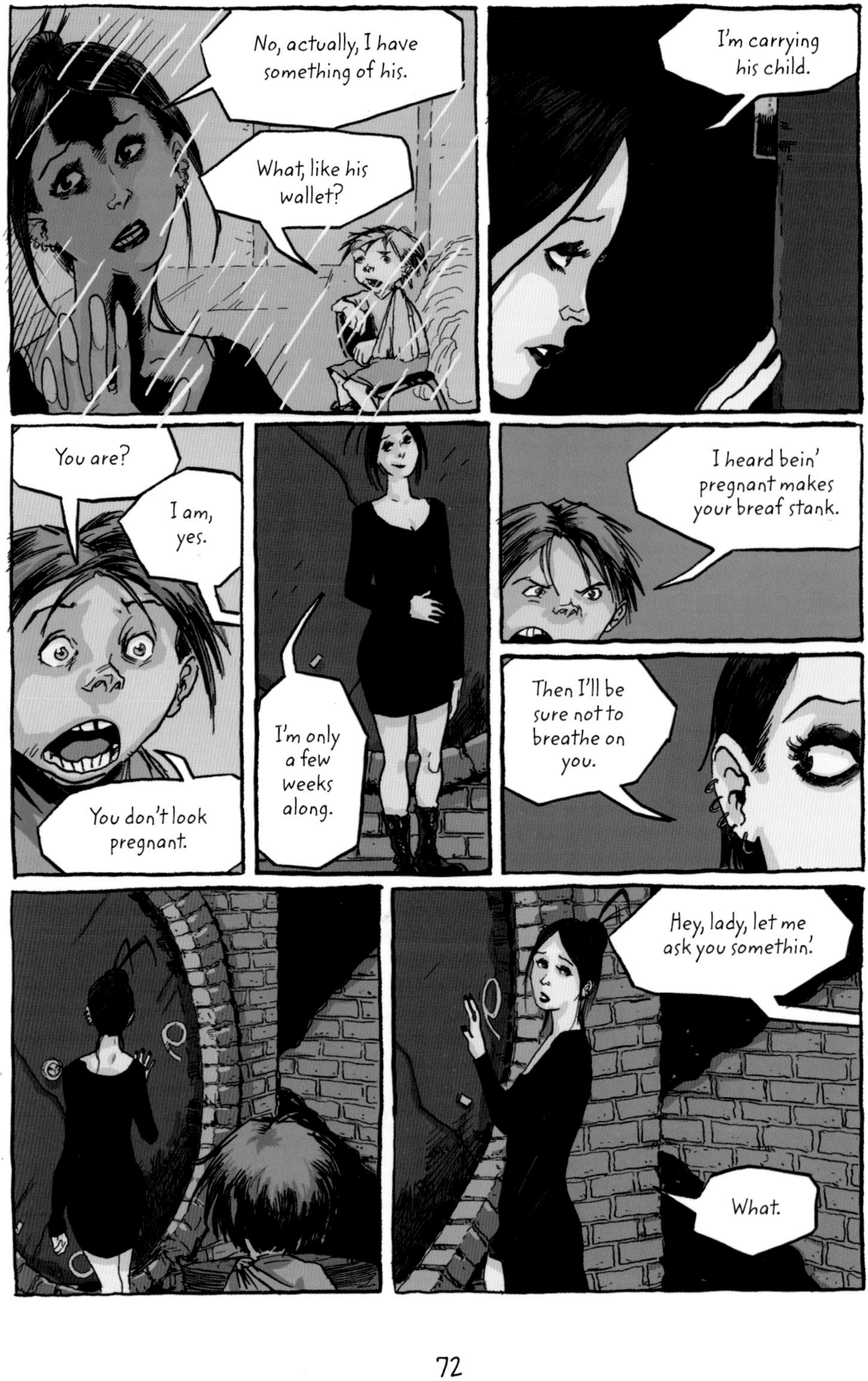
No, actually, I have something of his.
What, like his wallet?
I'm carrying his child.
You are?
I am, yes.
You don't look pregnant.
I'm only a few weeks along.
I heard bein' pregnant makes your breaf stank.
Then I'll be sure not to breathe on you.
Hey, lady, let me ask you somethin'.
What.

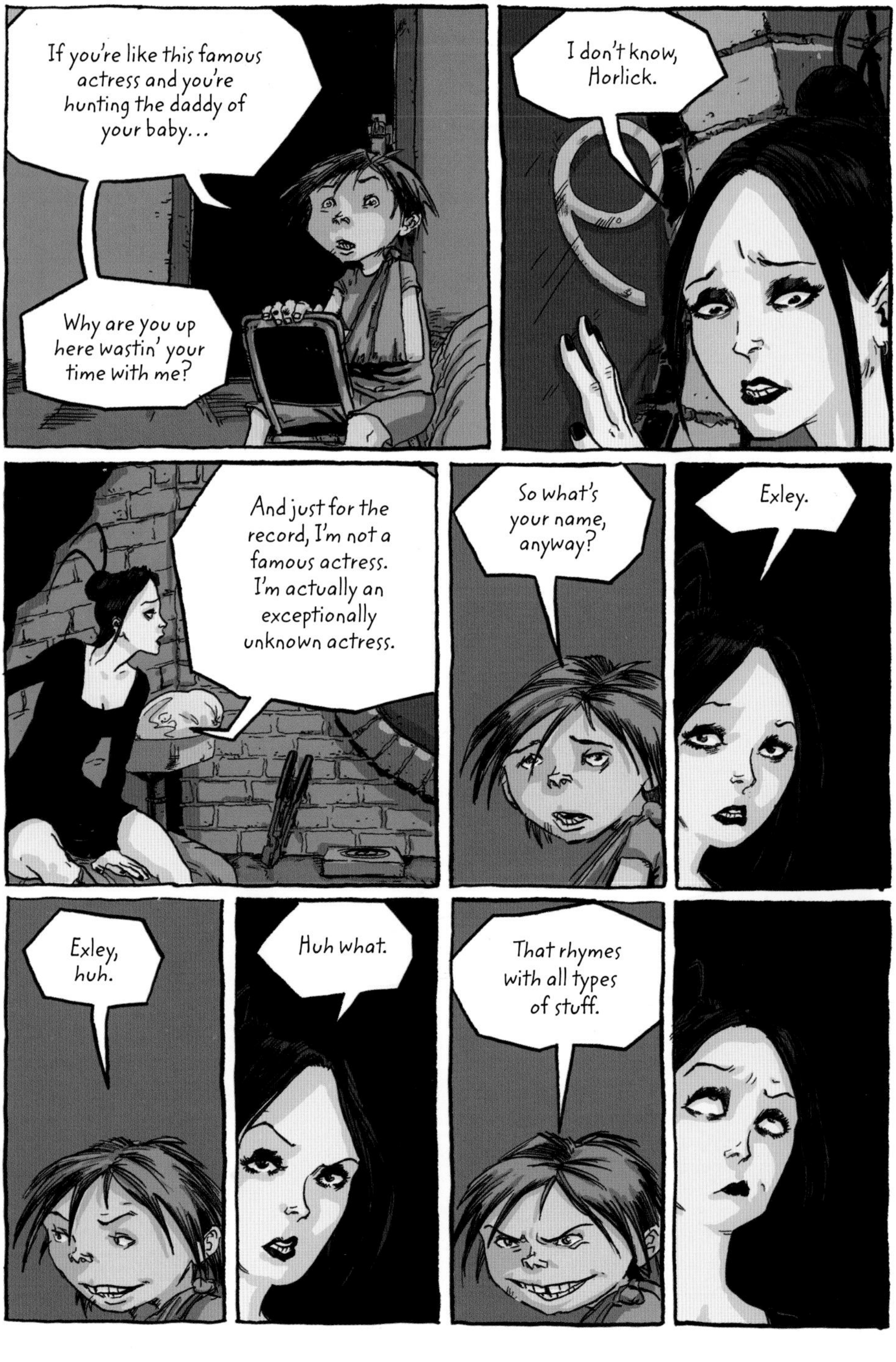
If you're like this famous actress and you're hunting the daddy of your baby...
Why are you up here wastin' your time with me?
I don't know, Horlick.
And just for the record, I'm not a famous actress. I'm actually an exceptionally unknown actress.
So what's your name, anyway?
Exley.
Exley, huh.
Huh what.
That rhymes with all types of stuff.

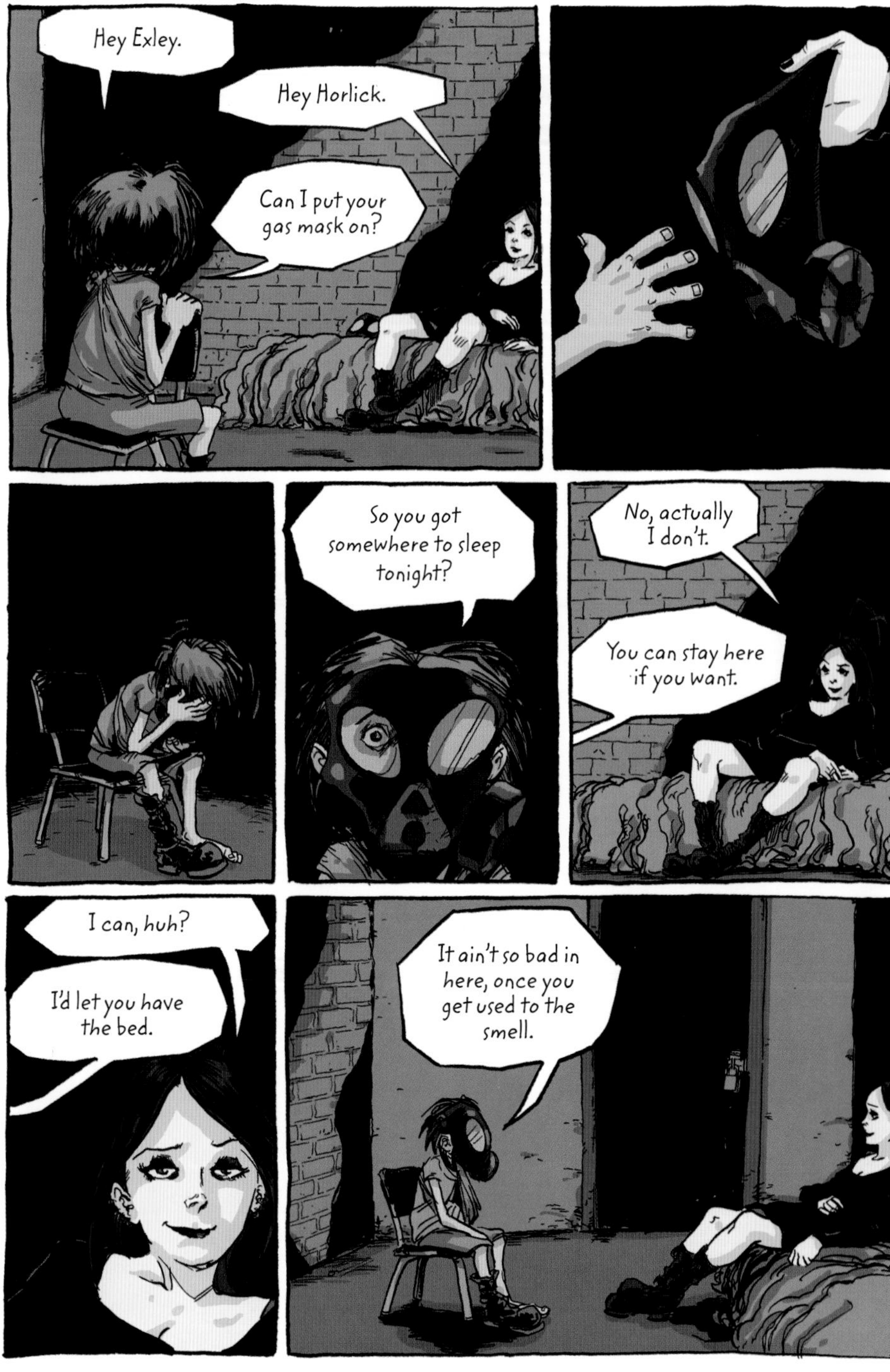
Hey Exley.
Hey Horlick.
Can I put your gas mask on?
So you got somewhere to sleep tonight?
No, actually I don't.
You can stay here if you want.
I can, huh?
I'd let you have the bed.
It ain't so bad in here, once you get used to the smell.

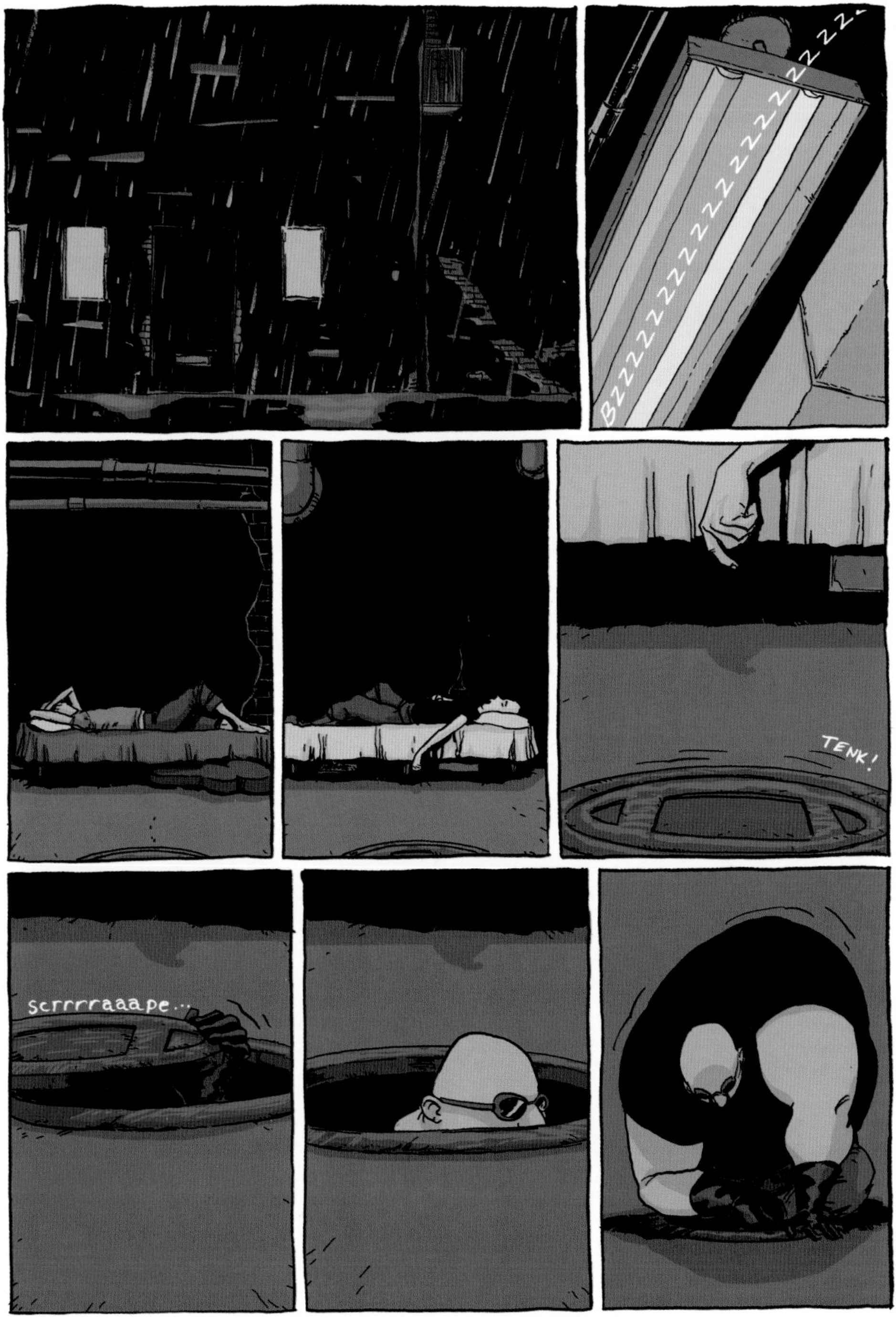
BZZZZZZZZZZZZZZZZZZZ
TENK!
scrrrraaape...

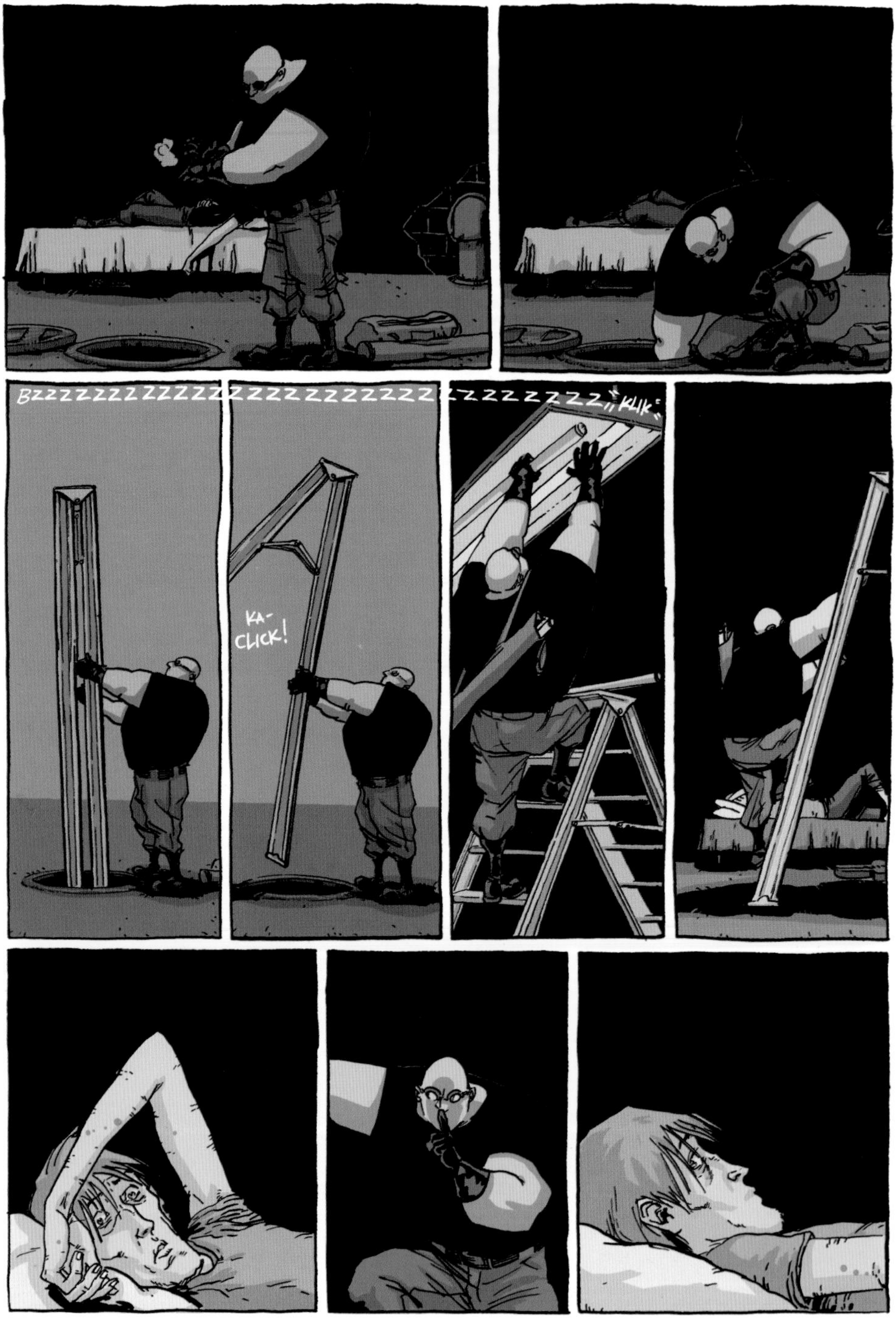
BZZZZZZZZZZZZZZZZZZZZZZZZZZZZZZZZZ
KA-CLICK!
KLIK

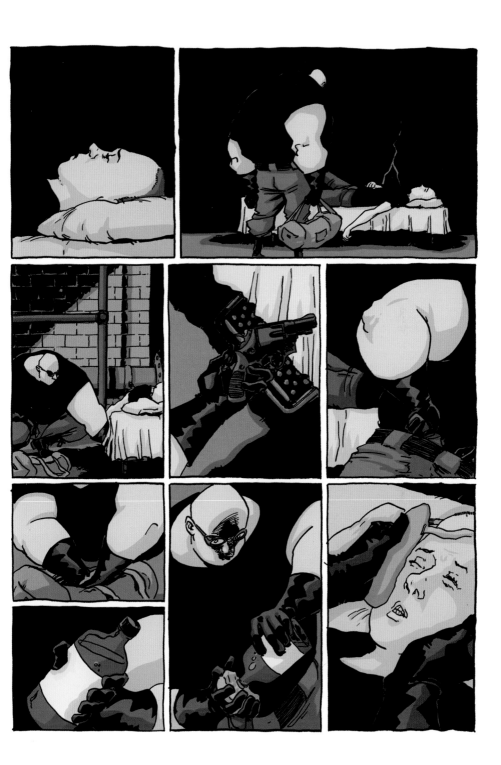

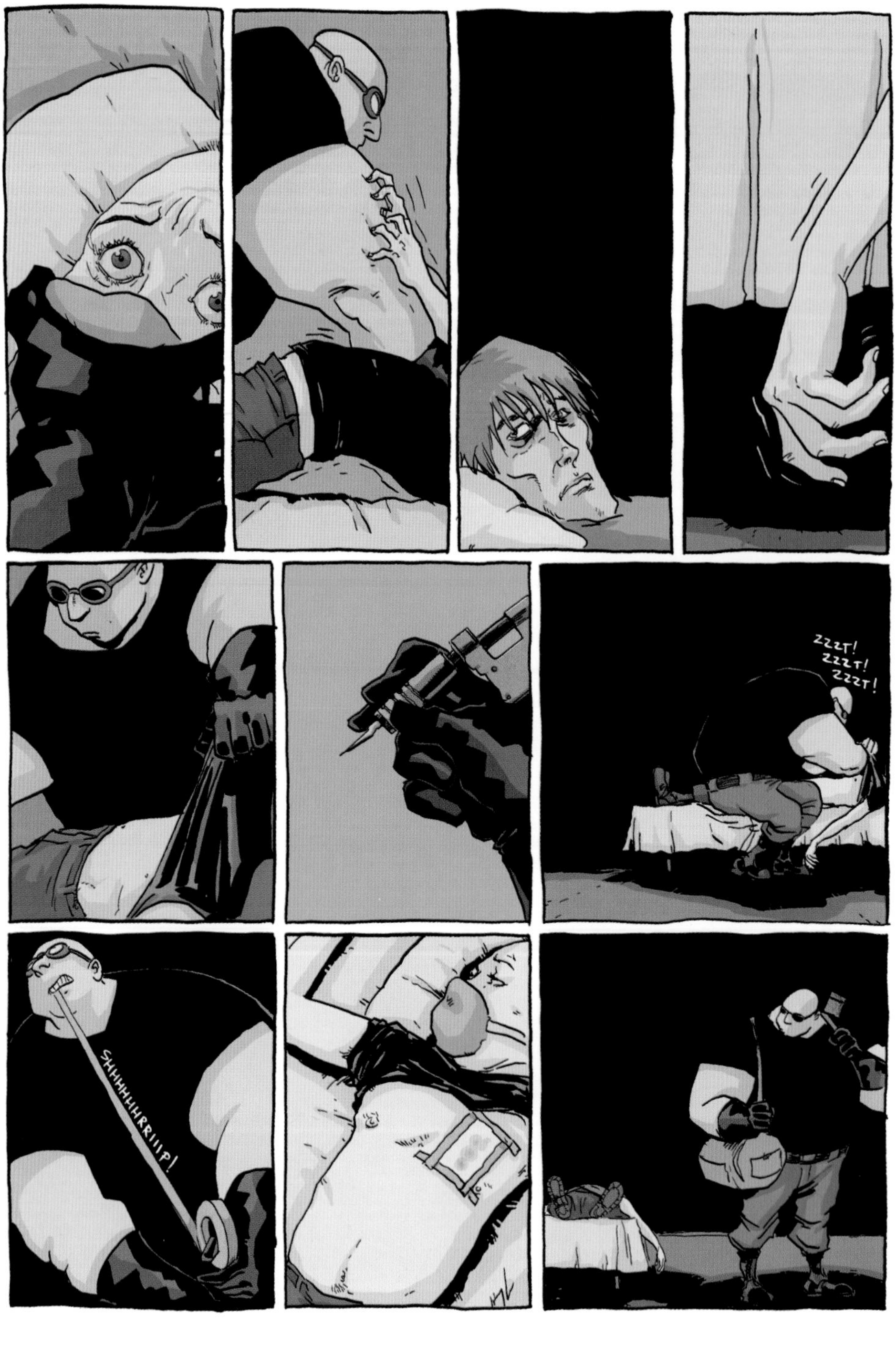
ZZZT!
ZZZT!
ZZZT!
SHHHHHHRRIIIP!

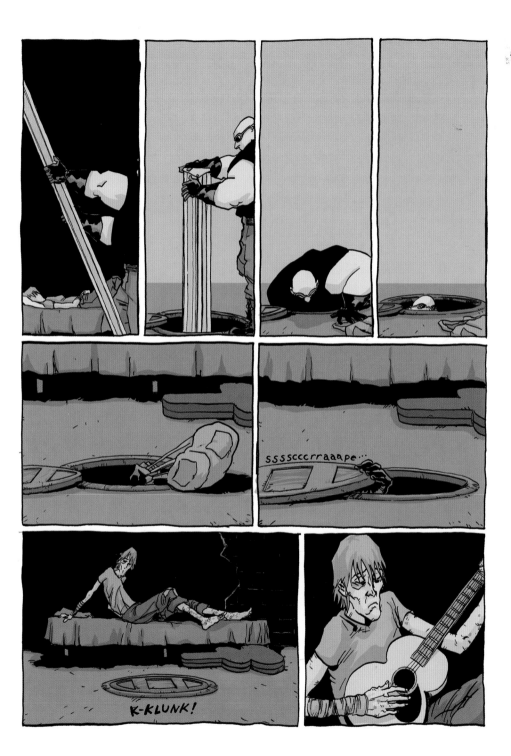

SSSSCCCRRAAAPE...

K-KLUNK!

79

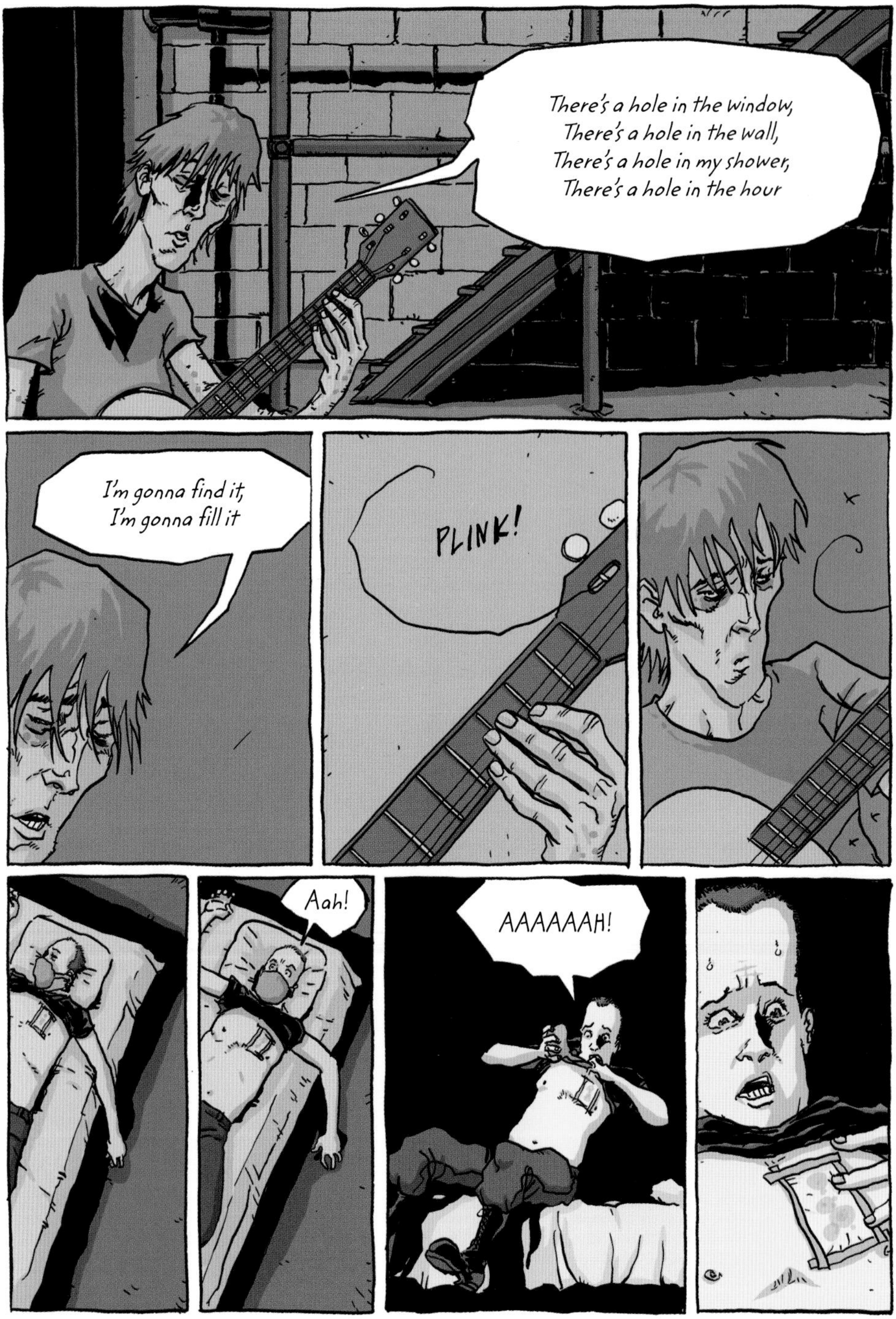

There's a hole in the window,
There's a hole in the wall,
There's a hole in my shower,
There's a hole in the hour
I'm gonna find it,
I'm gonna fill it
PLINK!
Aah!
AAAAAAH!

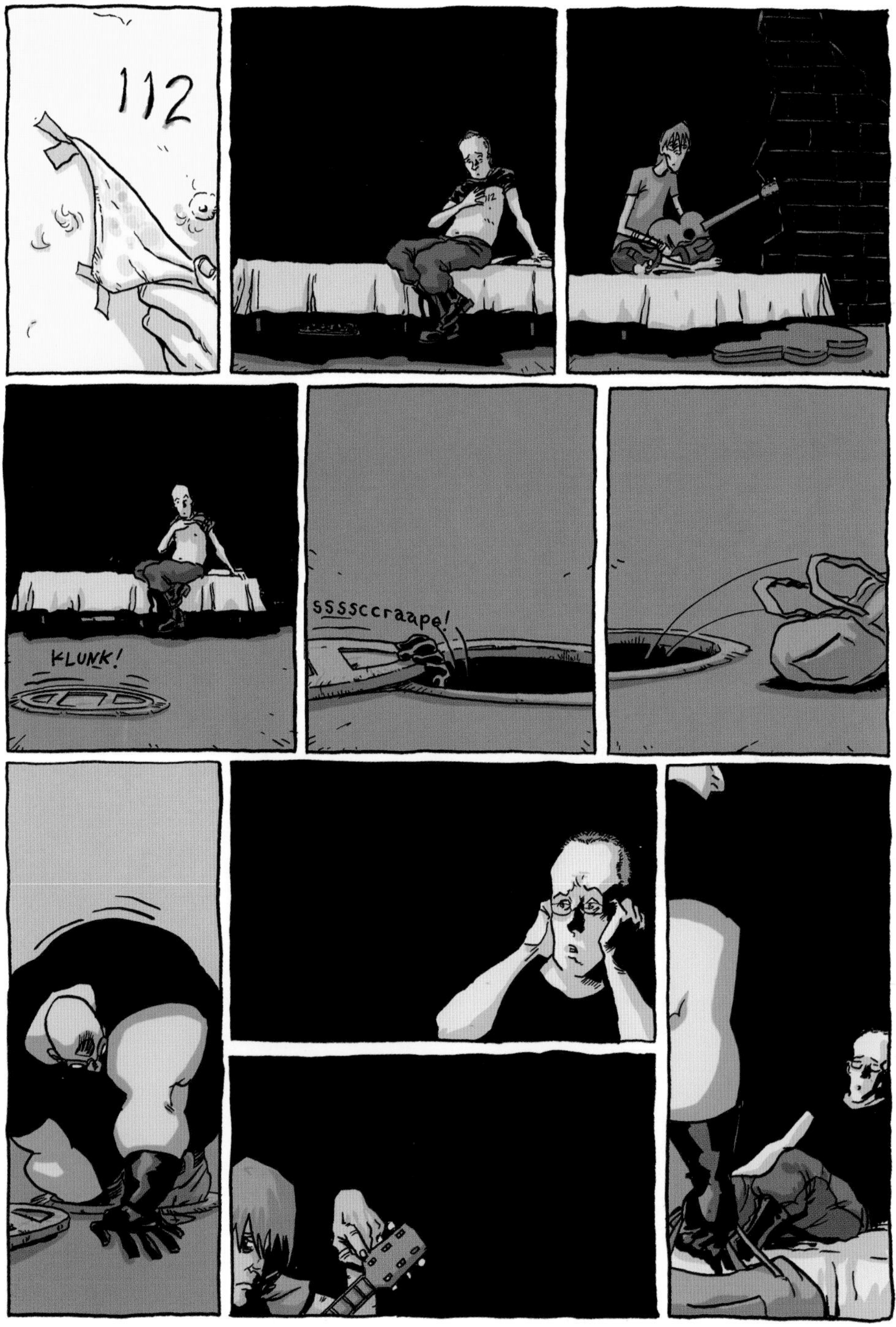
112
KLUNK!
sssssccraape!

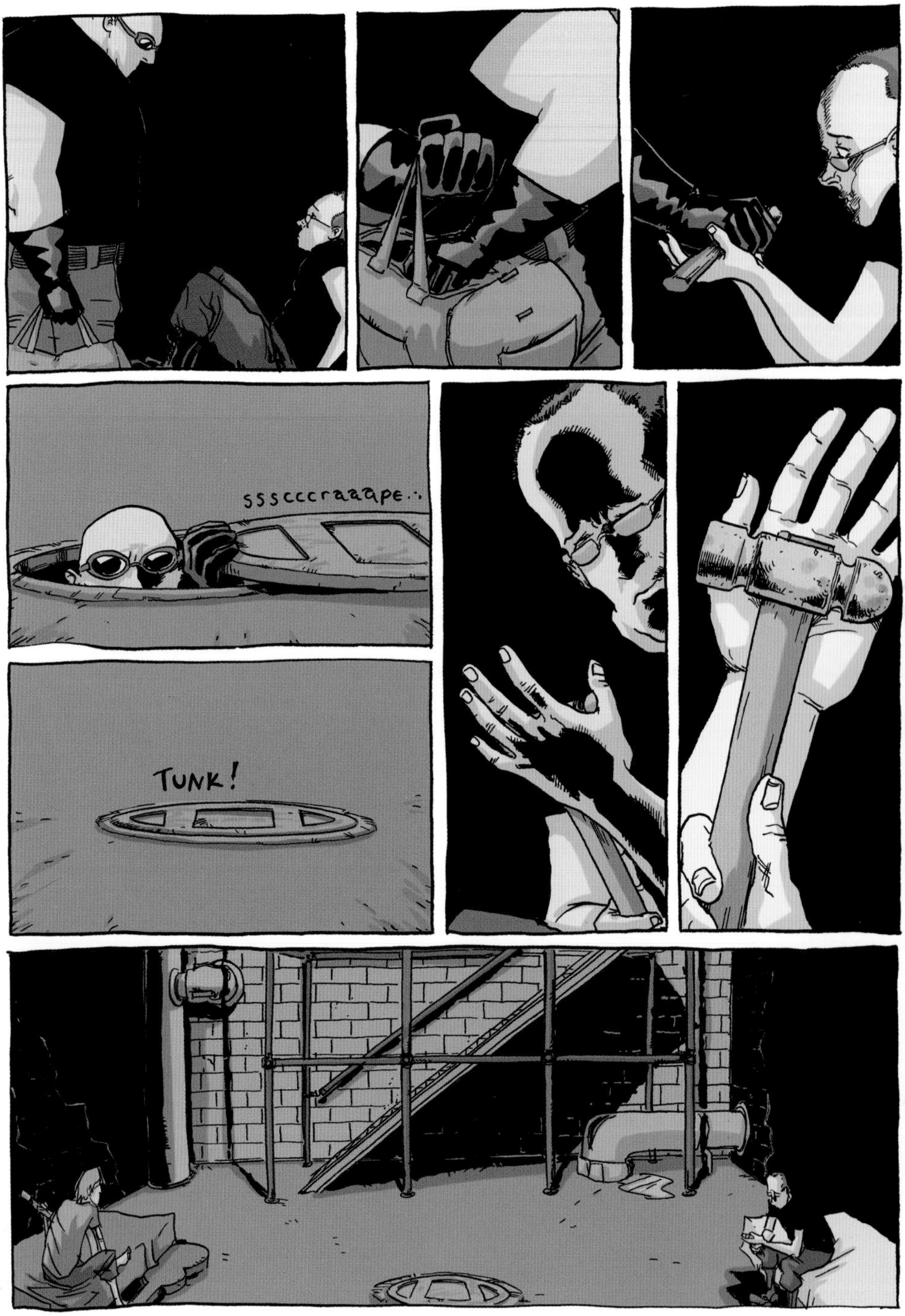
sssscccraaape...
TUNK!

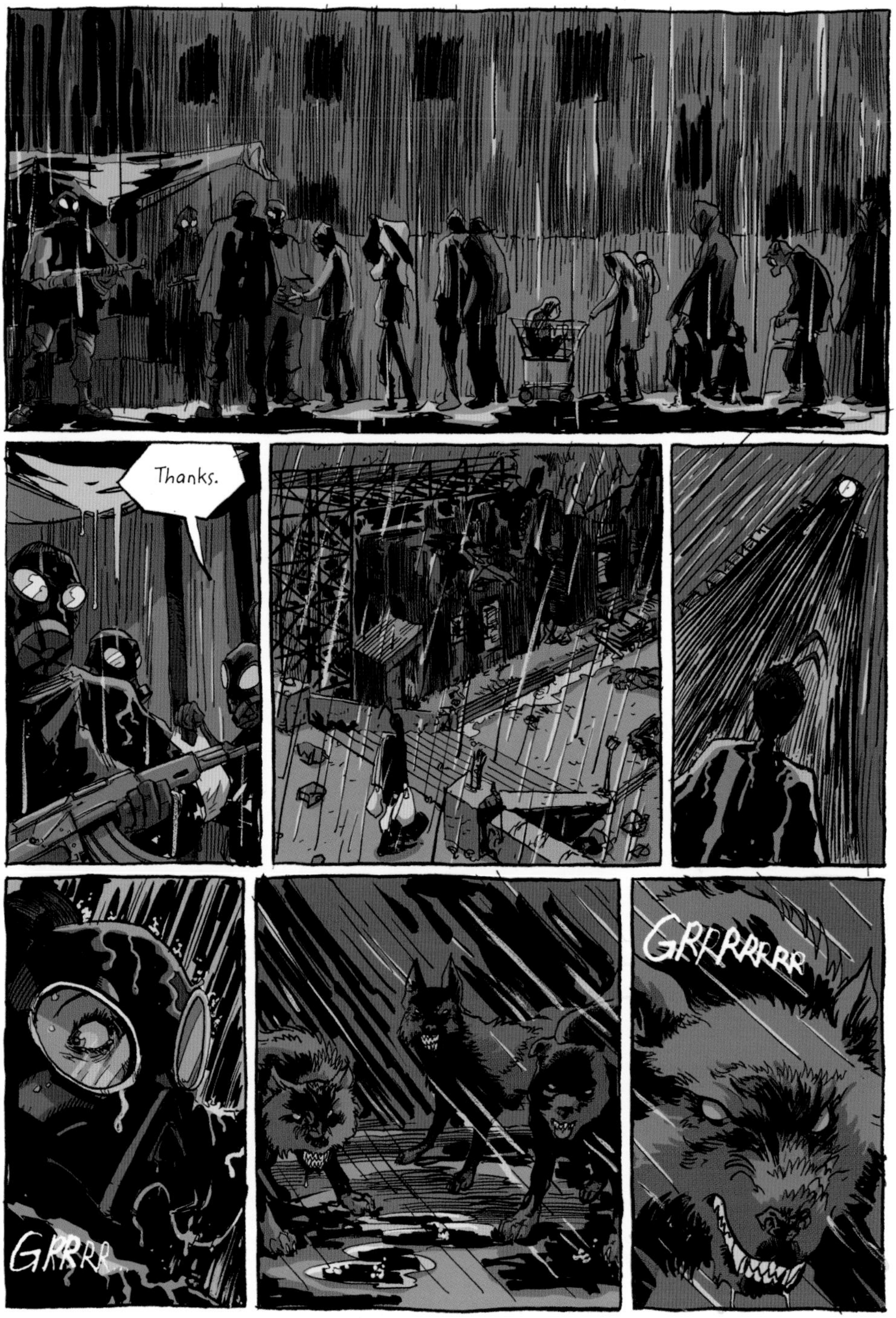
Thanks.
GRRRR...
GRRRRRRRR

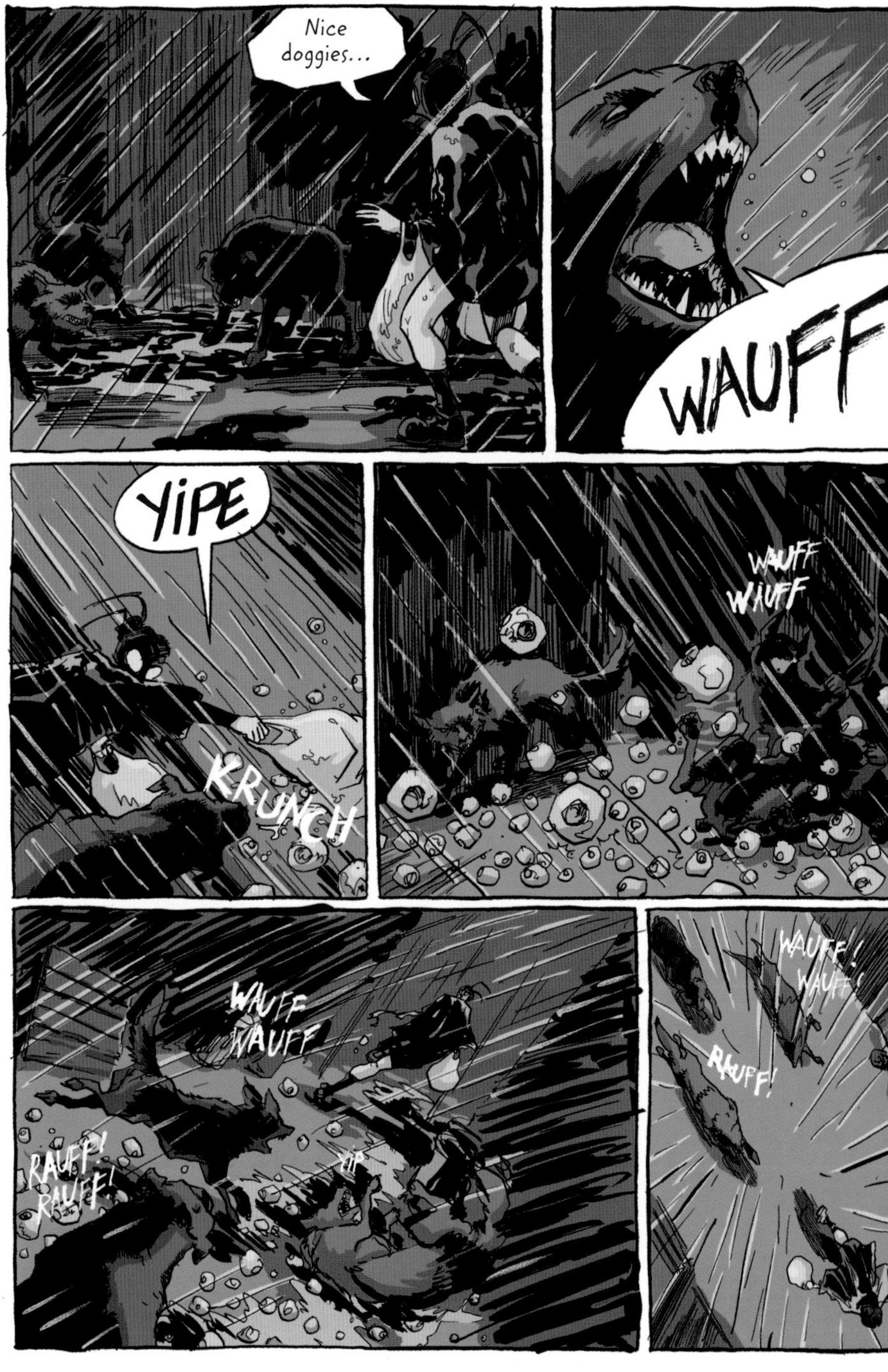
Nice doggies...
WAUFF
YIPE
KRUNCH
WAUFF
WAUFF
WAUFF
WAUFF
RAUFF! RAUFF!
YIP
WAUFF!
WAUFF!
RAUFF!

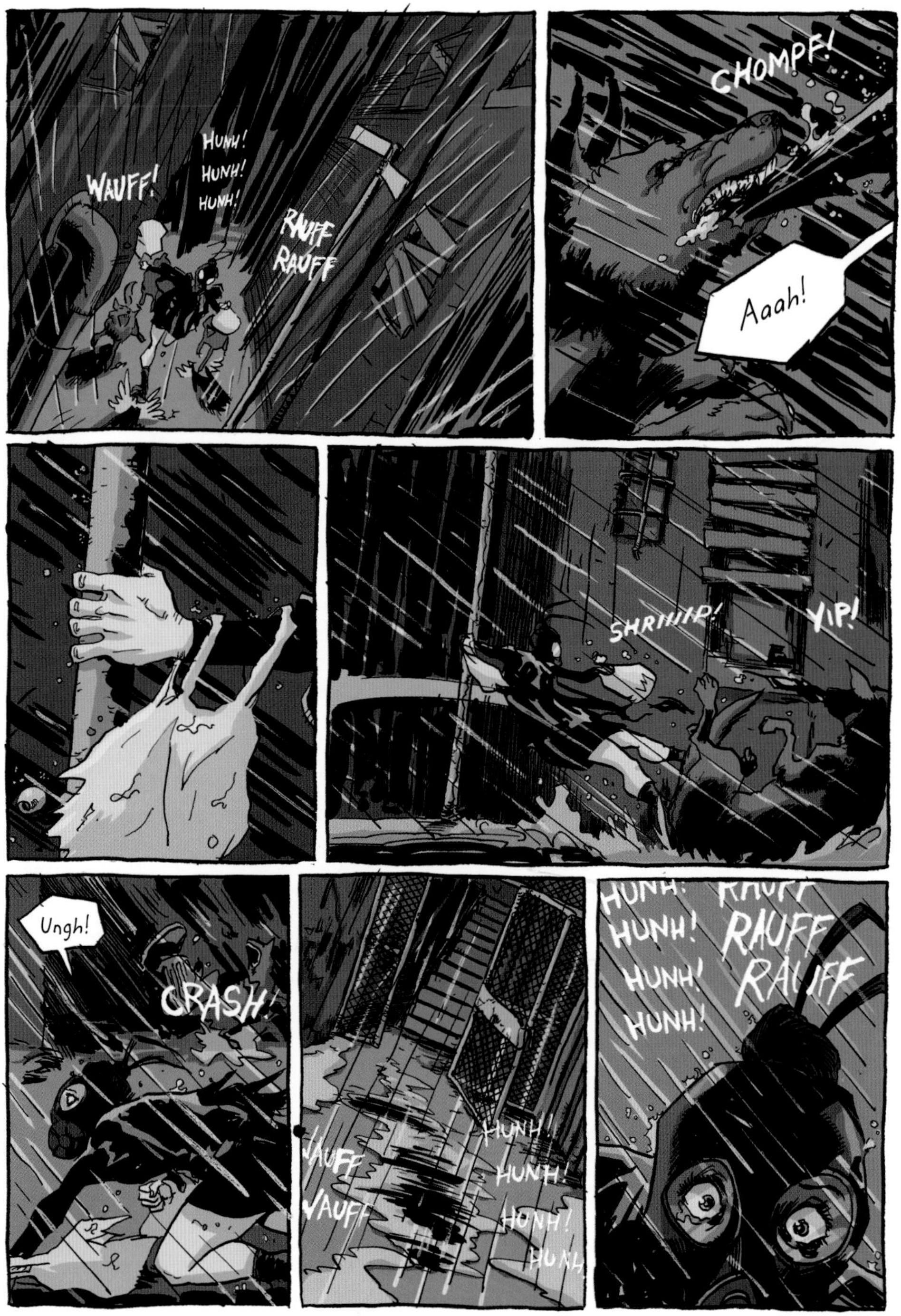
WAUFF!
HUNH!
HUNH!
HUNH!
RAUFF
RAUFF
CHOMPF!
Aaah!
SHRIIIIP!
YIP!
Ungh!
CRASH!
WAUFF
WAUFF
HUNH!
HUNH!
HUNH!
HUNH
HUNH!
HUNH!
HUNH!
HUNH!
RAUFF
RAUFF
RAUFF

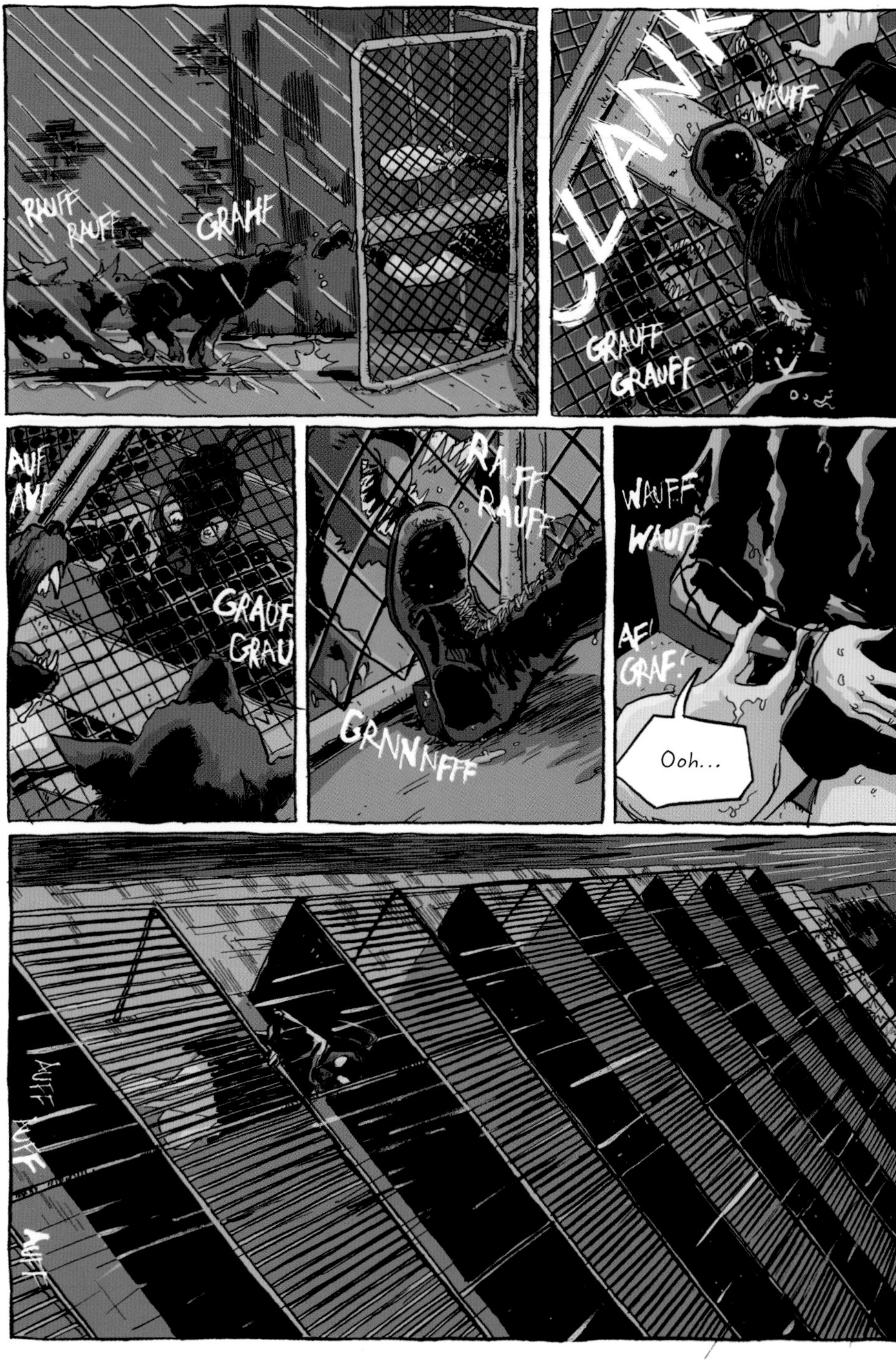
RAUFF
RAUFF
GRAHF
CLANK
WAUFF
GRAUFF
GRAUFF
AUF
AUF
GRAUF
GRAU
RAUFF
RAUFF
GRNNNFFF
WAUFF
WAUFF
AF!
GRAF!
Ooh...
AUFF
AUFF
AUFF

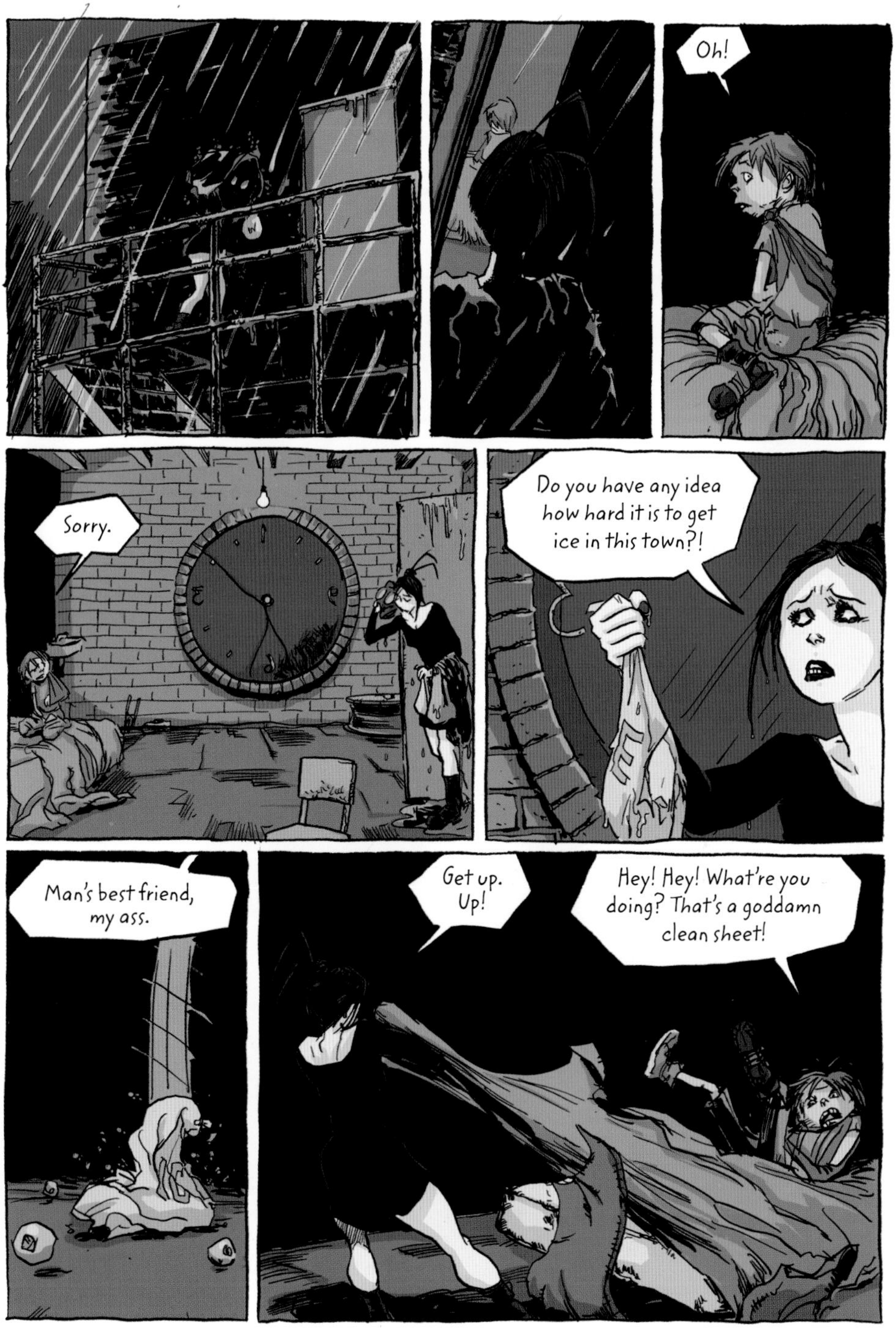
Oh!
Sorry.
Do you have any idea how hard it is to get ice in this town?!
Man's best friend, my ass.
Get up. Up!
Hey! Hey! What're you doing? That's a goddamn clean sheet!

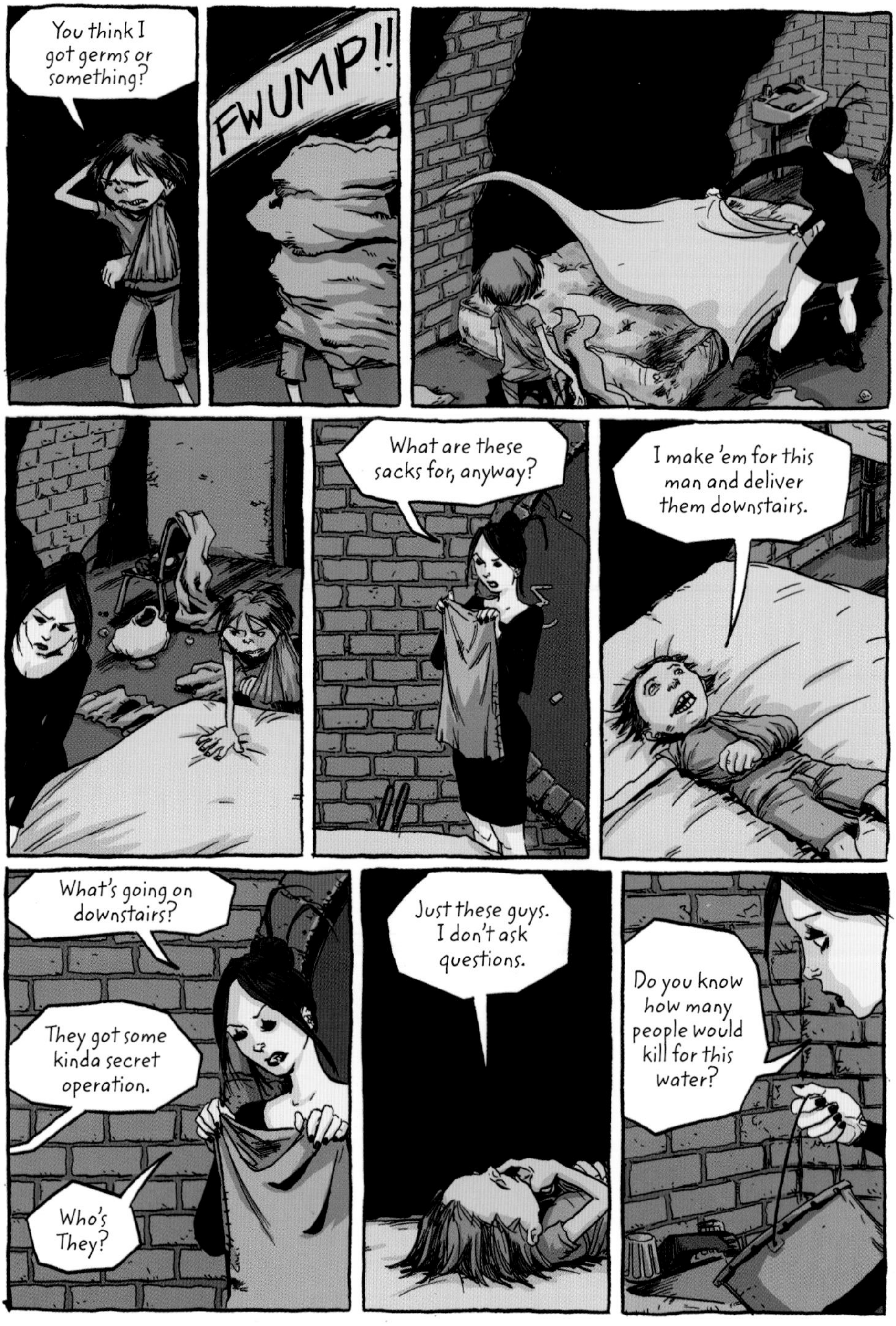
You think I got germs or something?
FWUMP!!
What are these sacks for, anyway?
I make 'em for this man and deliver them downstairs.
What's going on downstairs?
They got some kinda secret operation.
Who's They?
Just these guys. I don't ask questions.
Do you know how many people would kill for this water?

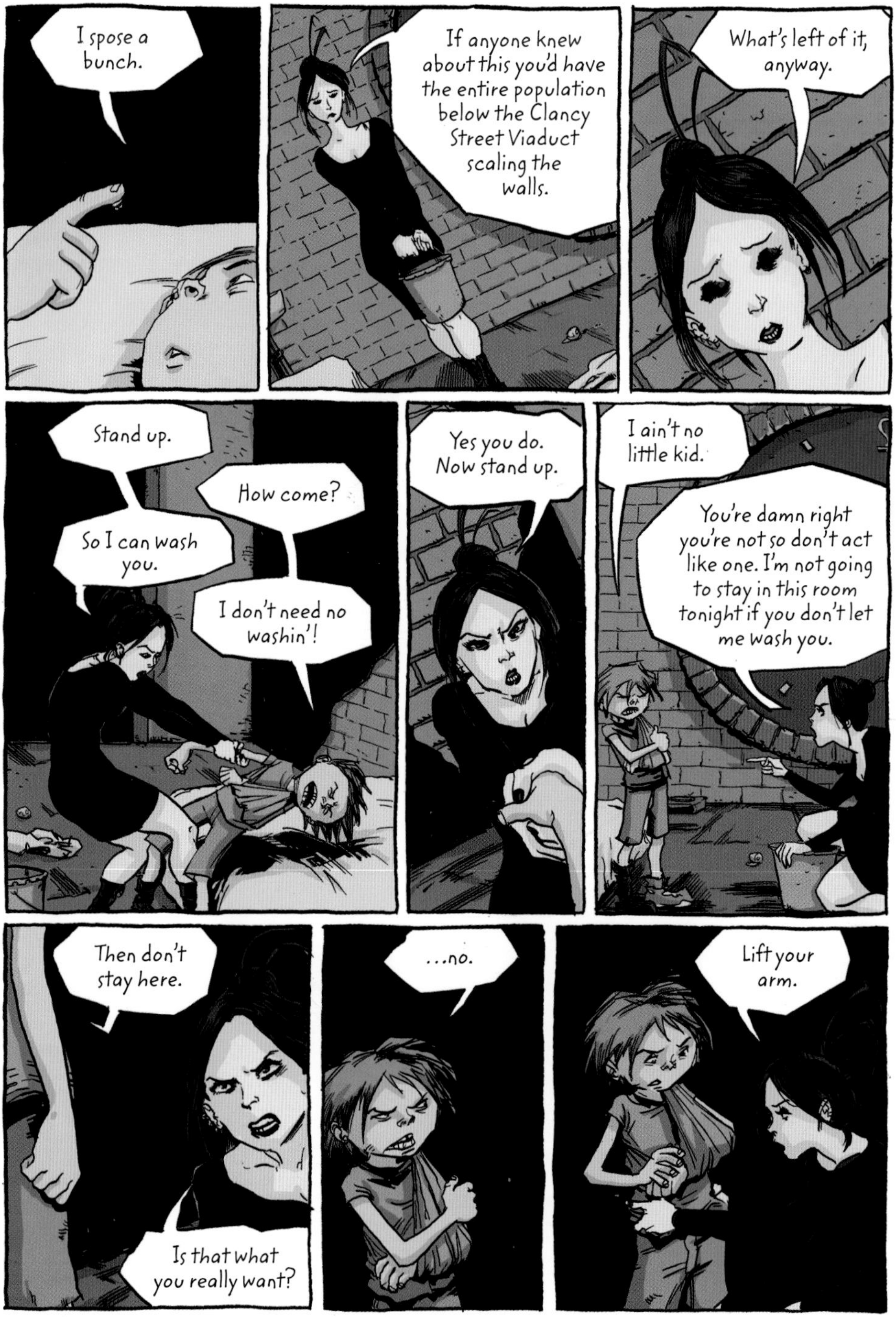
I spose a bunch.
If anyone knew about this you'd have the entire population below the Clancy Street Viaduct scaling the walls.
What's left of it, anyway.
Stand up.
How come?
So I can wash you.
I don't need no washin'!
Yes you do. Now stand up.
I ain't no little kid.
You're damn right you're not so don't act like one. I'm not going to stay in this room tonight if you don't let me wash you.
Then don't stay here.
Is that what you really want?
...no.
Lift your arm.

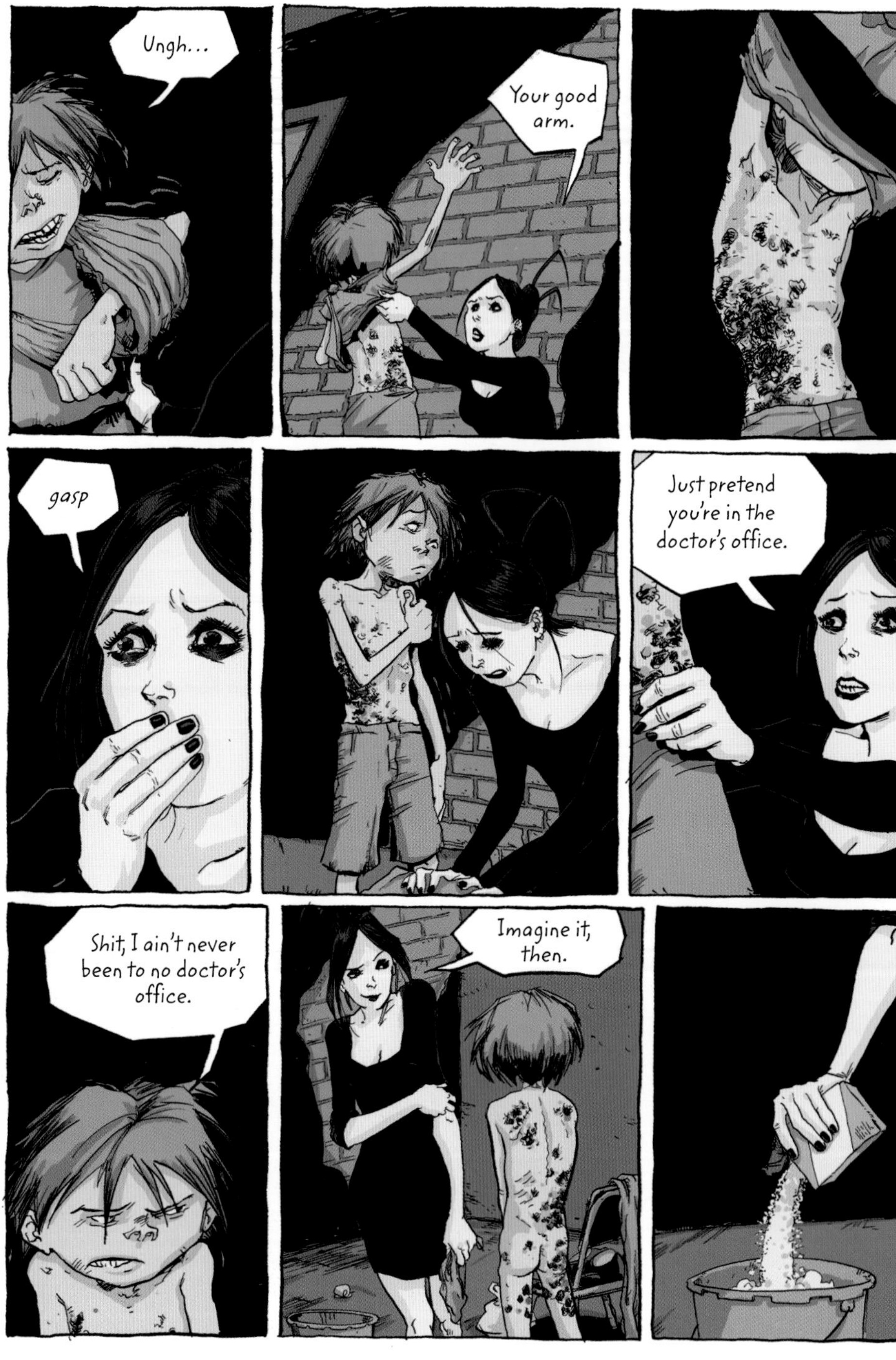

Ungh...
Your good arm.
gasp
Just pretend you're in the doctor's office.
Shit, I ain't never been to no doctor's office.
Imagine it, then.

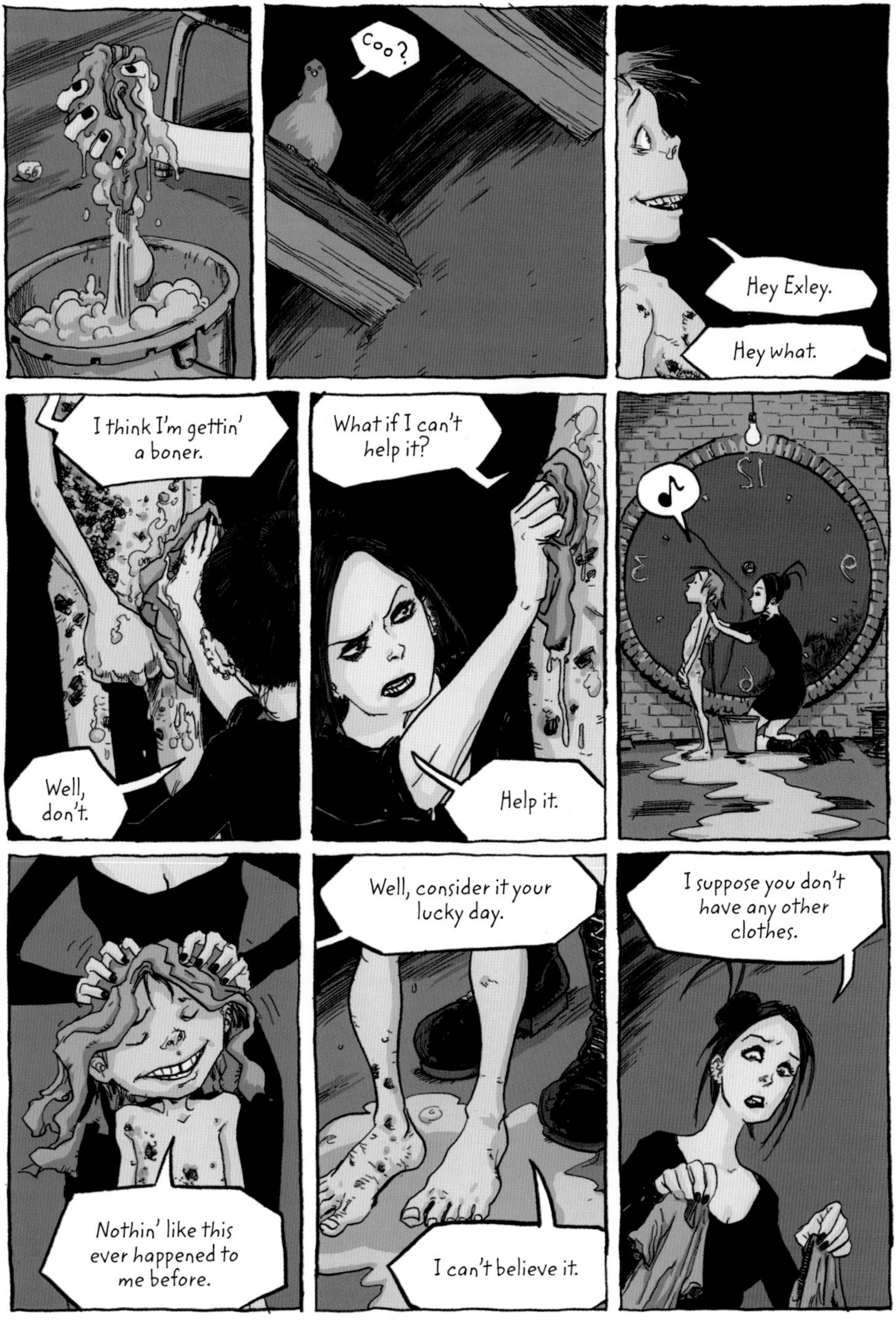
Coo?
Hey Exley.
Hey what.
I think I'm gettin' a boner.
Well, don't.
What if I can't help it?
Help it.
Nothin' like this ever happened to me before.
Well, consider it your lucky day.
I can't believe it.
I suppose you don't have any other clothes.

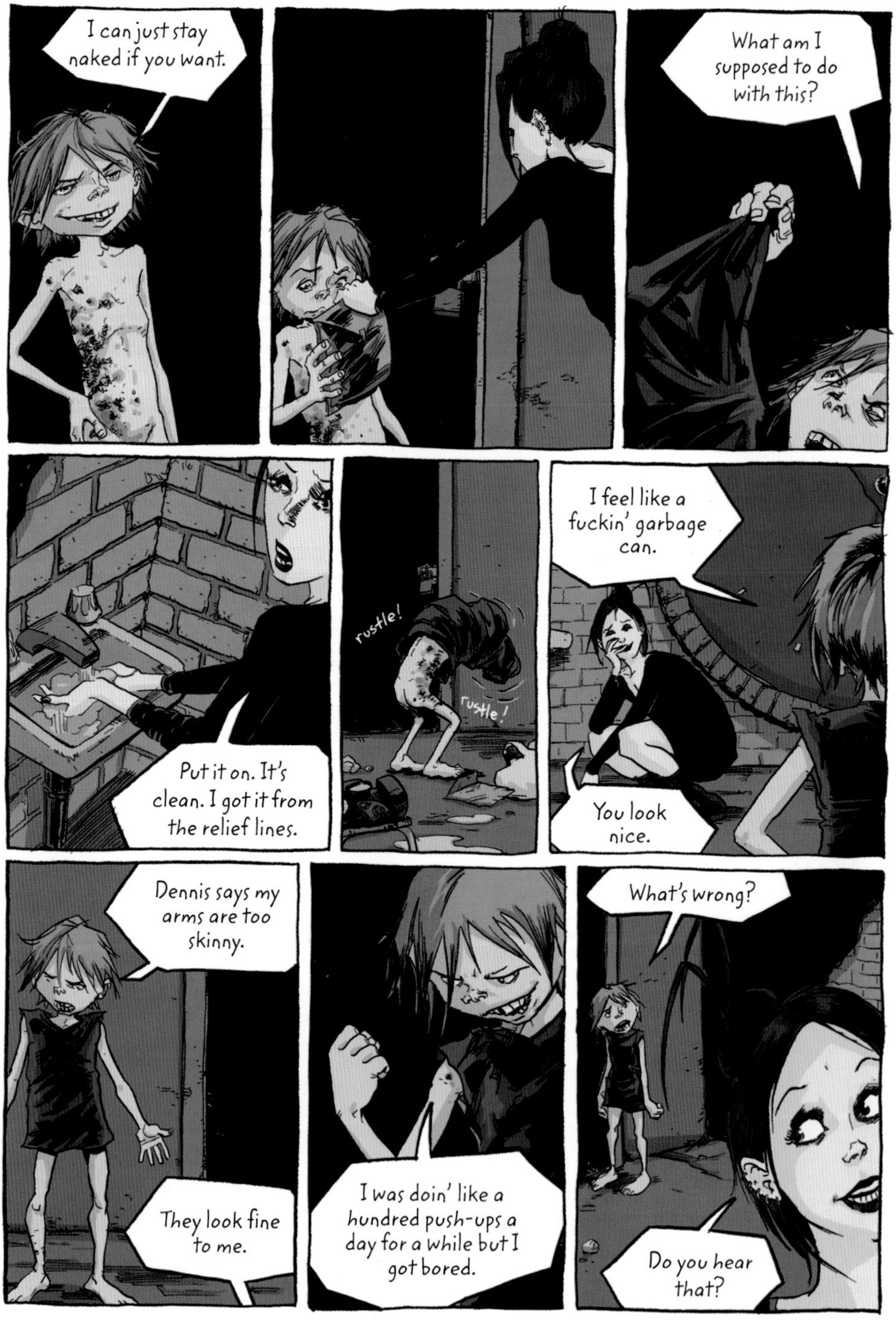
I can just stay naked if you want.
What am I supposed to do with this?
Put it on. It's clean. I got it from the relief lines.
rustle!
rustle!
I feel like a fuckin' garbage can.
You look nice.
Dennis says my arms are too skinny.
They look fine to me.
I was doin' like a hundred push-ups a day for a while but I got bored.
What's wrong?
Do you hear that?

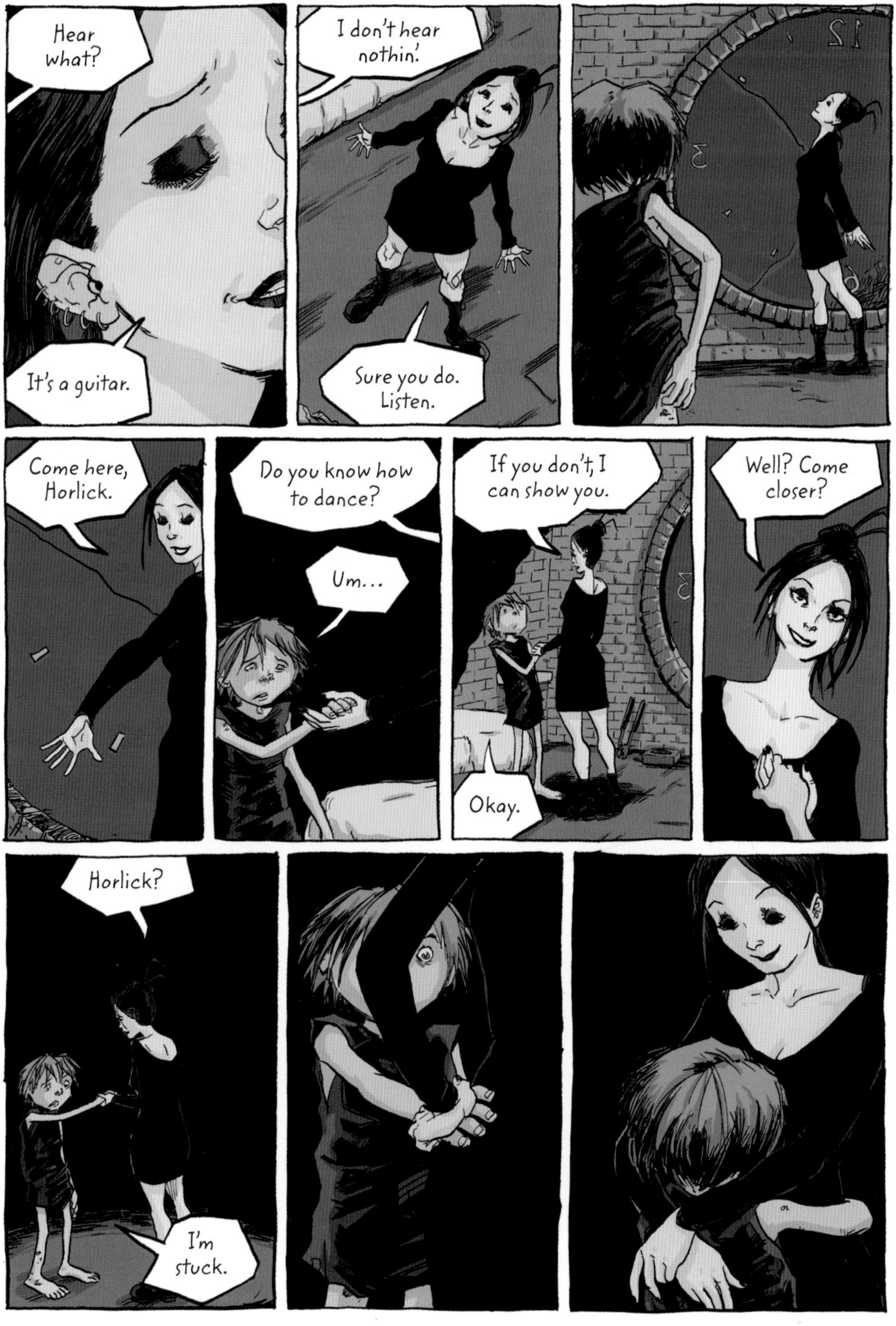
Hear what?
It's a guitar.
I don't hear nothin.'
Sure you do. Listen.
Come here, Horlick.
Do you know how to dance?
Um...
If you don't, I can show you.
Okay.
Well? Come closer?
Horlick?
I'm stuck.

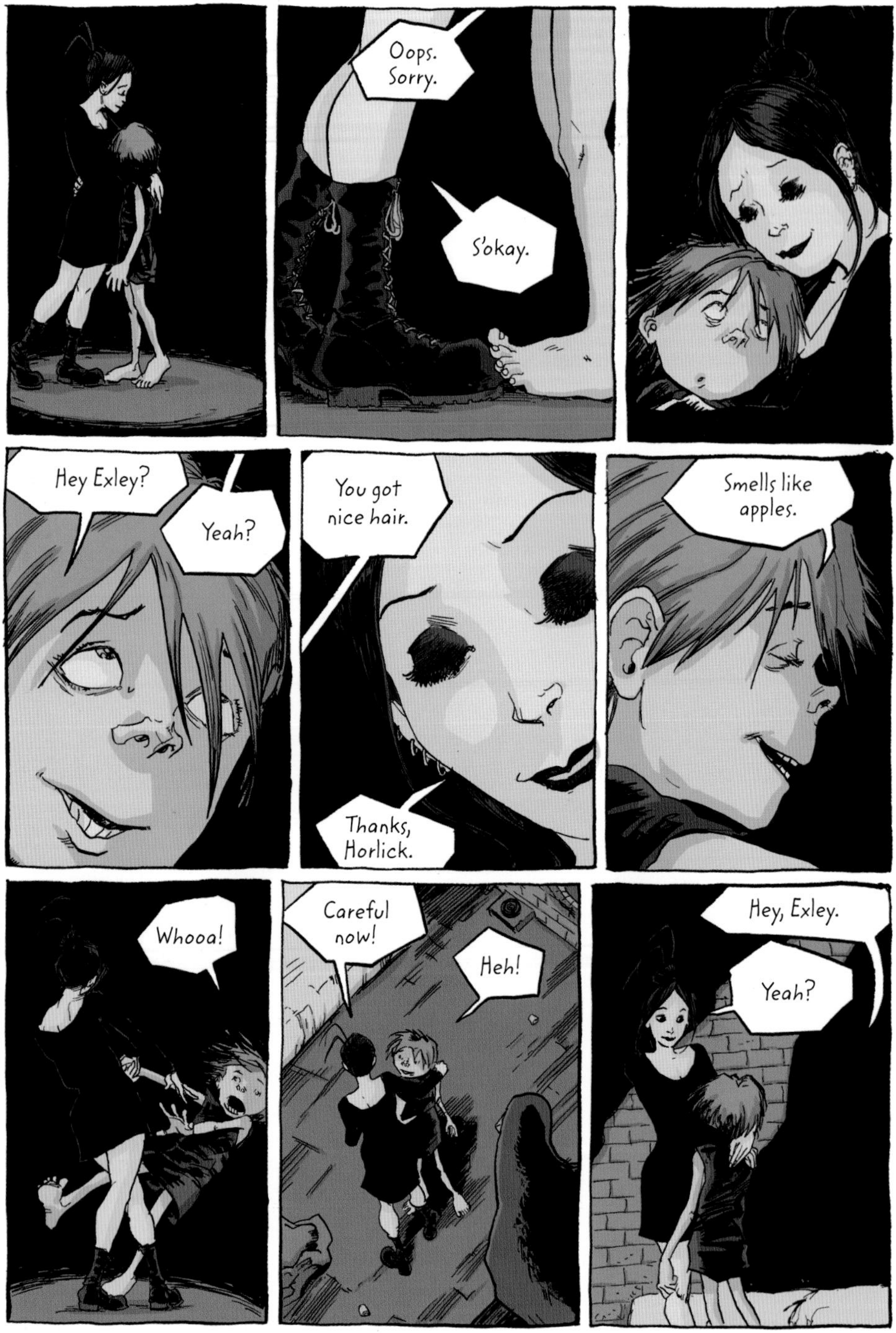
Oops. Sorry.
S'okay.
Hey Exley?
Yeah?
You got nice hair.
Thanks, Horlick.
Smells like apples.
Whooa!
Careful now!
Heh!
Hey, Exley.
Yeah?

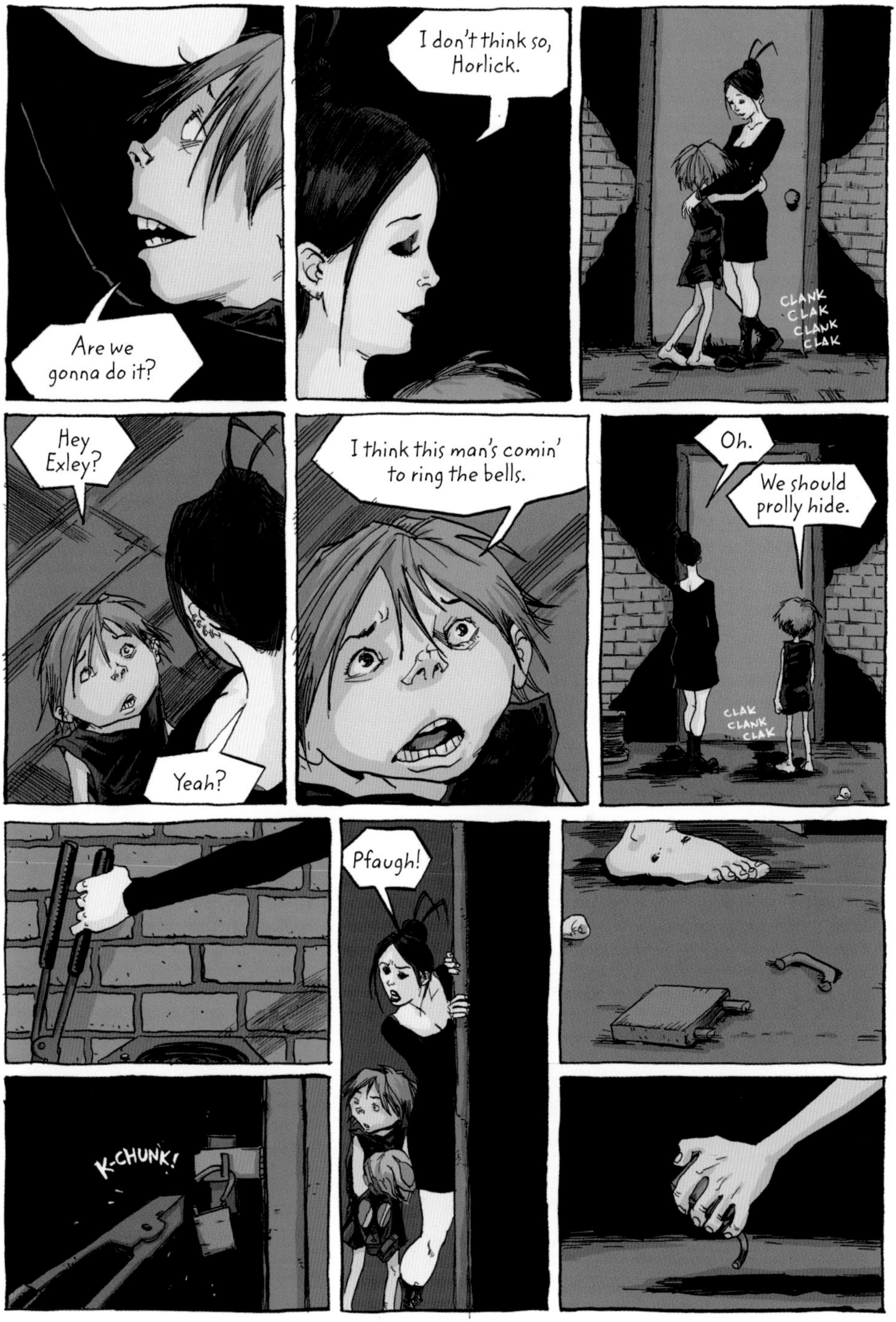
Are we gonna do it?
I don't think so, Horlick.
CLANK CLAK CLANK CLAK
Hey Exley?
Yeah?
I think this man's comin' to ring the bells.
Oh.
We should prolly hide.
CLAK CLANK CLAK
Pfaugh!
K-CHUNK!

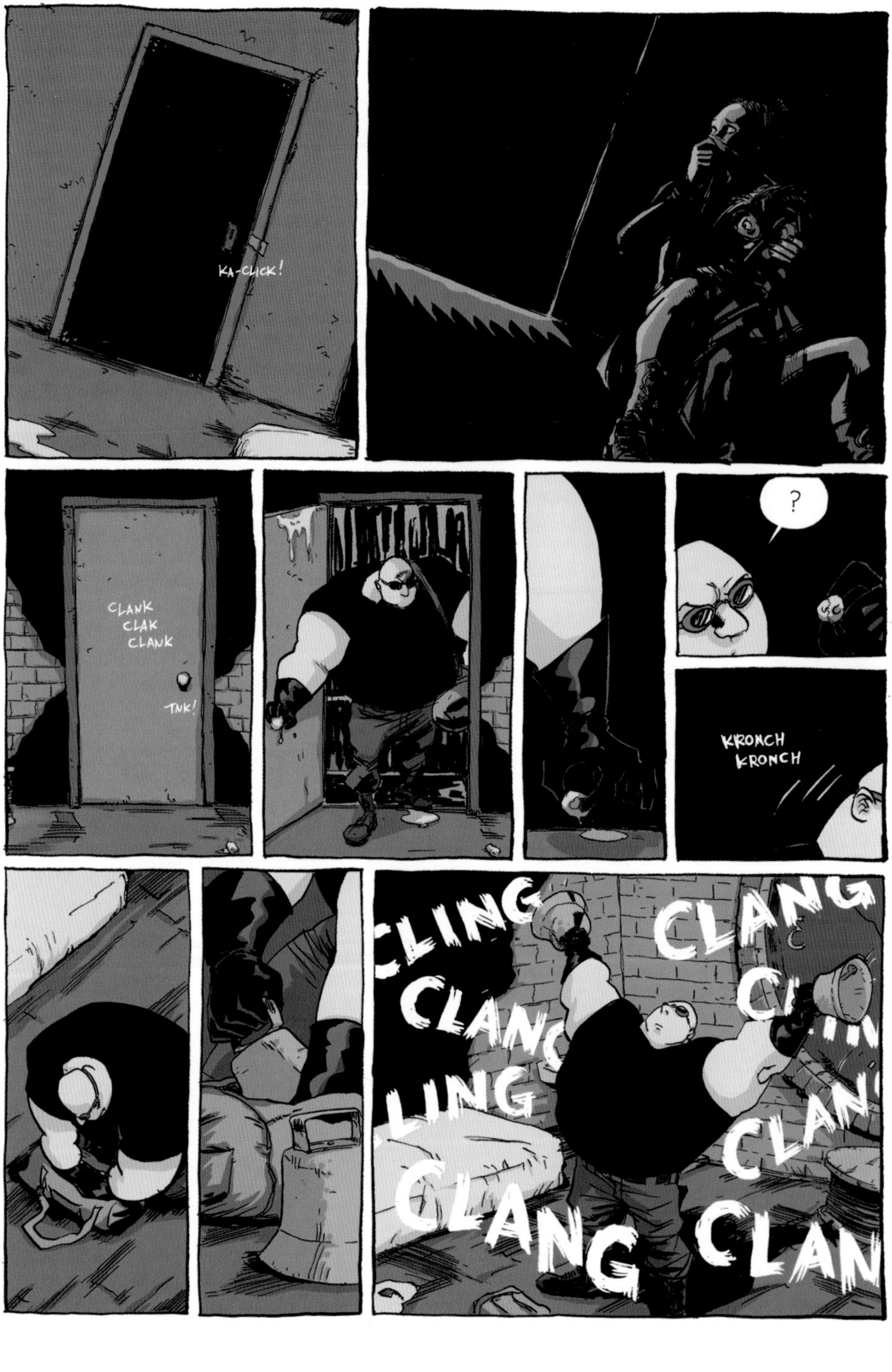
KA-CLICK!
CLANK
CLAK
CLANK
TNK!
?
KRONCH
KRONCH
CLING
CLANG
CLANG
LING
CLANG
CLANG
CLANG
CLANG
CLANG
CLAN

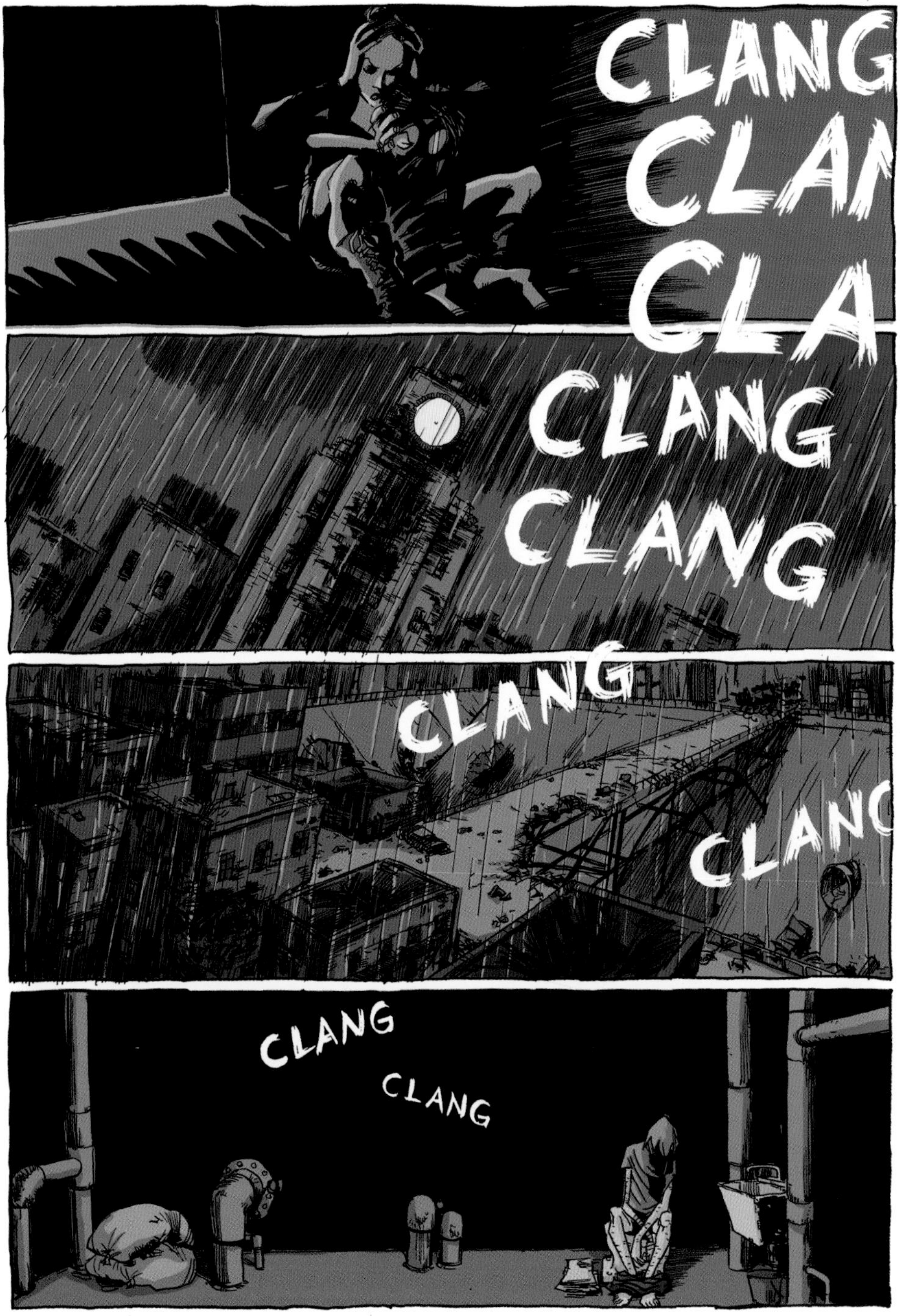
CLANG
CLAN
CLA
CLANG
CLANG
CLANG
CLAN
CLANG
CLANG

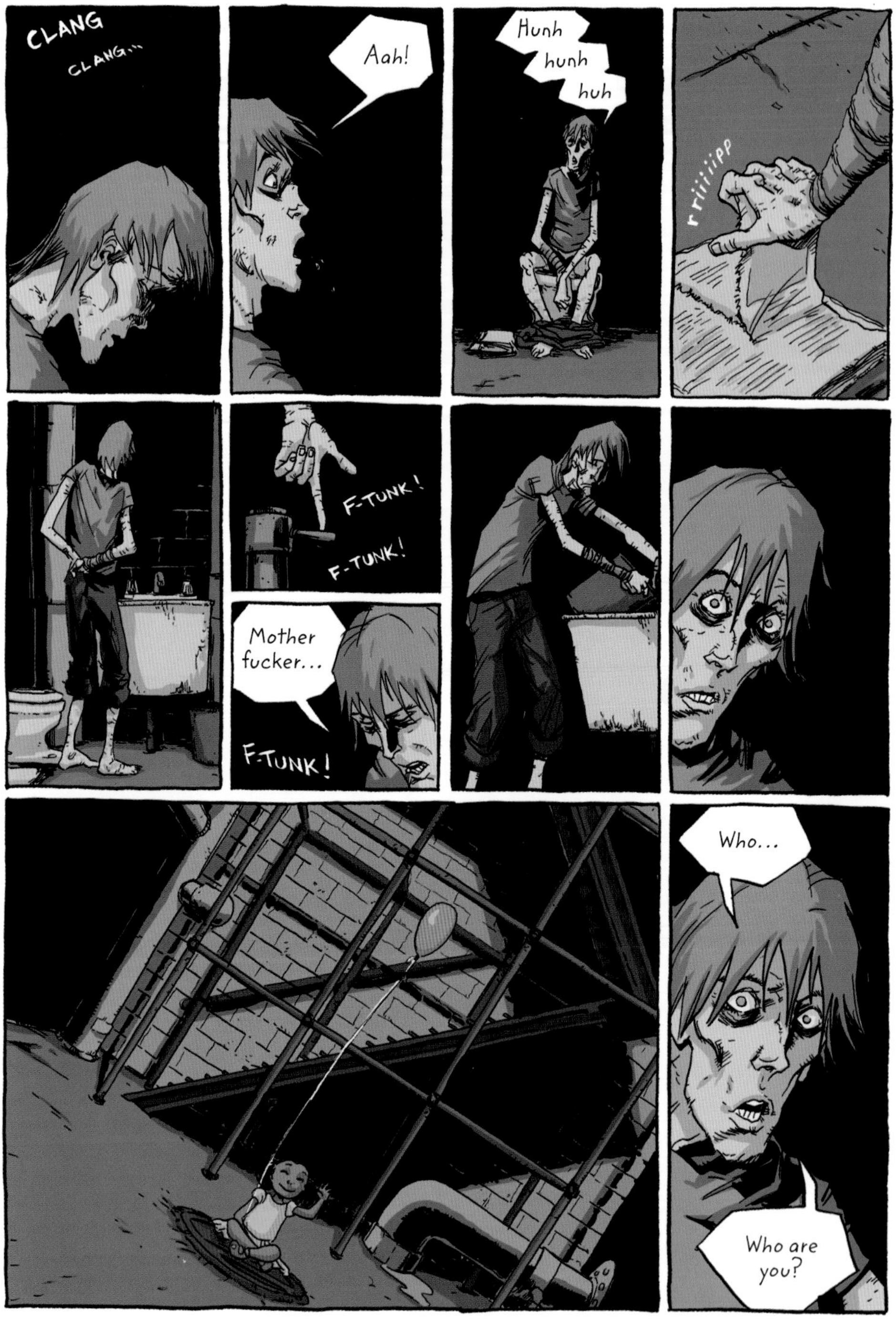
CLANG
CLANG...
Aah!
Hunh hunh huh
rriiiiiipp
F-TUNK!
F-TUNK!
Mother fucker...
F-TUNK!
Who...
Who are you?

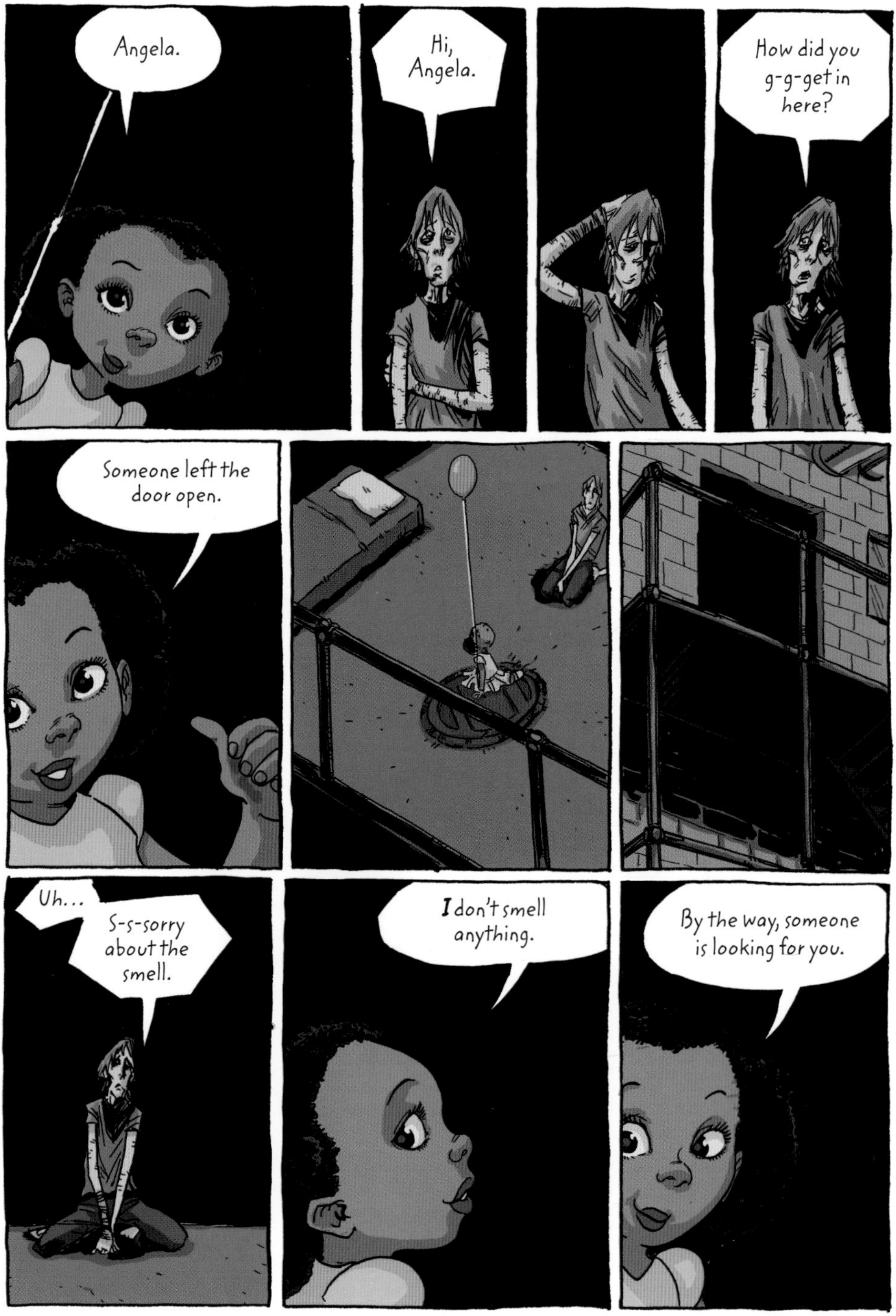
Angela.
Hi, Angela.
How did you g-g-get in here?
Someone left the door open.
Uh...
S-s-sorry about the smell.
I don't smell anything.
By the way, someone is looking for you.

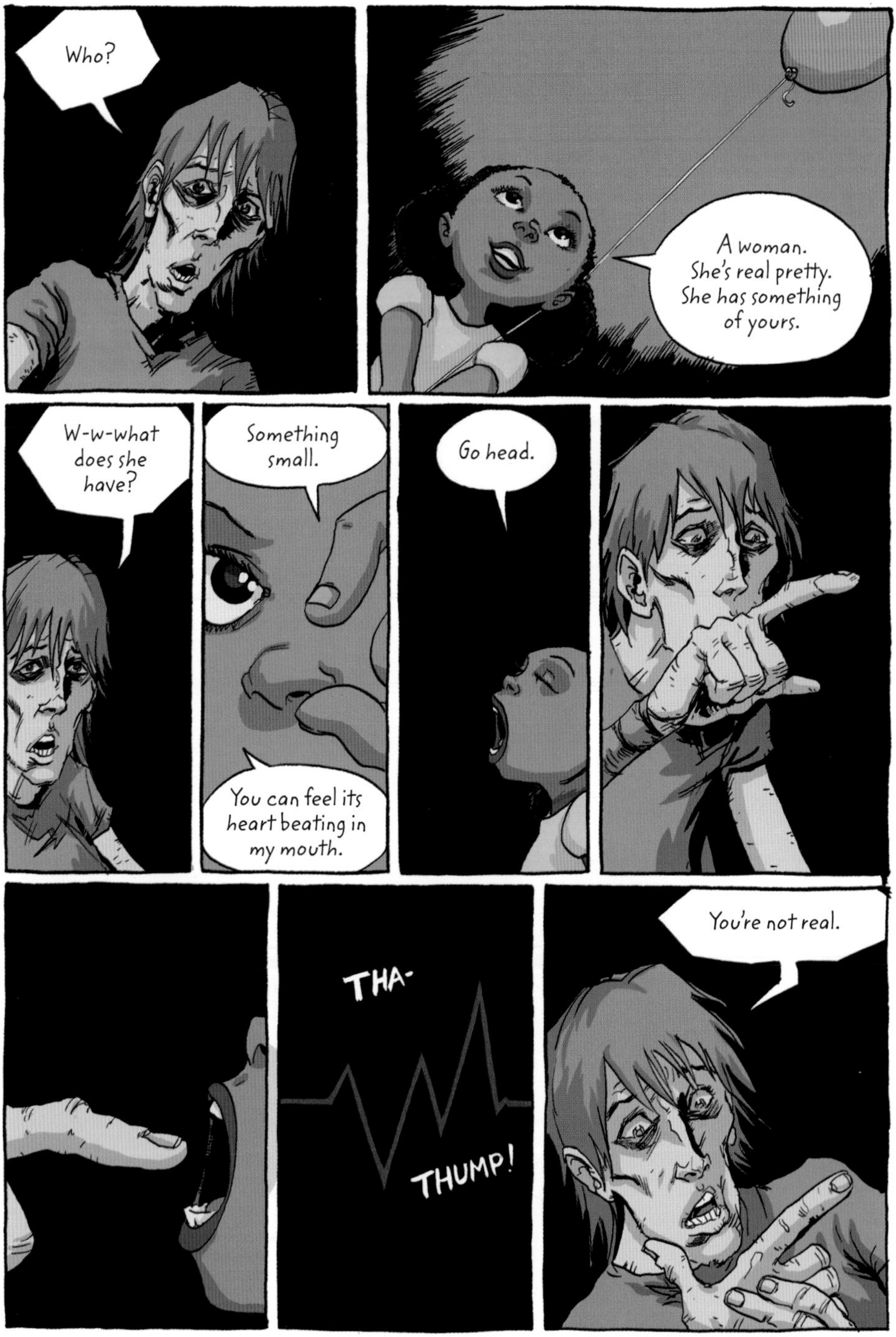
Who?
A woman. She's real pretty. She has something of yours.
W-w-what does she have?
Something small.
You can feel its heart beating in my mouth.
Go head.
THA-
THUMP!
You're not real.

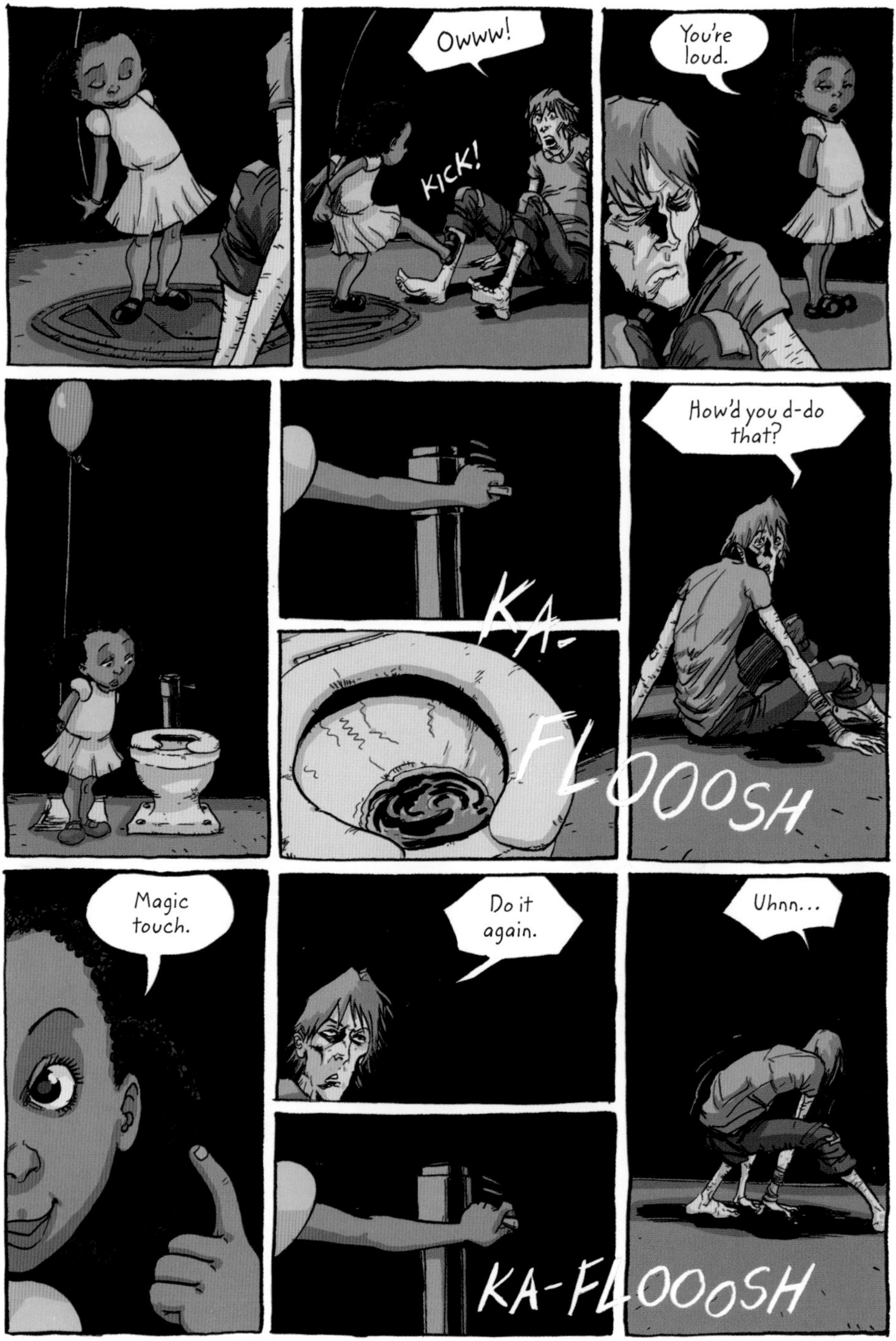
Owww!
KICK!
You're loud.
How'd you d-do that?
KA-
FLOOOSH
Magic touch.
Do it again.
Uhnn...
KA-FLOOOSH

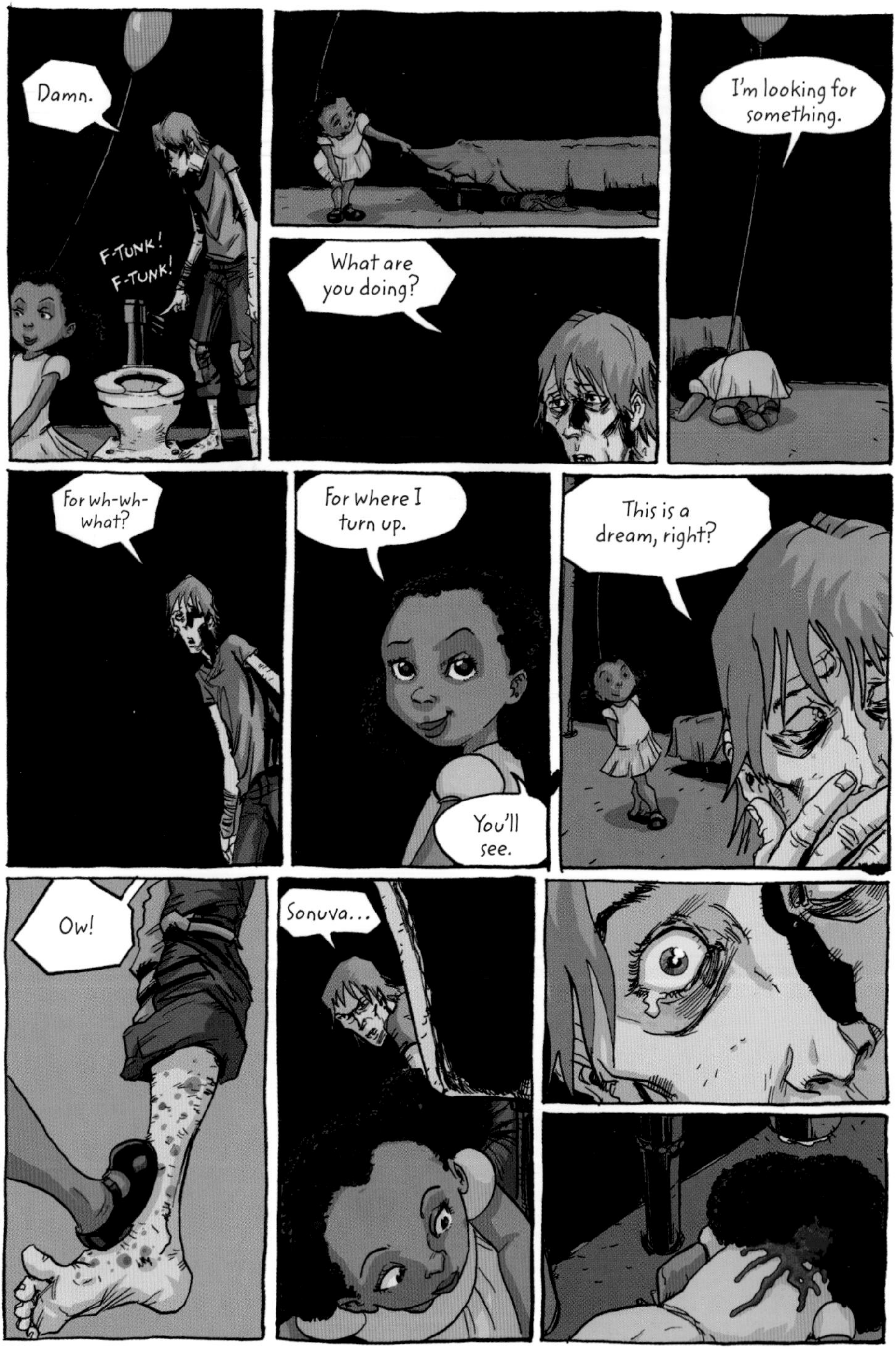
Damn.
F-TUNK! F-TUNK!
I'm looking for something.
What are you doing?
For wh-wh-what?
For where I turn up.
You'll see.
This is a dream, right?
Ow!
Sonuva...

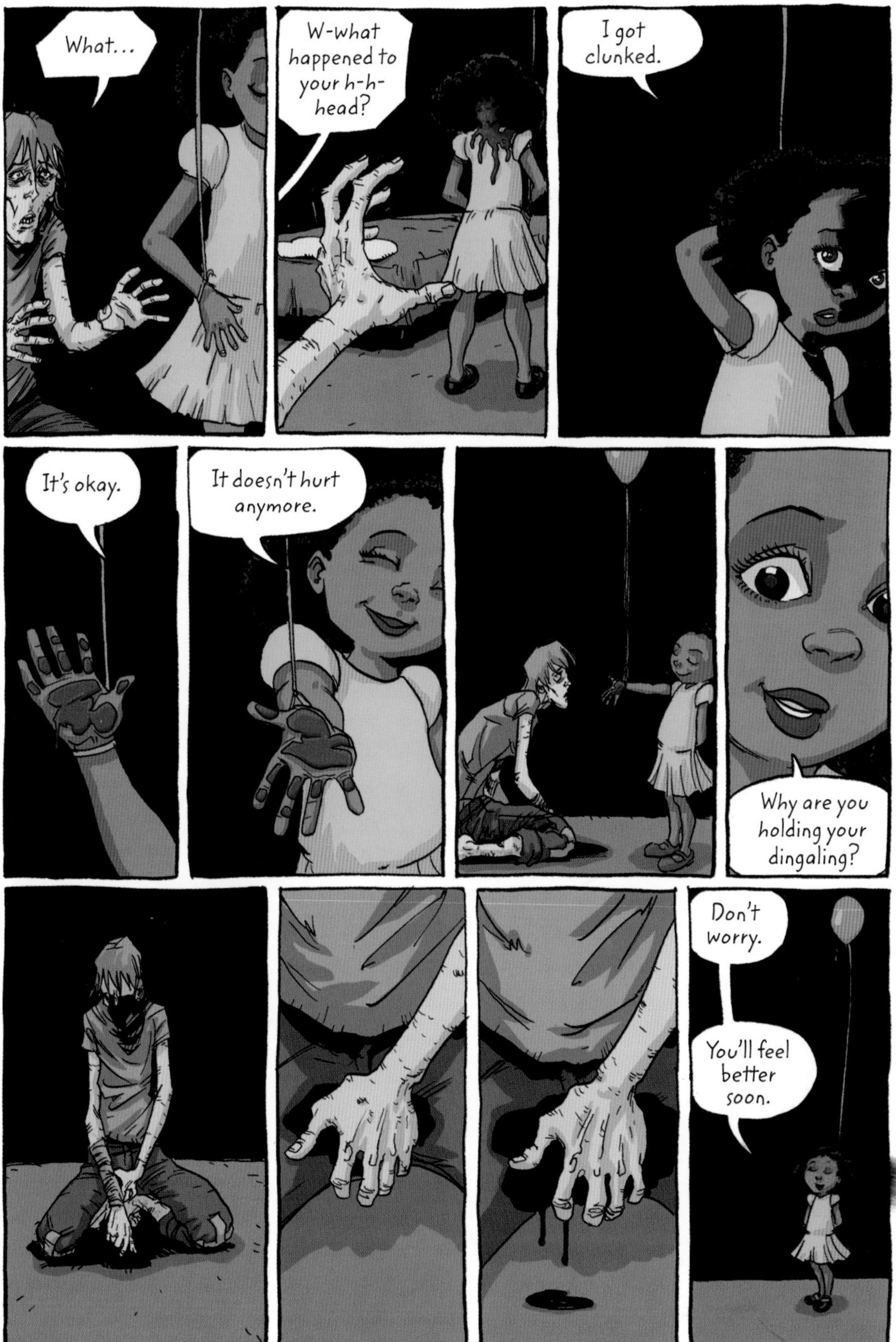
What...
W-what happened to your h-h-head?
I got clunked.
It's okay.
It doesn't hurt anymore.
Why are you holding your dingaling?
Don't worry.
You'll feel better soon.

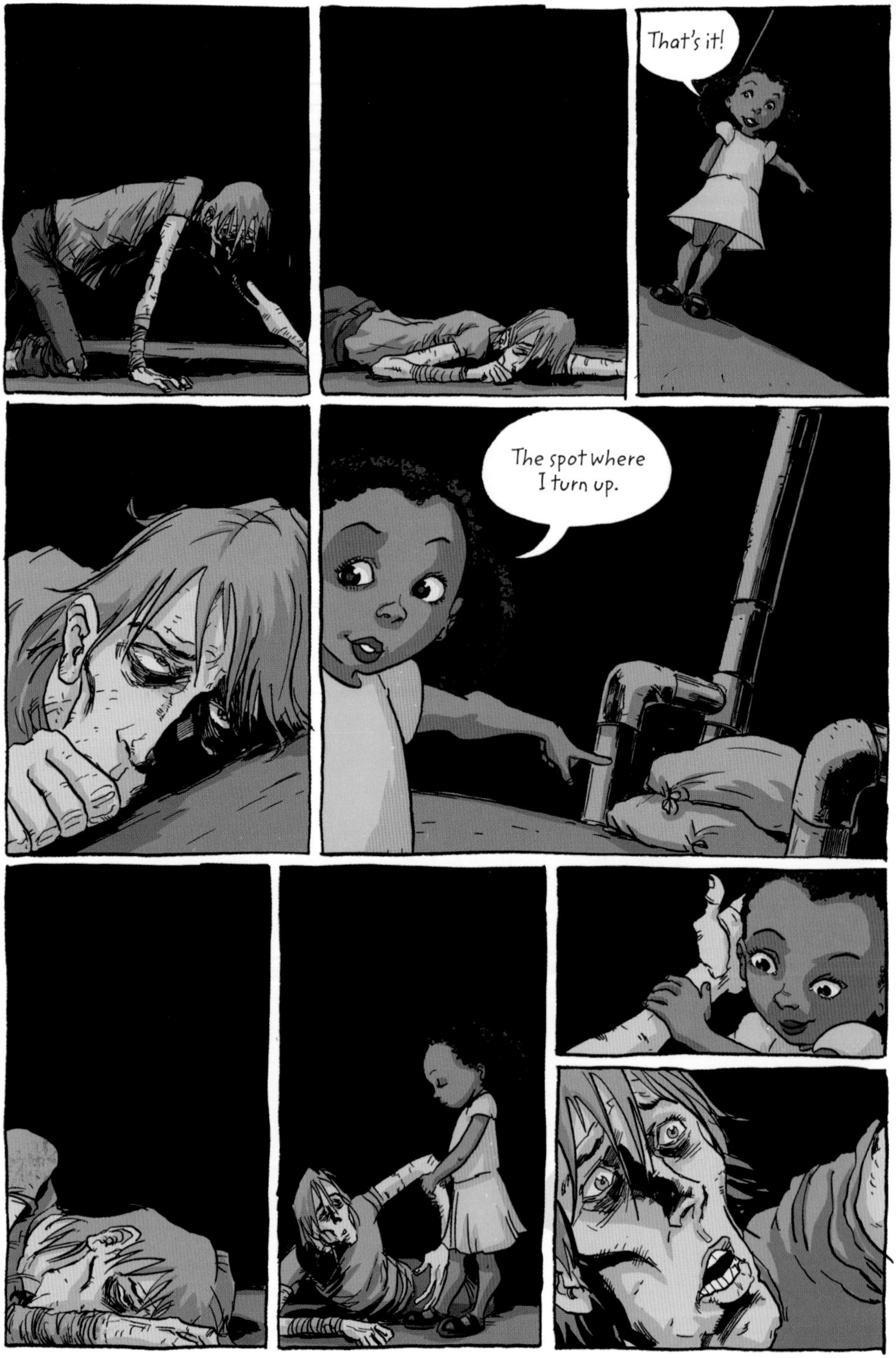
That's it!
The spot where I turn up.

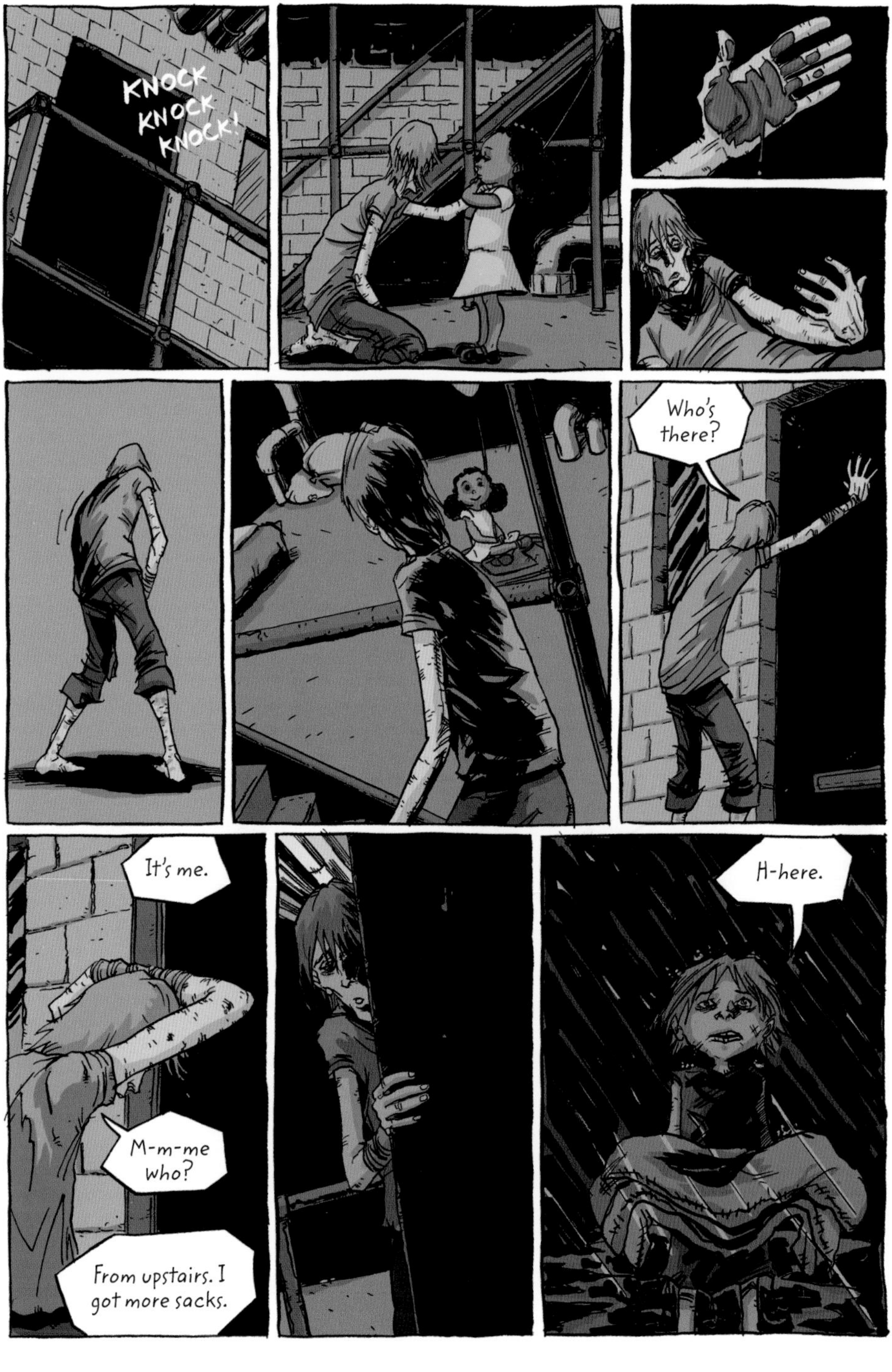
KNOCK KNOCK KNOCK!
Who's there?
It's me.
M-m-me who?
From upstairs. I got more sacks.
H-here.

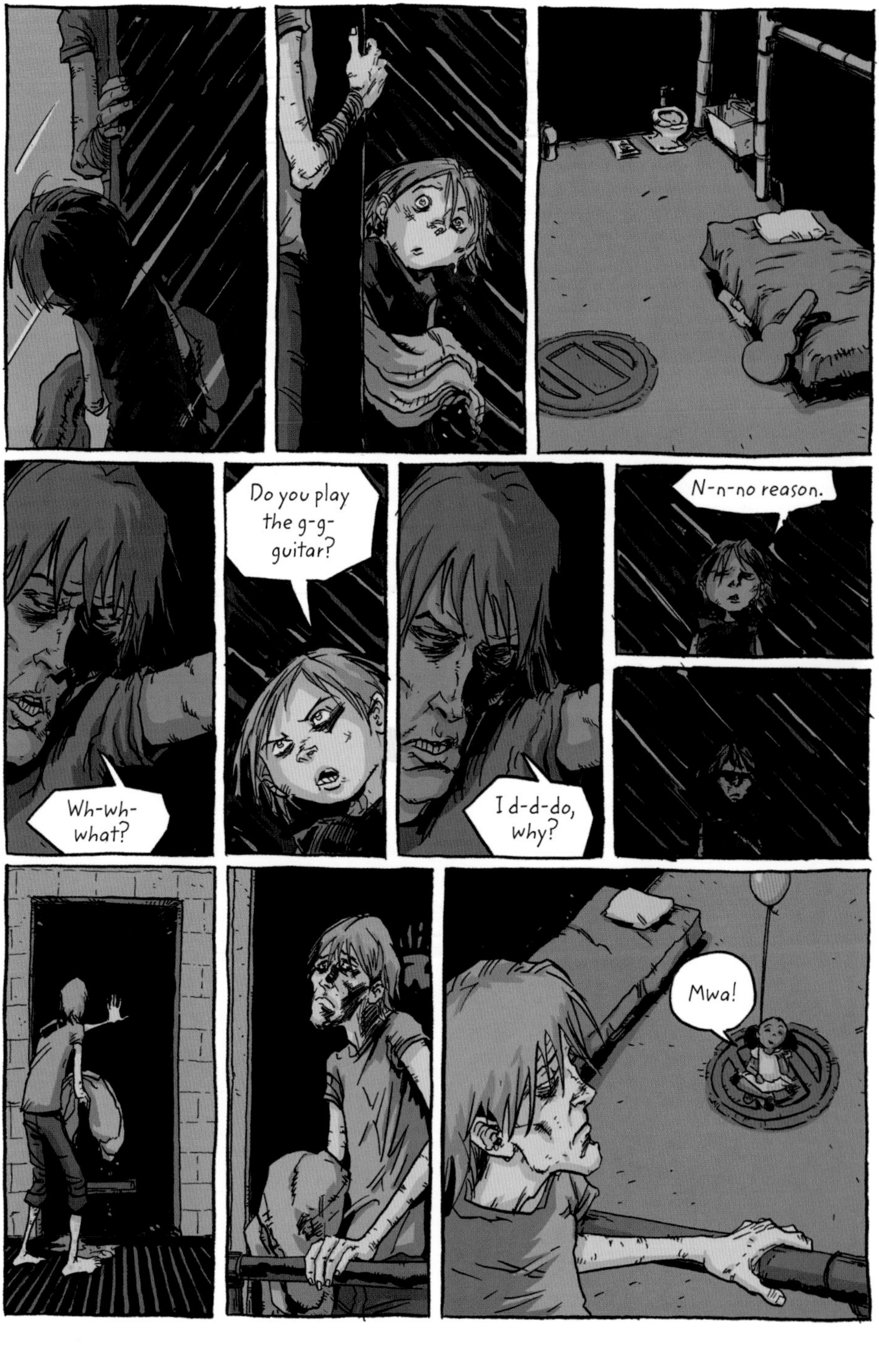
Wh-wh-what?
Do you play the g-g-guitar?
I d-d-do, why?
N-n-no reason.
Mwa!

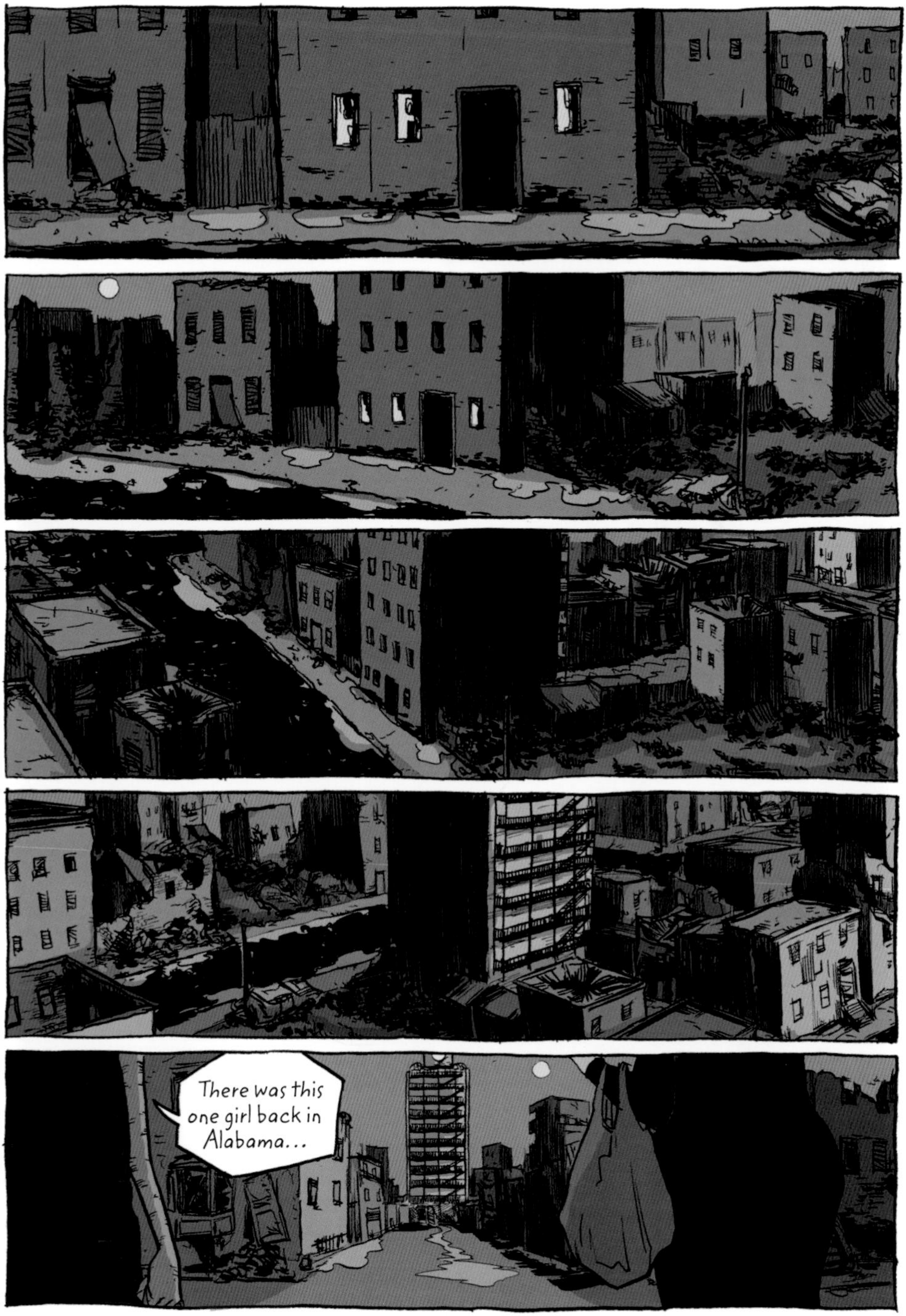
There was this one girl back in Alabama...

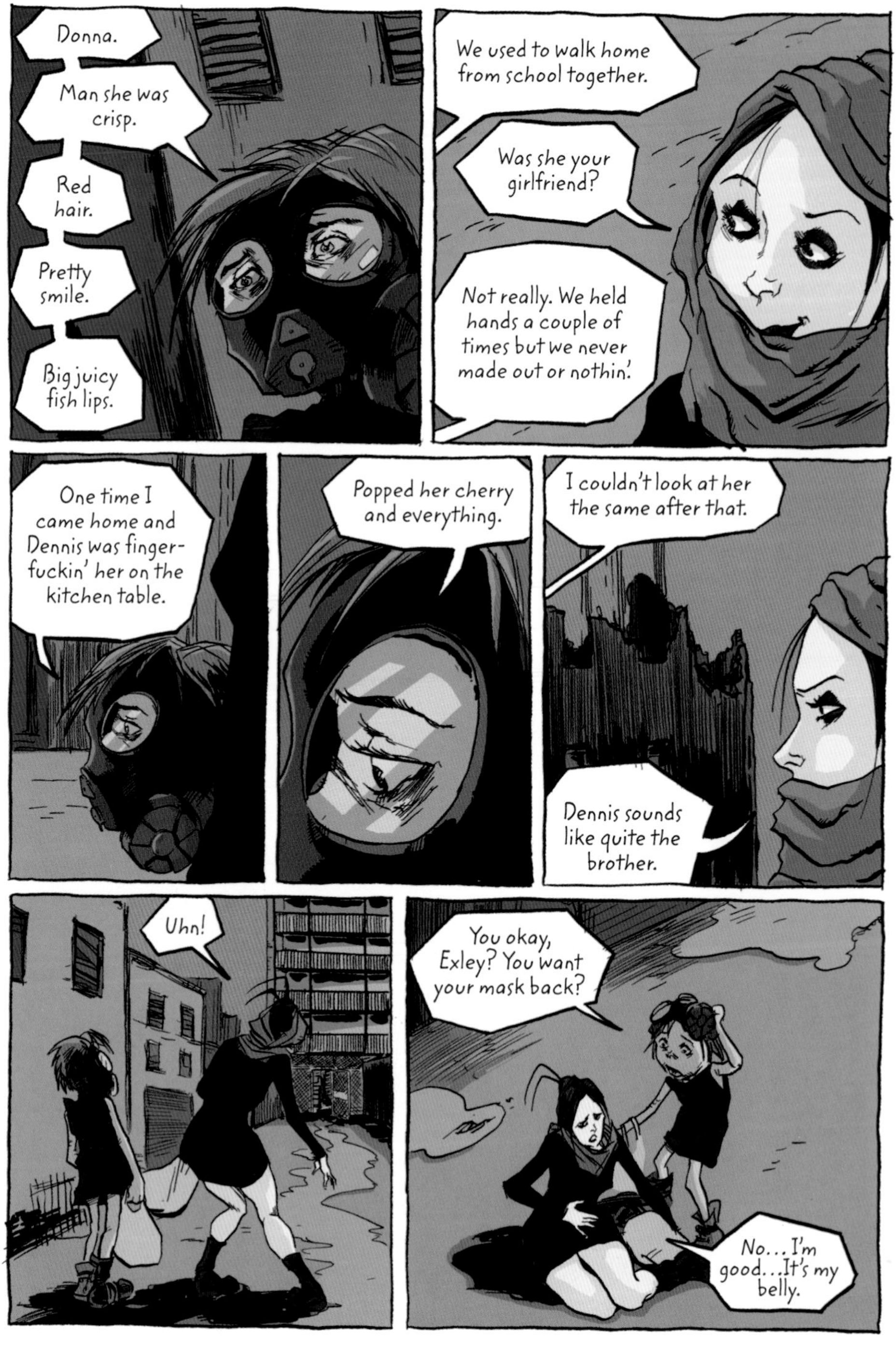

Donna.
Man she was crisp.
Red hair.
Pretty smile.
Big juicy fish lips.
We used to walk home from school together.
Was she your girlfriend?
Not really. We held hands a couple of times but we never made out or nothin'.
One time I came home and Dennis was finger-fuckin' her on the kitchen table.
Popped her cherry and everything.
I couldn't look at her the same after that.
Dennis sounds like quite the brother.
Uhn!
You okay, Exley? You want your mask back?
No... I'm good... It's my belly.

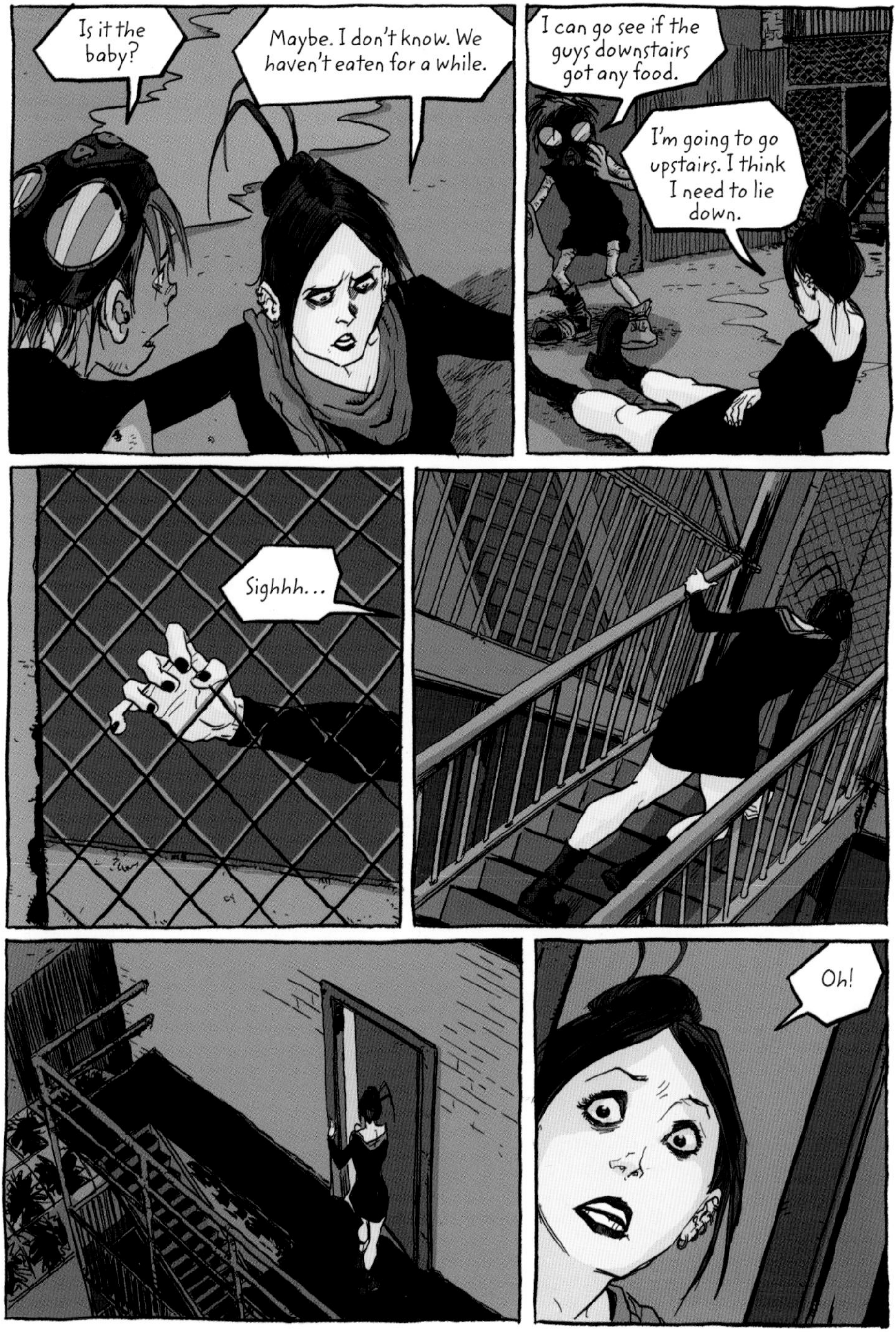
Is it the baby?
Maybe. I don't know. We haven't eaten for a while.
I can go see if the guys downstairs got any food.
I'm going to go upstairs. I think I need to lie down.
Sighhh...
Oh!

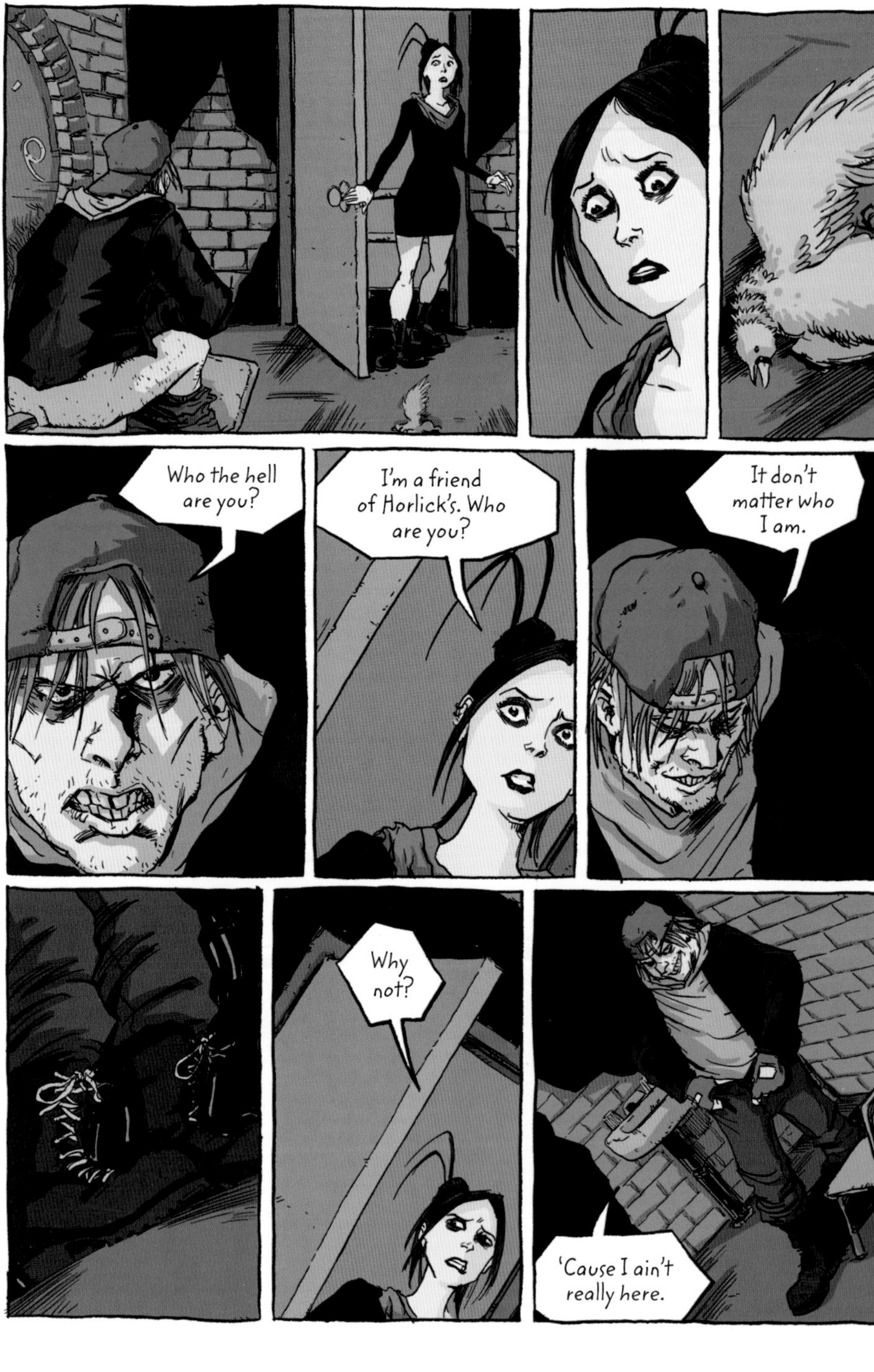
Who the hell are you?
I'm a friend of Horlick's. Who are you?
It don't matter who I am.
Why not?
'Cause I ain't really here.

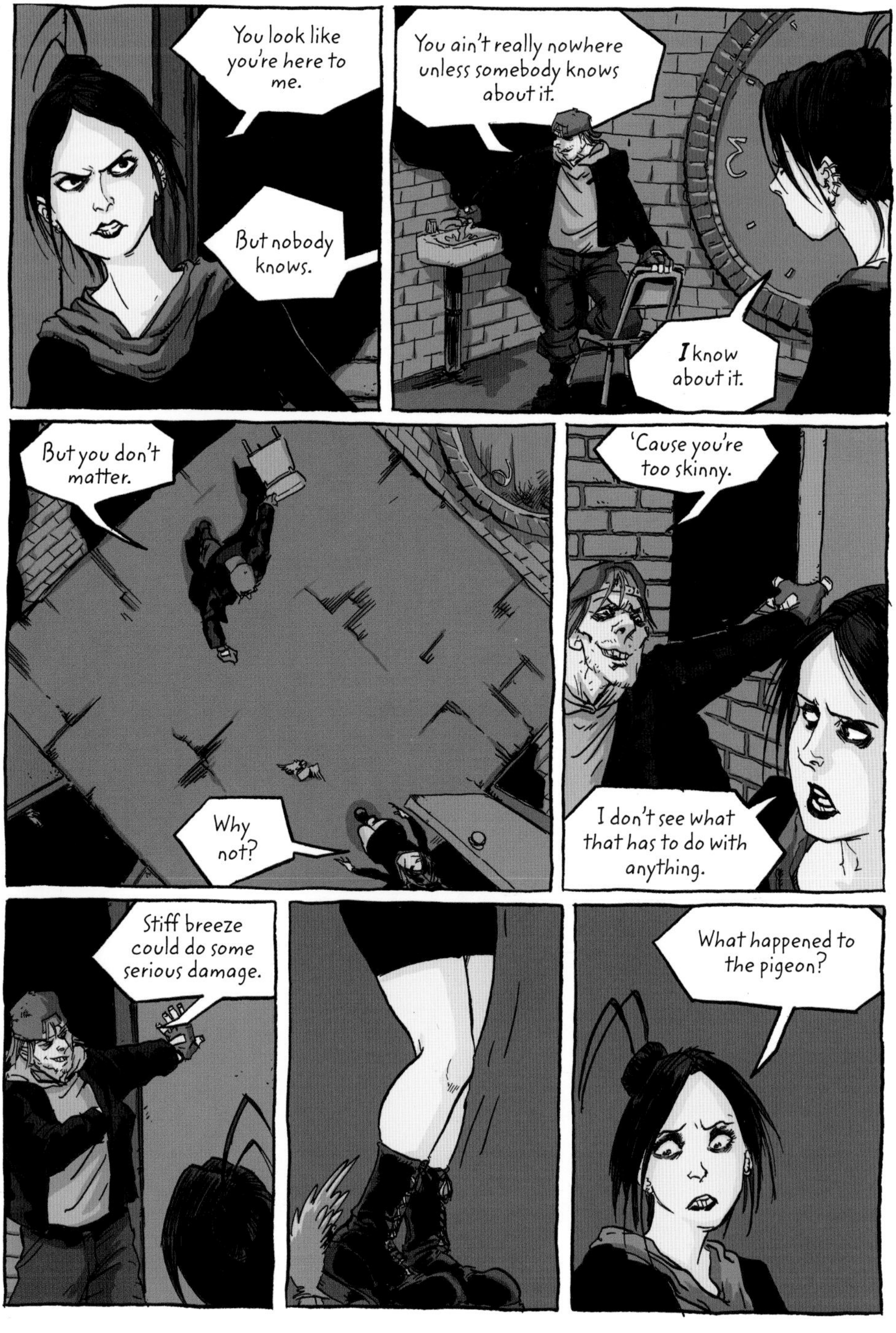
You look like you're here to me.
But nobody knows.
You ain't really nowhere unless somebody knows about it.
I know about it.
But you don't matter.
Why not?
'Cause you're too skinny.
I don't see what that has to do with anything.
Stiff breeze could do some serious damage.
What happened to the pigeon?

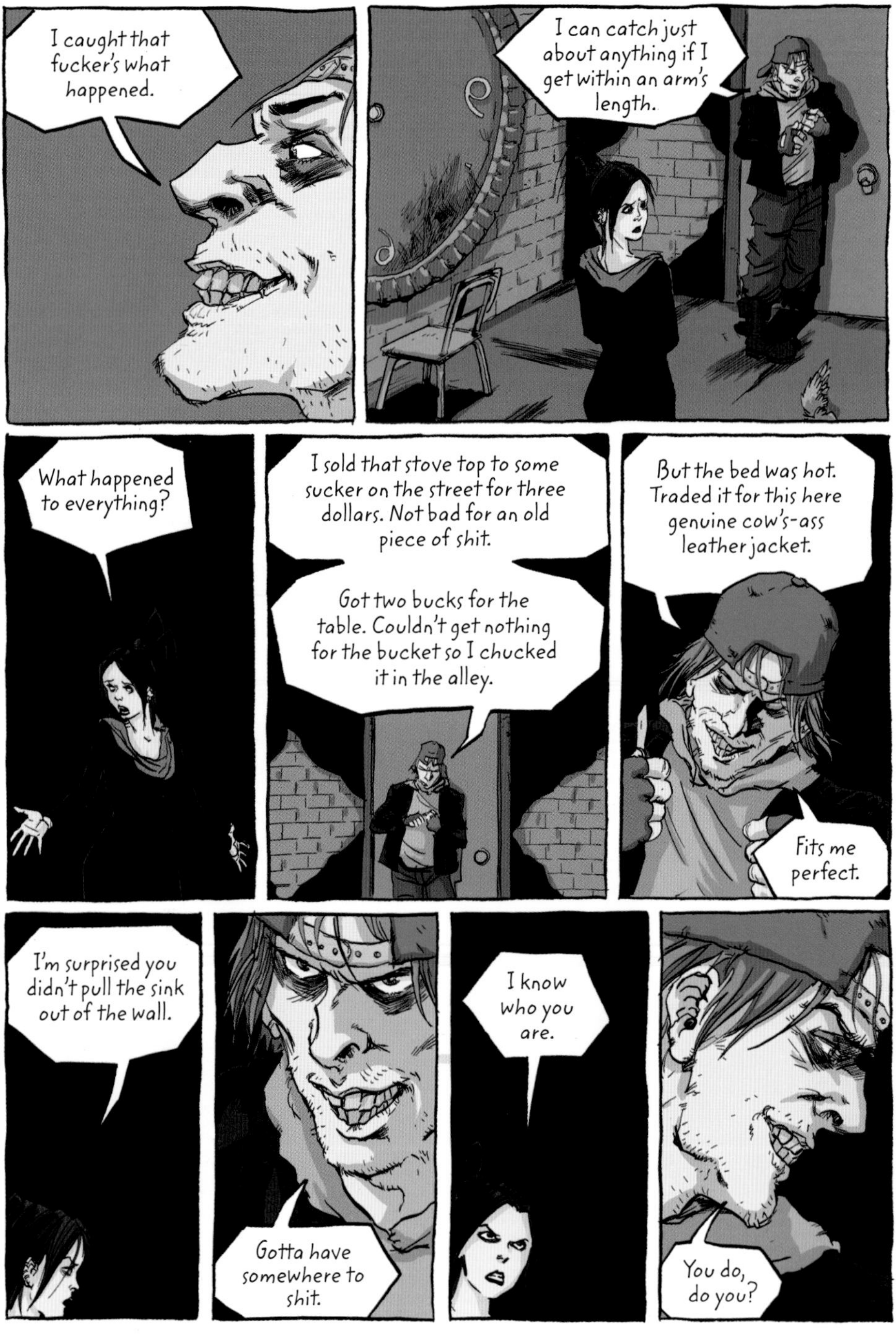

I caught that fucker's what happened.
I can catch just about anything if I get within an arm's length.
What happened to everything?
I sold that stove top to some sucker on the street for three dollars. Not bad for an old piece of shit.
Got two bucks for the table. Couldn't get nothing for the bucket so I chucked it in the alley.
But the bed was hot. Traded it for this here genuine cow's-ass leather jacket.
Fits me perfect.
I'm surprised you didn't pull the sink out of the wall.
Gotta have somewhere to shit.
I know who you are.
You do, do you?

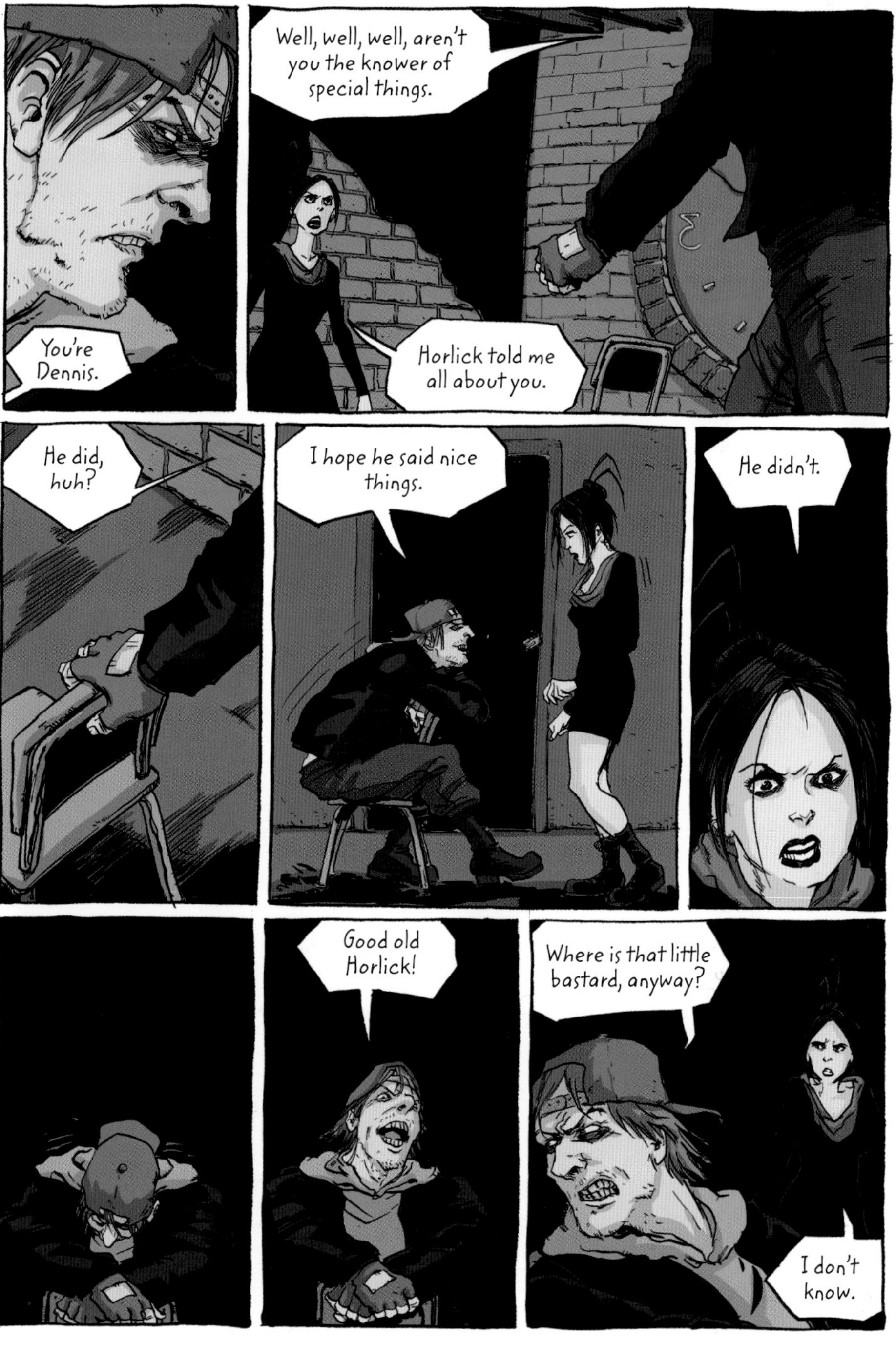
Well, well, well, aren't you the knower of special things.
You're Dennis.
Horlick told me all about you.
He did, huh?
I hope he said nice things.
He didn't.
Good old Horlick!
Where is that little bastard, anyway?
I don't know.

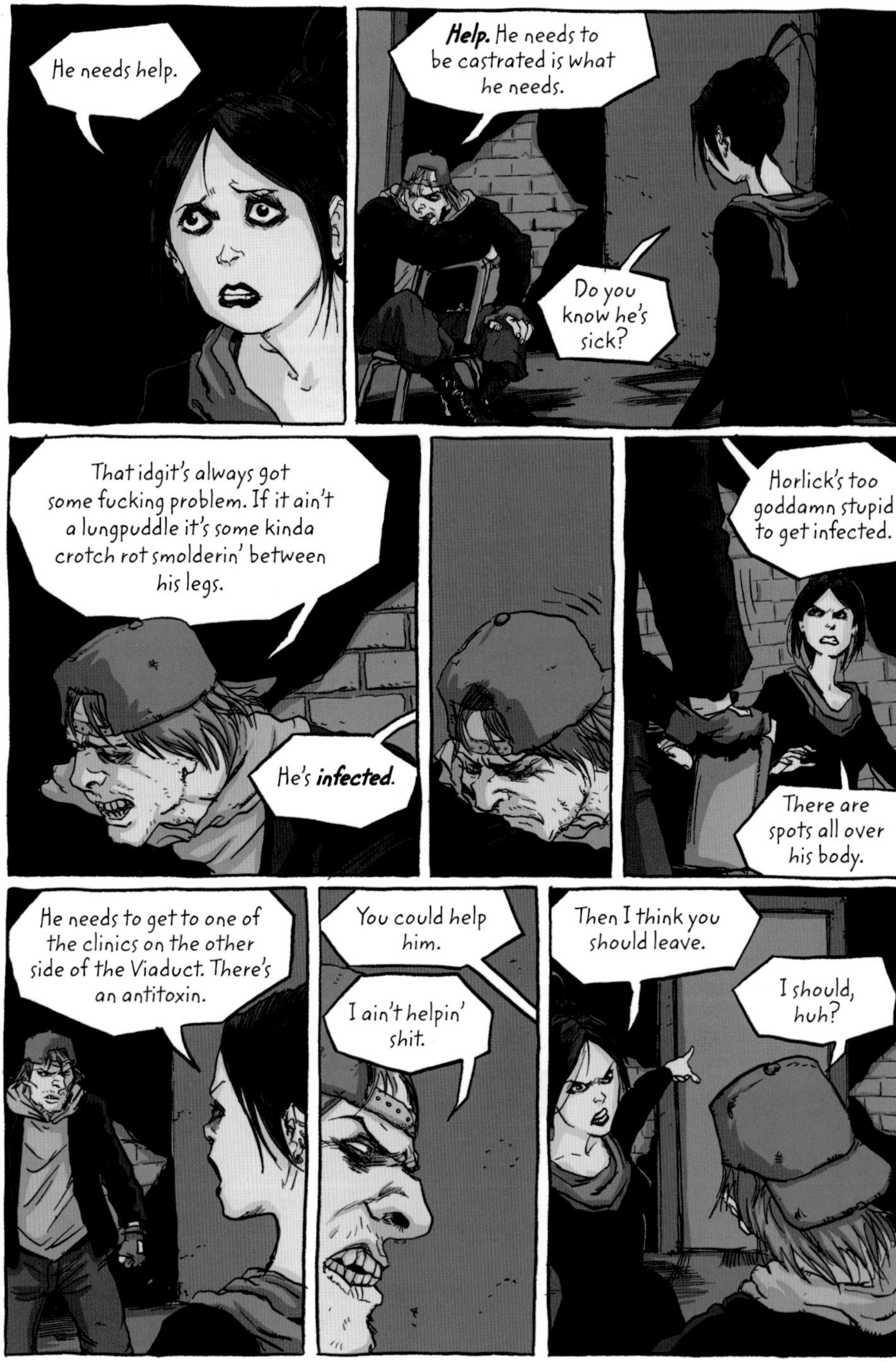
He needs help.
Help. He needs to be castrated is what he needs.
Do you know he's sick?
That idgit's always got some fucking problem. If it ain't a lungpuddle it's some kinda crotch rot smolderin' between his legs.
He's ***infected.***
Horlick's too goddamn stupid to get infected.
There are spots all over his body.
He needs to get to one of the clinics on the other side of the Viaduct. There's an antitoxin.
You could help him.
I ain't helpin' shit.
Then I think you should leave.
I should, huh?

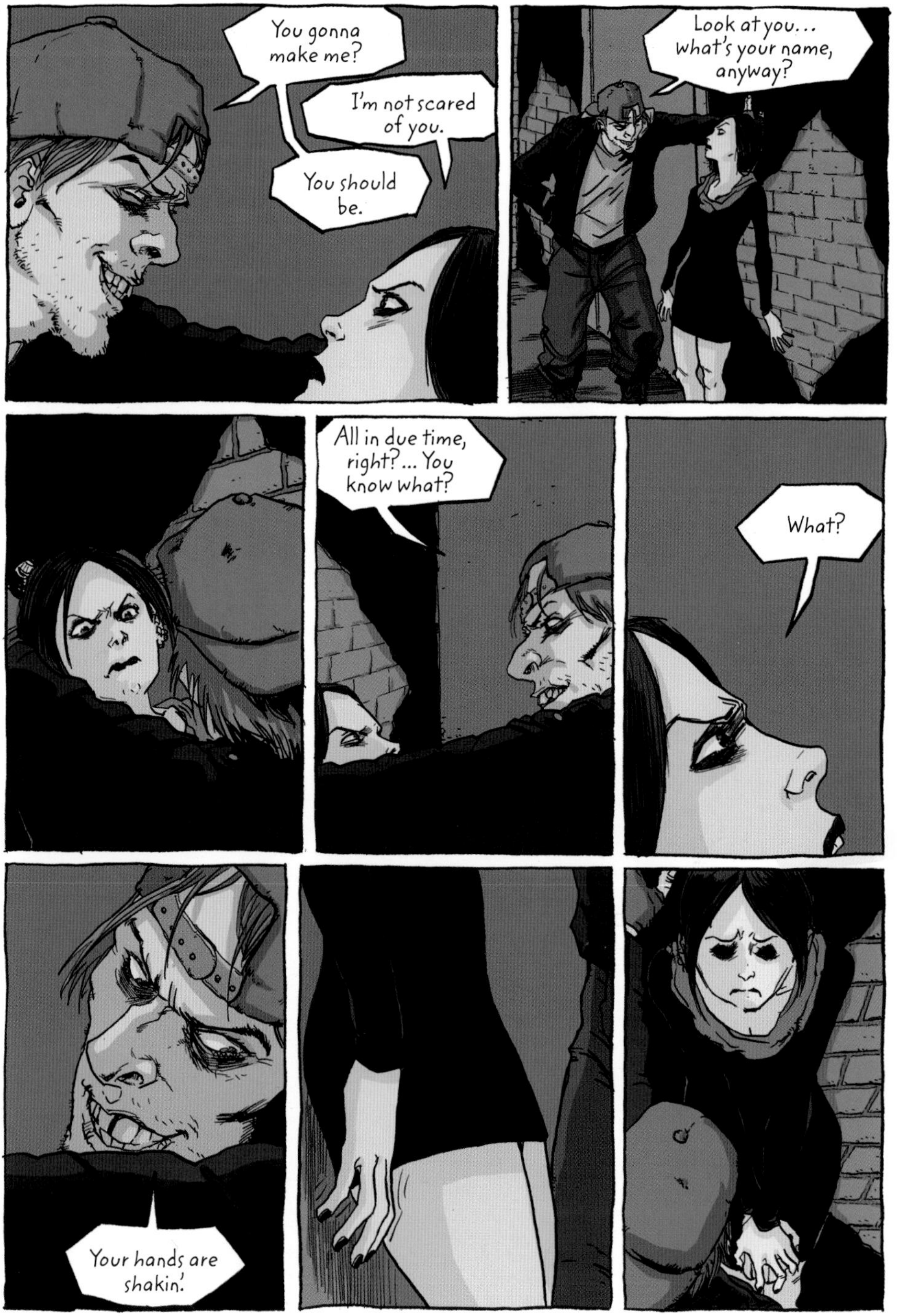
You gonna make me?
I'm not scared of you.
You should be.
Look at you... what's your name, anyway?
All in due time, right?... You know what?
What?
Your hands are shakin'.

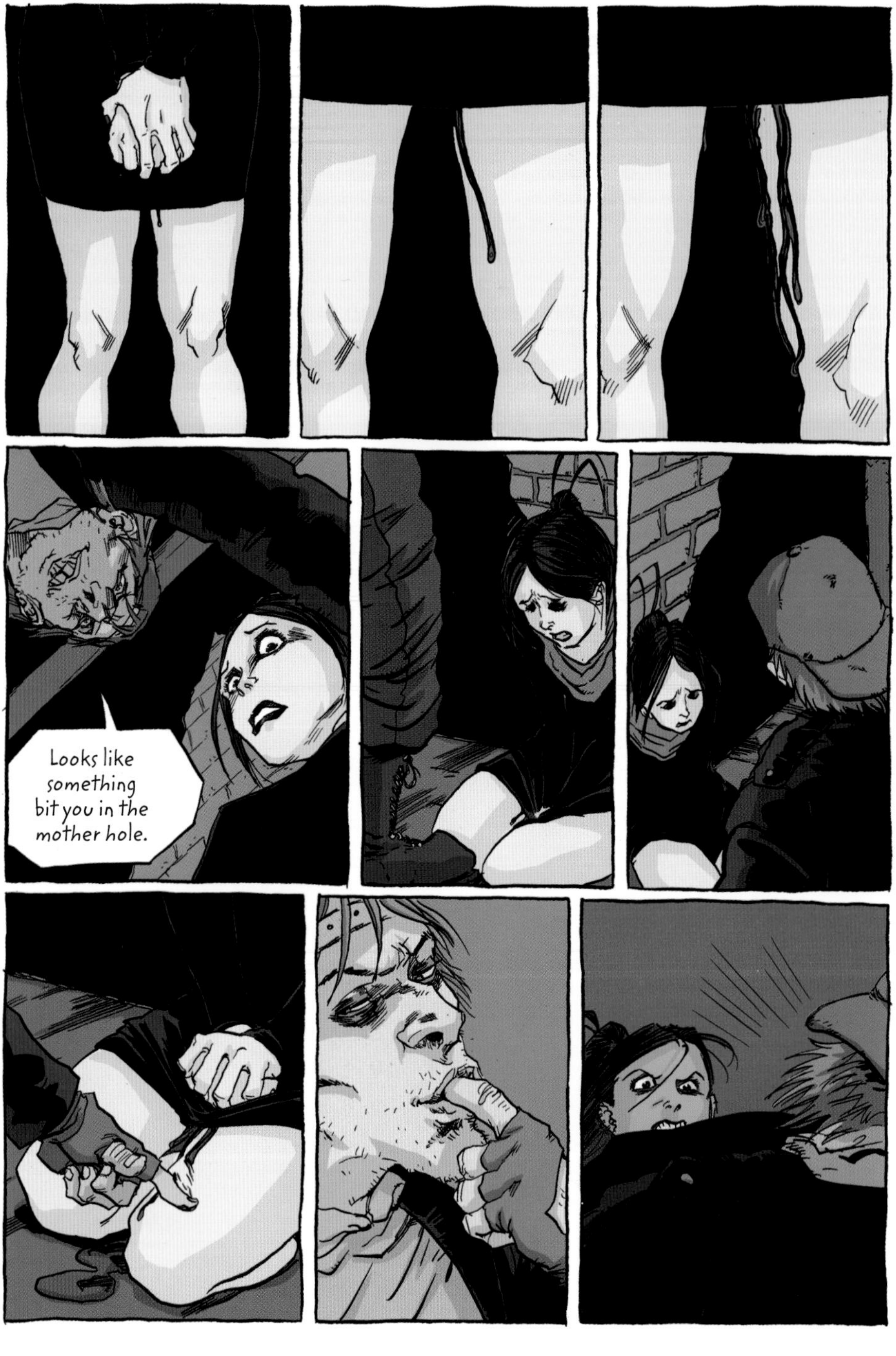
Looks like something bit you in the mother hole.

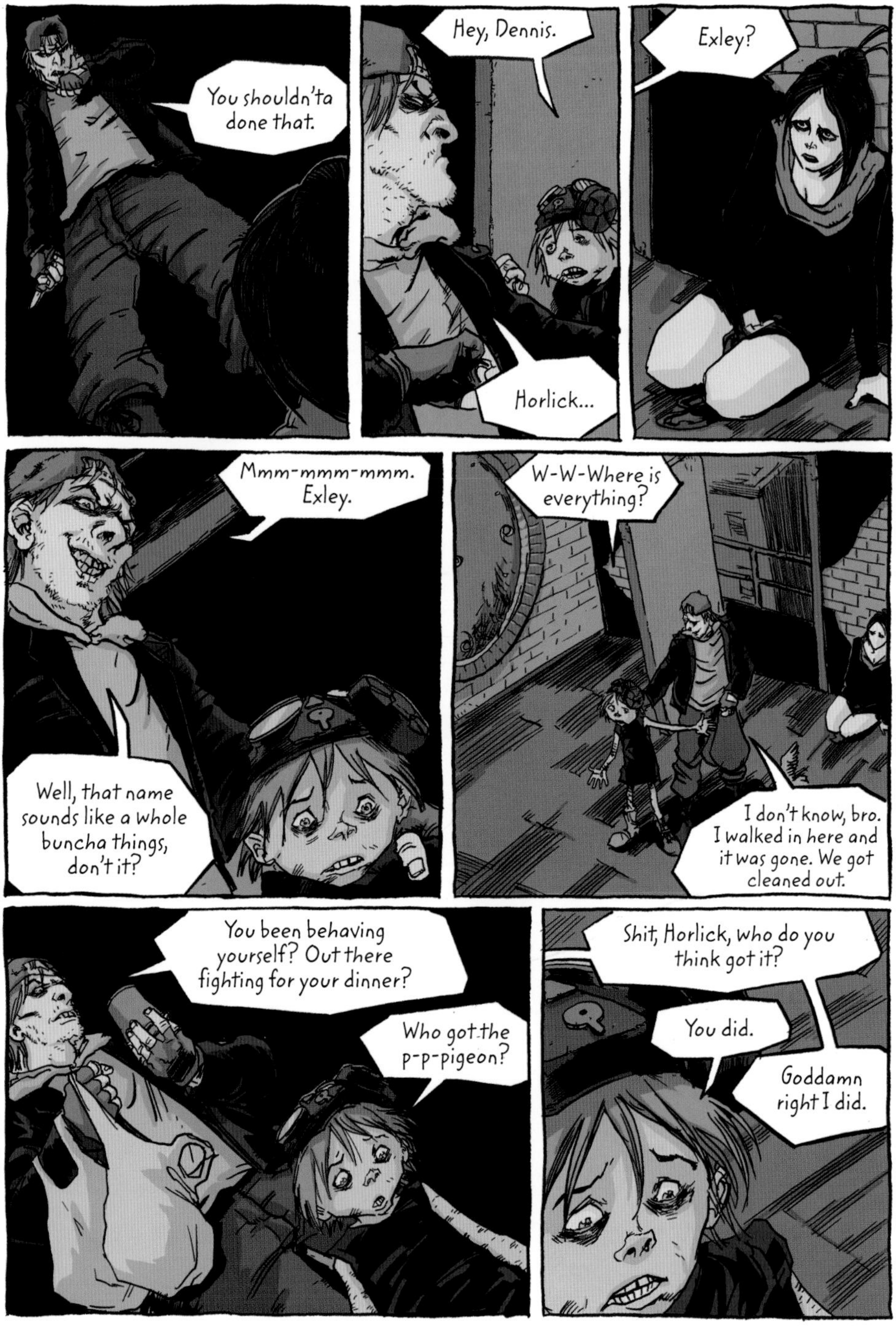
You shouldn'ta done that.
Hey, Dennis.
Horlick...
Exley?
Mmm-mmm-mmm. Exley.
Well, that name sounds like a whole buncha things, don't it?
W-W-Where is everything?
I don't know, bro. I walked in here and it was gone. We got cleaned out.
You been behaving yourself? Out there fighting for your dinner?
Who got the p-p-pigeon?
Shit, Horlick, who do you think got it?
You did.
Goddamn right I did.

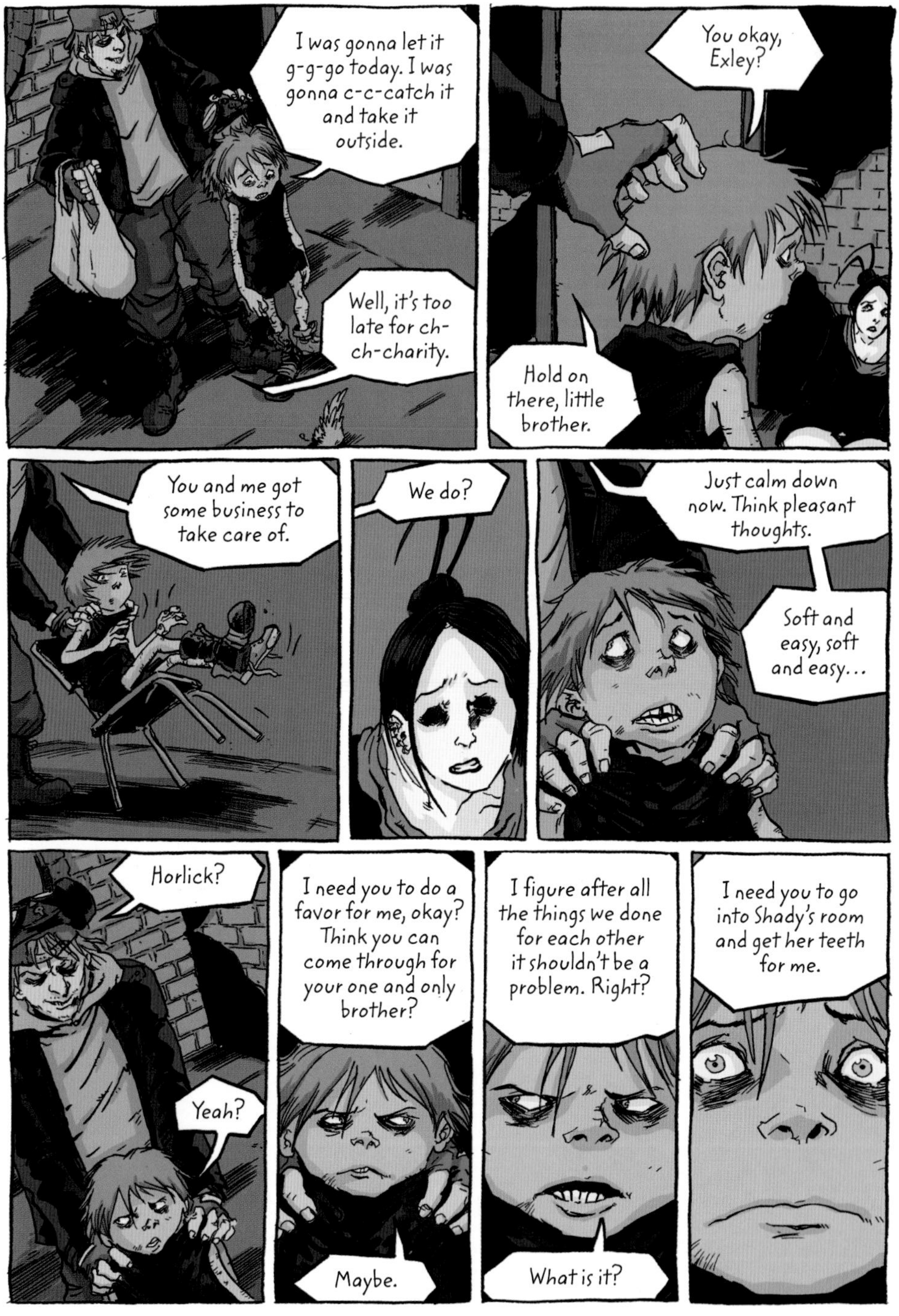
I was gonna let it g-g-go today. I was gonna c-c-catch it and take it outside.
Well, it's too late for ch-ch-charity.
You okay, Exley?
Hold on there, little brother.
You and me got some business to take care of.
We do?
Just calm down now. Think pleasant thoughts.
Soft and easy, soft and easy…
Horlick?
Yeah?
I need you to do a favor for me, okay? Think you can come through for your one and only brother?
Maybe.
I figure after all the things we done for each other it shouldn't be a problem. Right?
What is it?
I need you to go into Shady's room and get her teeth for me.

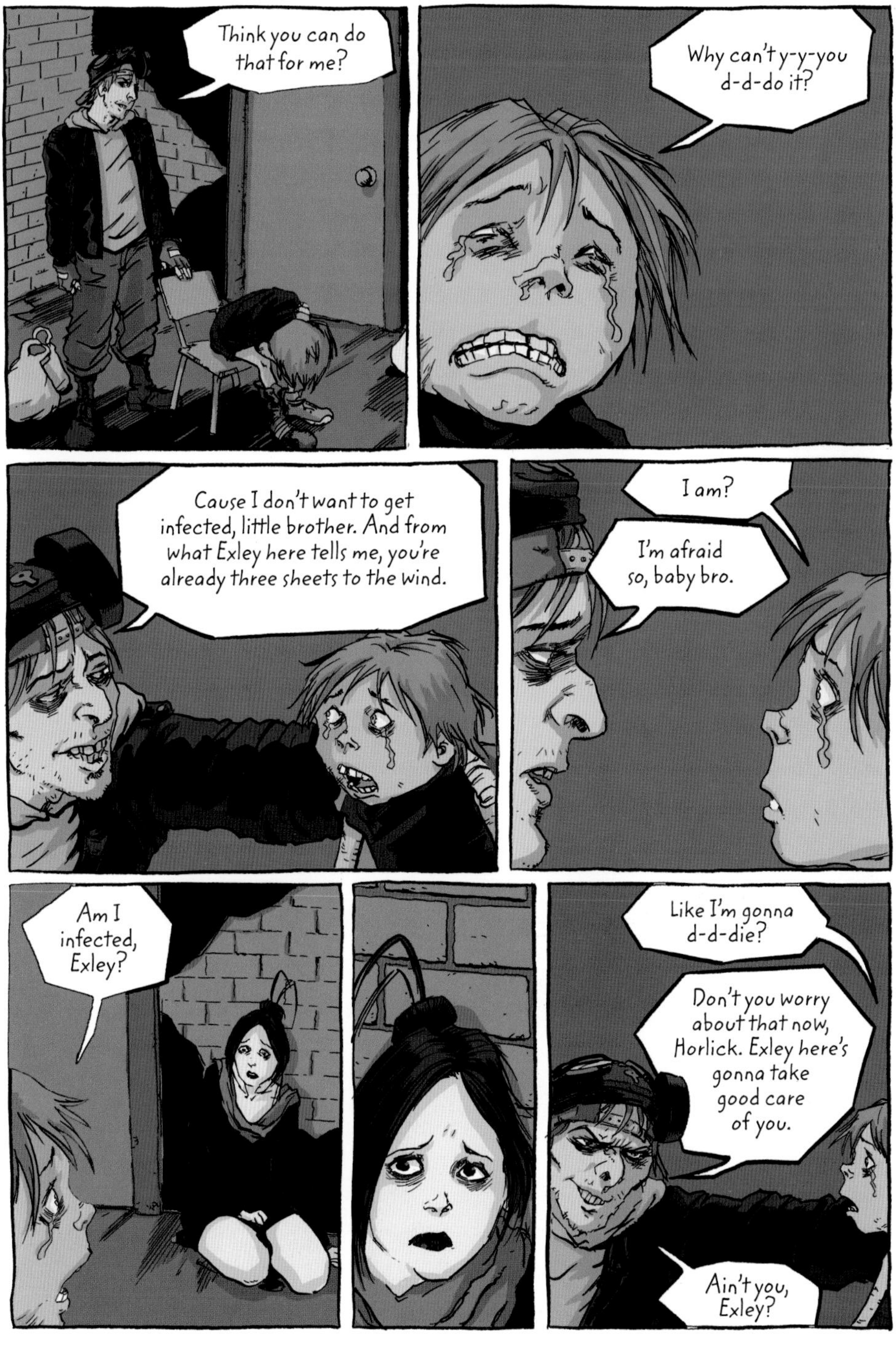
Think you can do that for me?
Why can't y-y-you d-d-do it?
Cause I don't want to get infected, little brother. And from what Exley here tells me, you're already three sheets to the wind.
I am?
I'm afraid so, baby bro.
Am I infected, Exley?
Like I'm gonna d-d-die?
Don't you worry about that now, Horlick. Exley here's gonna take good care of you.
Ain't you, Exley?

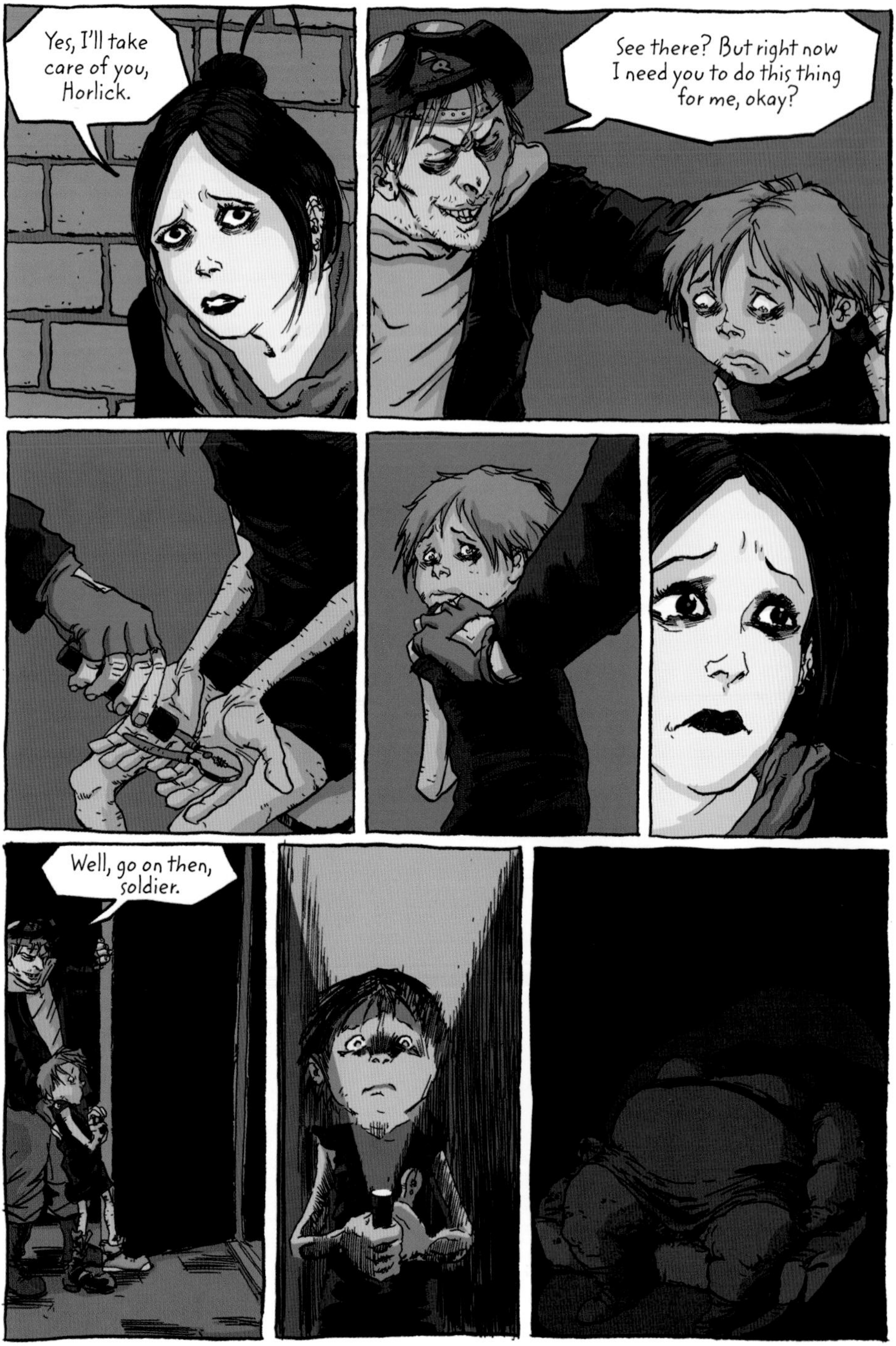
Yes, I'll take care of you, Horlick.
See there? But right now I need you to do this thing for me, okay?
Well, go on then, soldier.

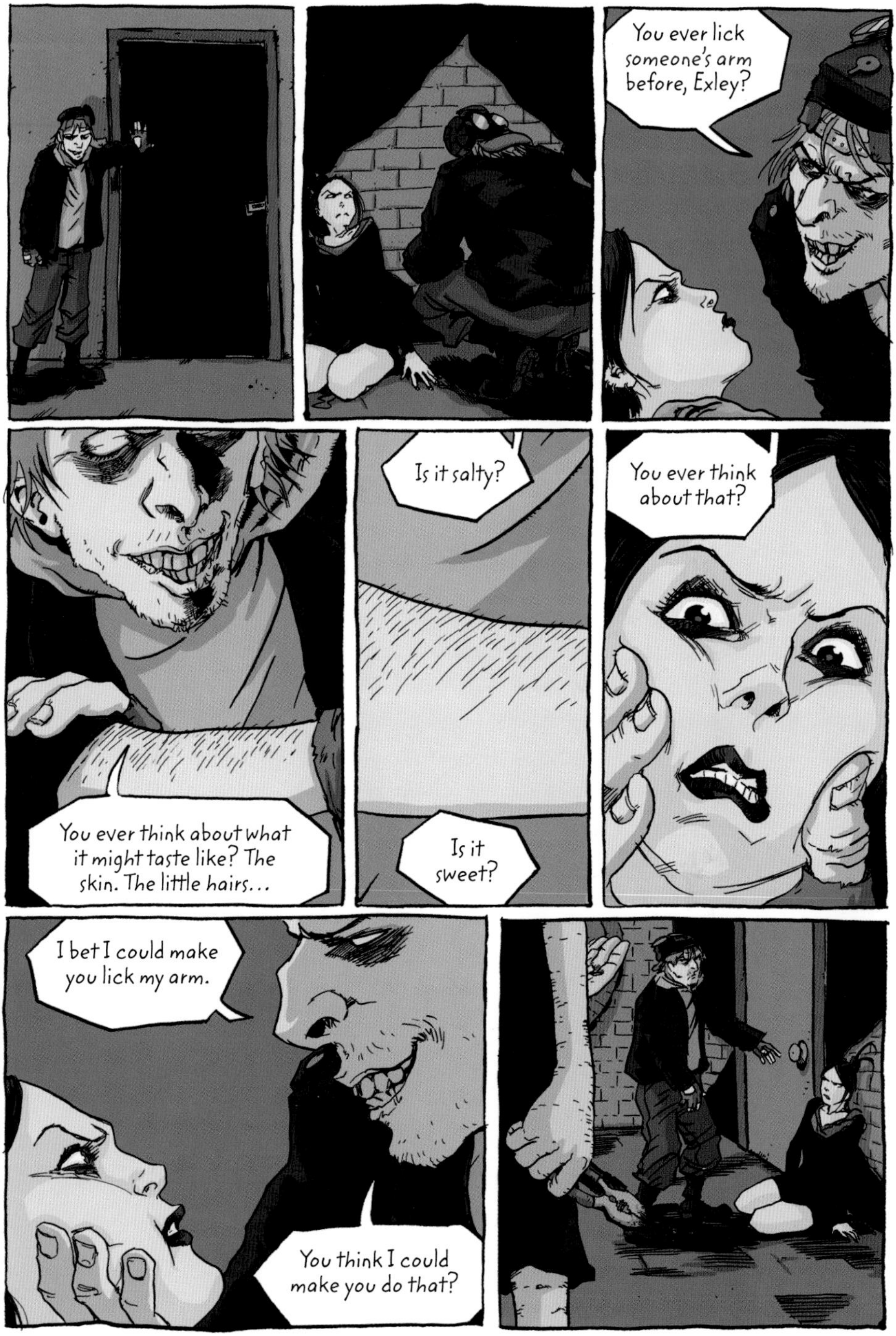
You ever lick someone's arm before, Exley?
You ever think about what it might taste like? The skin. The little hairs...
Is it salty?
Is it sweet?
You ever think about that?
I bet I could make you lick my arm.
You think I could make you do that?

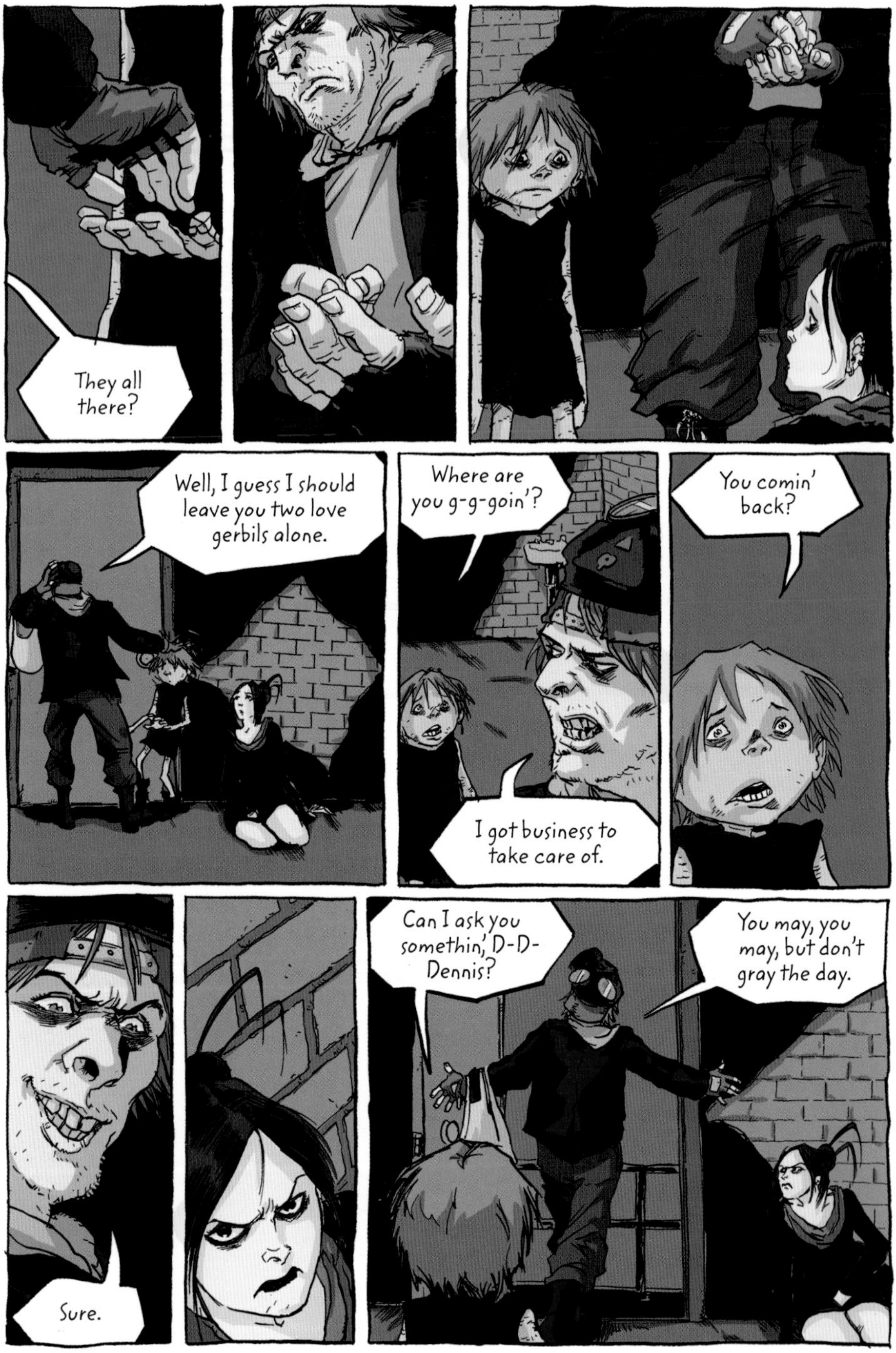
They all there?
Well, I guess I should leave you two love gerbils alone.
Where are you g-g-goin'?
I got business to take care of.
You comin' back?
Sure.
Can I ask you somethin,' D-D-Dennis?
You may, you may, but don't gray the day.

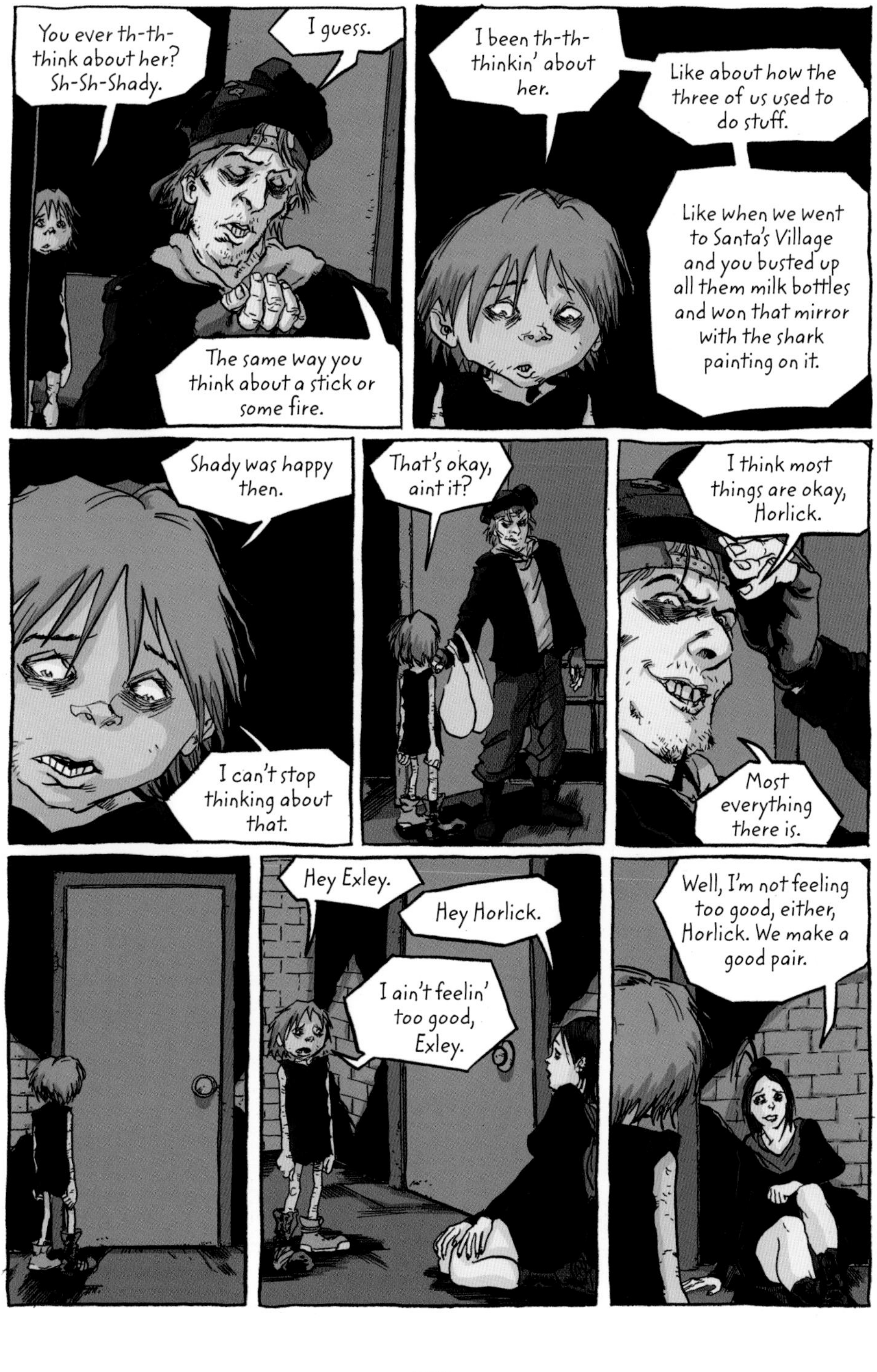

You ever th-th-think about her? Sh-Sh-Shady.
I guess.
The same way you think about a stick or some fire.
I been th-th-thinkin' about her.
Like about how the three of us used to do stuff.
Like when we went to Santa's Village and you busted up all them milk bottles and won that mirror with the shark painting on it.
Shady was happy then.
I can't stop thinking about that.
That's okay, aint it?
I think most things are okay, Horlick.
Most everything there is.
Hey Exley.
Hey Horlick.
I ain't feelin' too good, Exley.
Well, I'm not feeling too good, either, Horlick. We make a good pair.

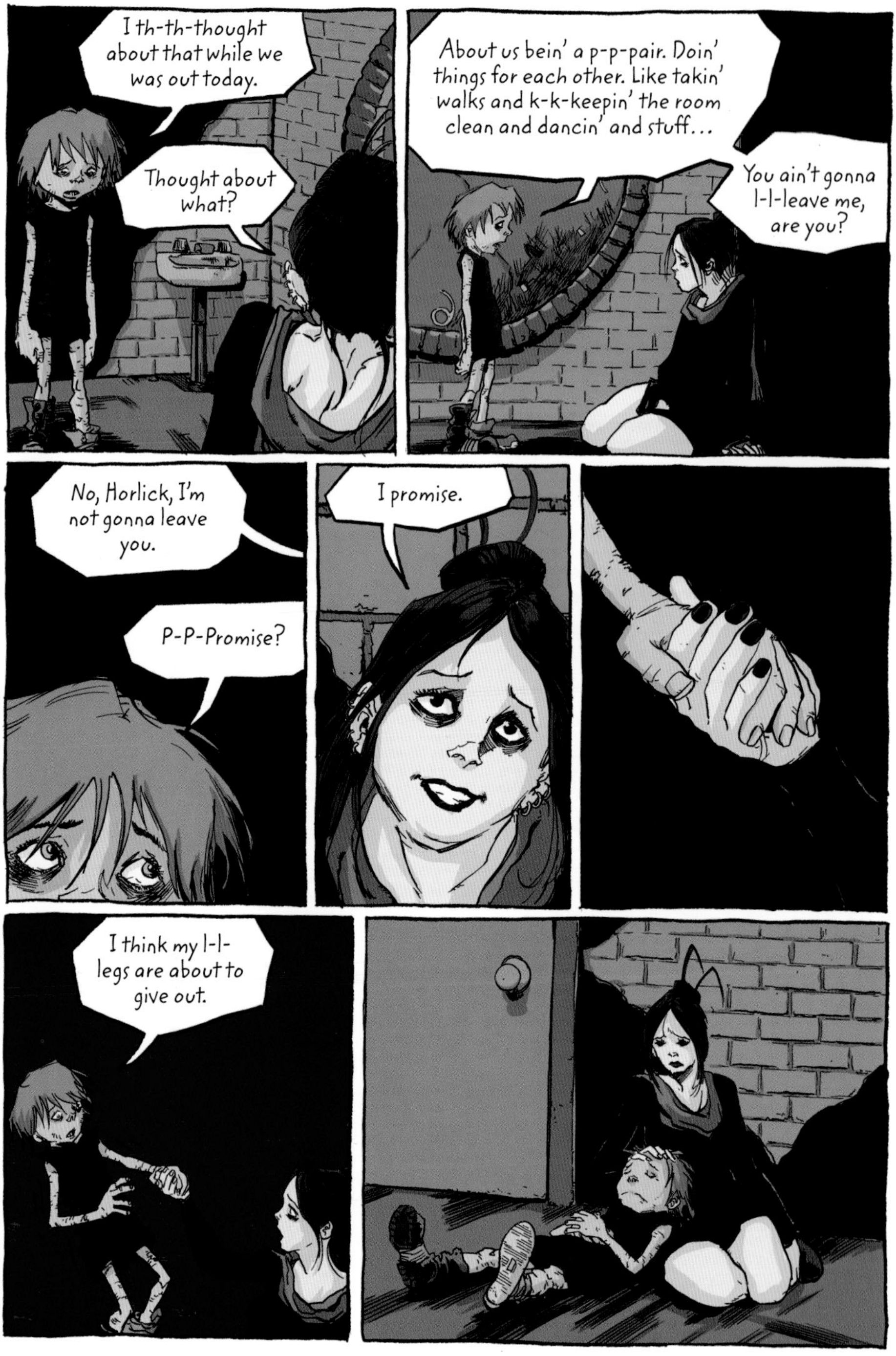

I th-th-thought about that while we was out today.
Thought about what?
About us bein' a p-p-pair. Doin' things for each other. Like takin' walks and k-k-keepin' the room clean and dancin' and stuff...
You ain't gonna l-l-leave me, are you?
No, Horlick, I'm not gonna leave you.
P-P-Promise?
I promise.
I think my l-l-legs are about to give out.

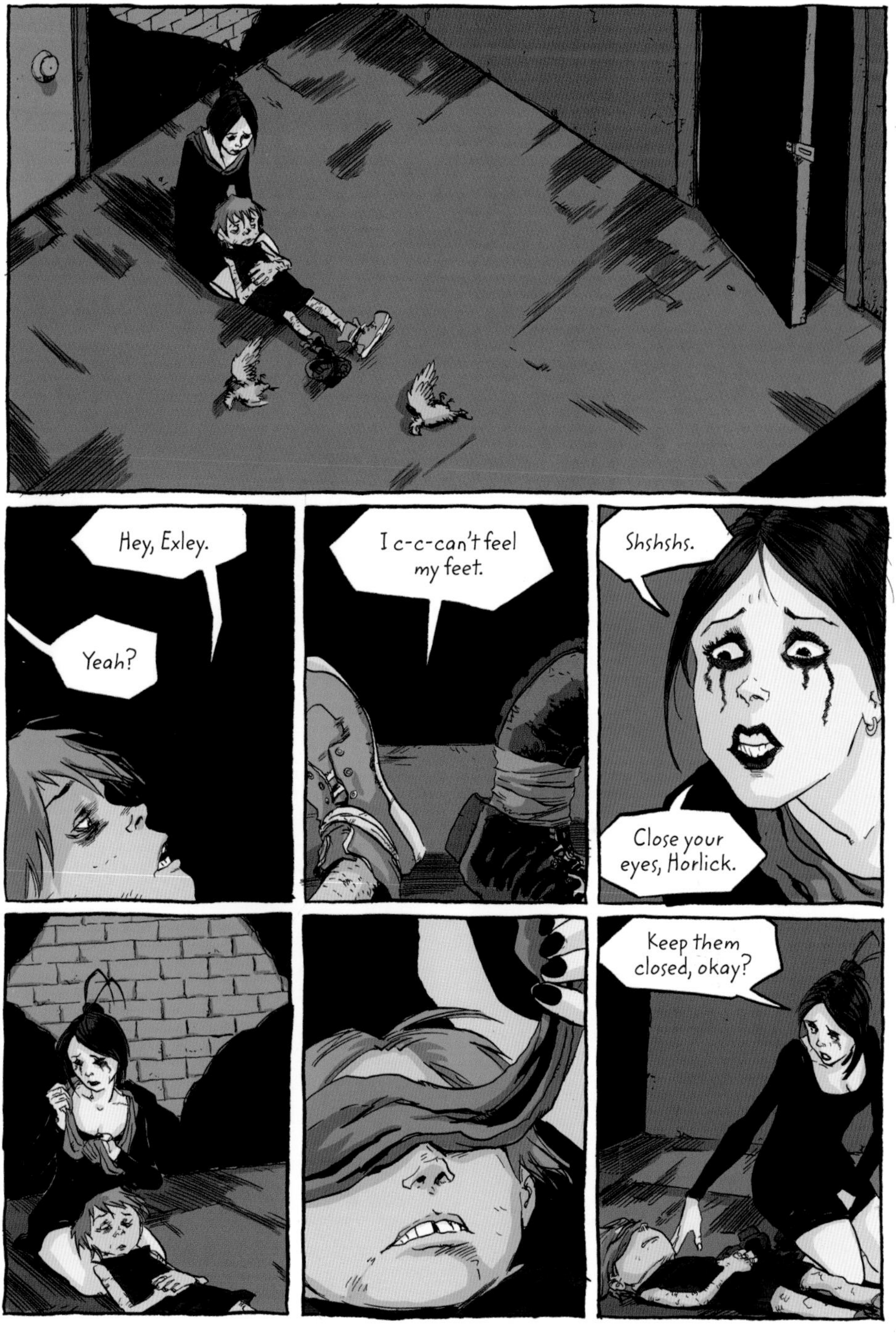
Hey, Exley.
Yeah?
I c-c-can't feel my feet.
Shshshs.
Close your eyes, Horlick.
Keep them closed, okay?

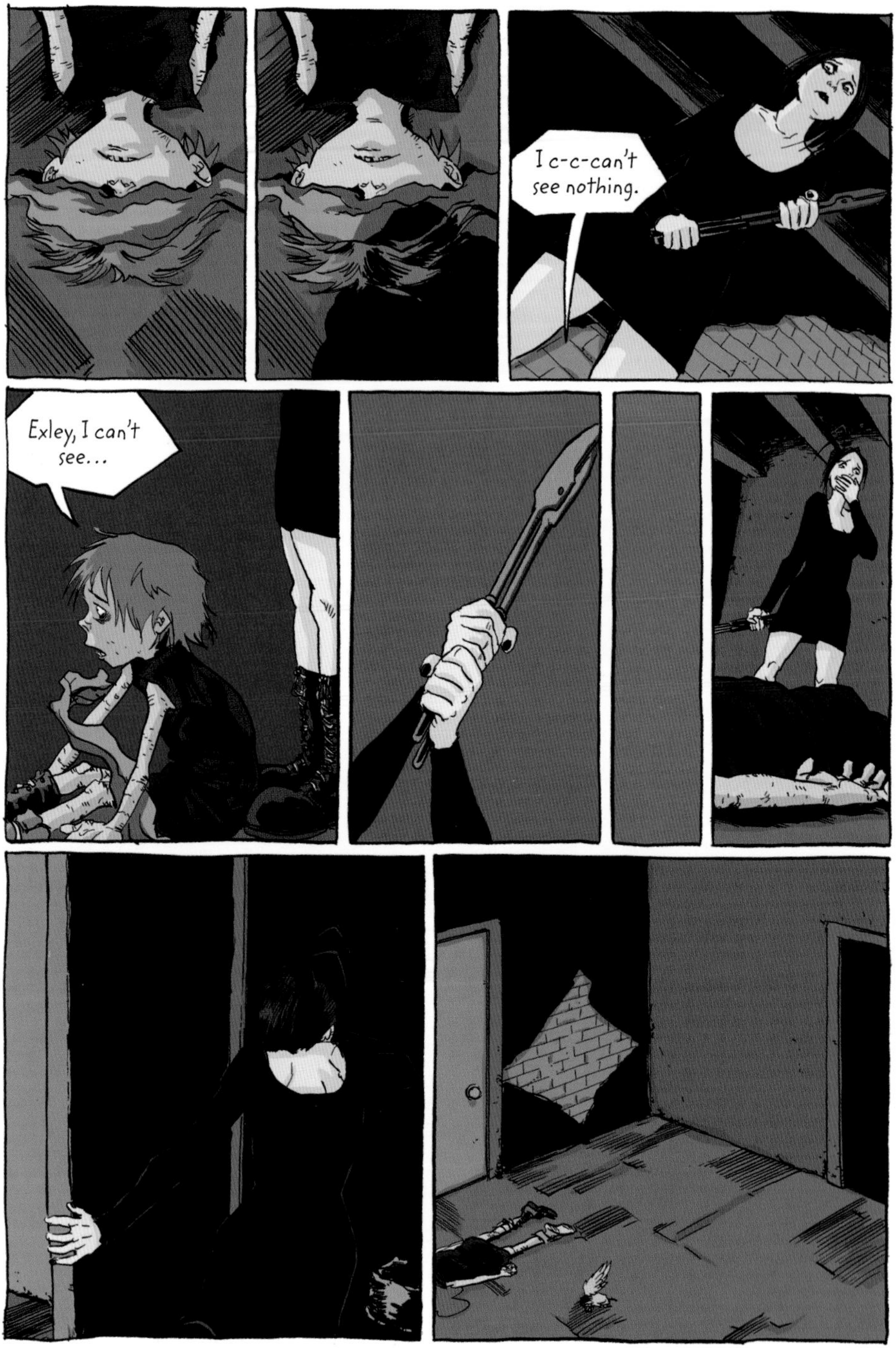
I c-c-can't see nothing.
Exley, I can't see...

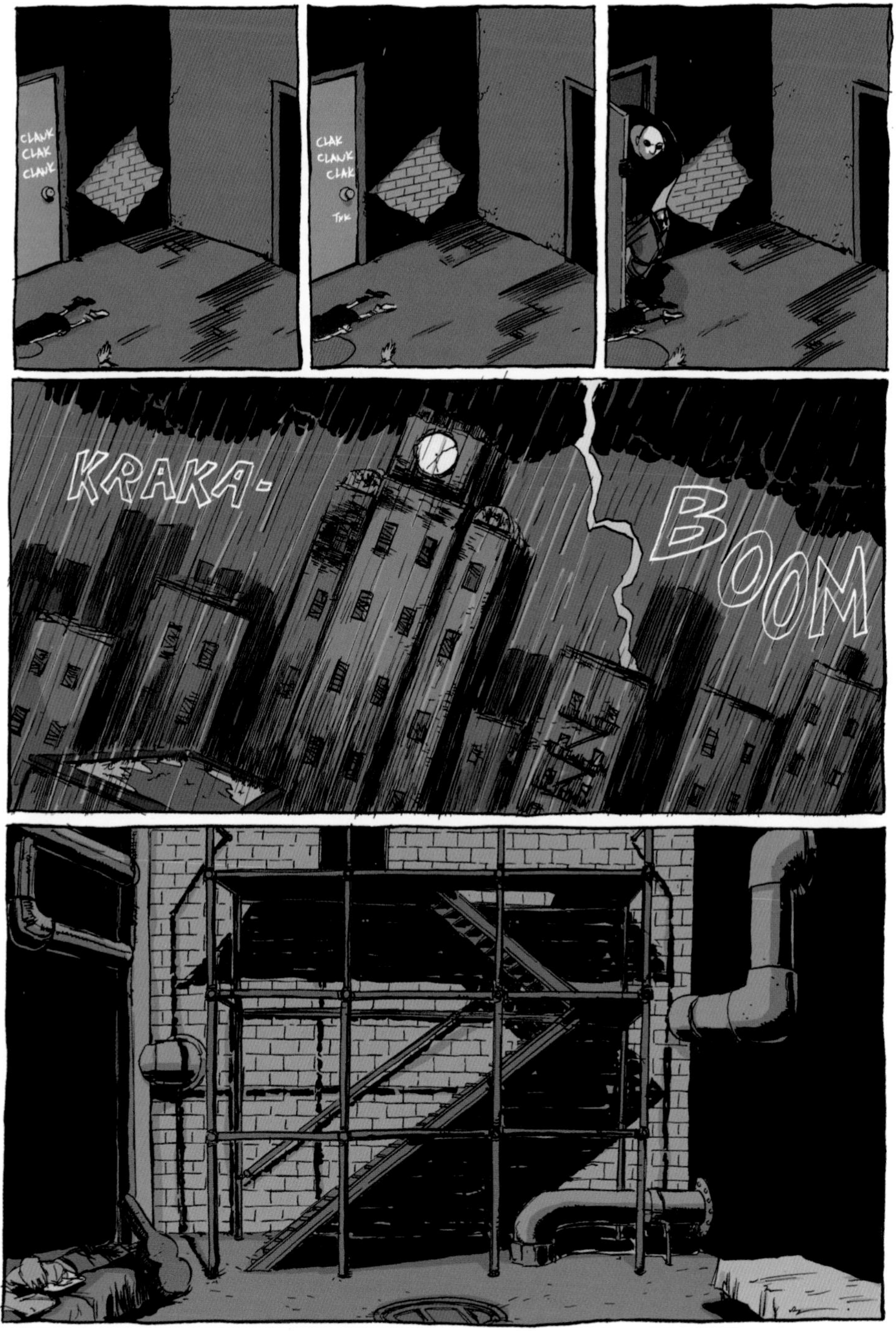
CLANK
CLAK
CLANK
CLAK
CLANK
CLAK
TNK
KRAKA-
BOOM

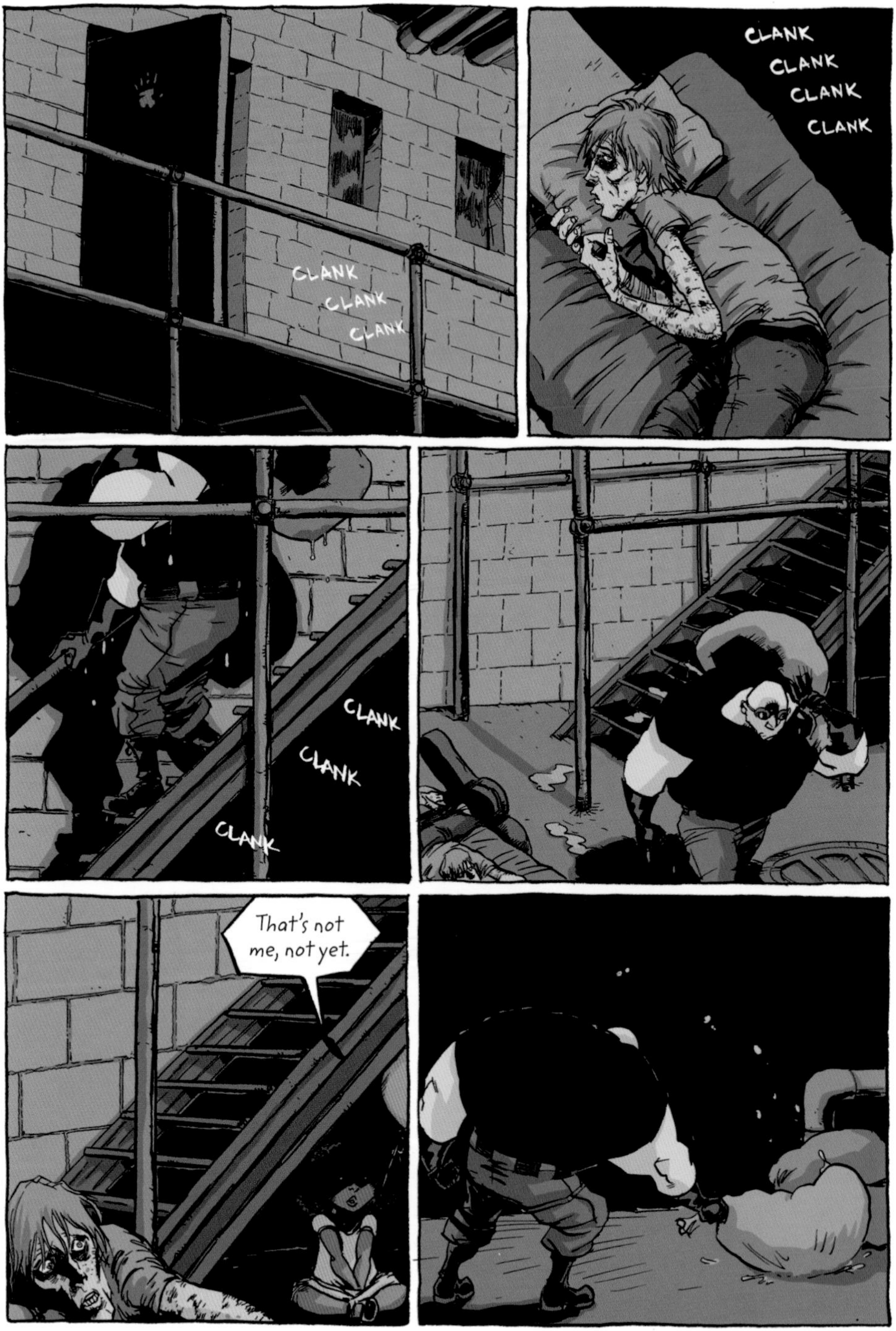
CLANK
CLANK
CLANK
CLANK
CLANK
CLANK
CLANK
CLANK
CLANK
CLANK
That's not me, not yet.

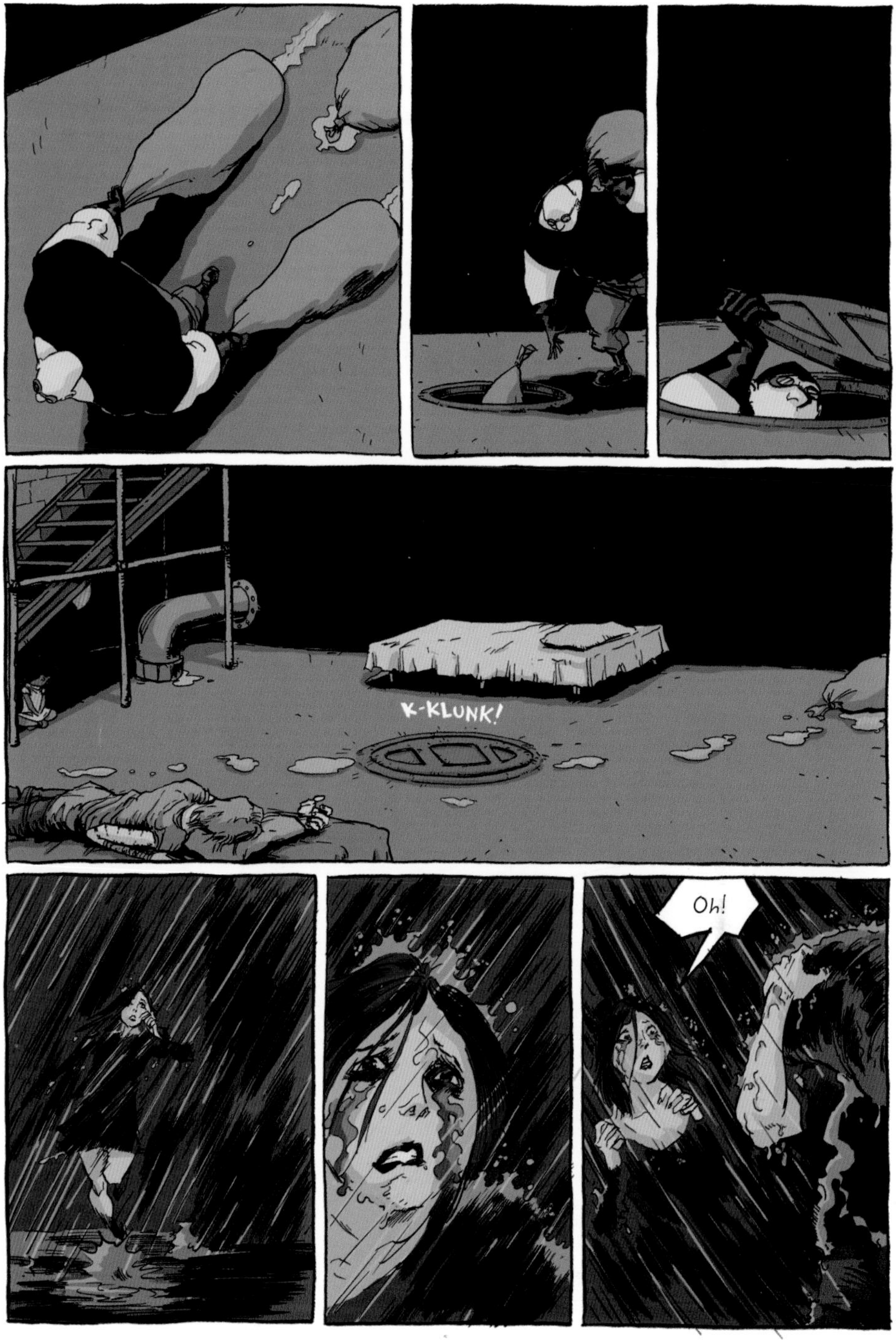
K-KLUNK!
Oh!

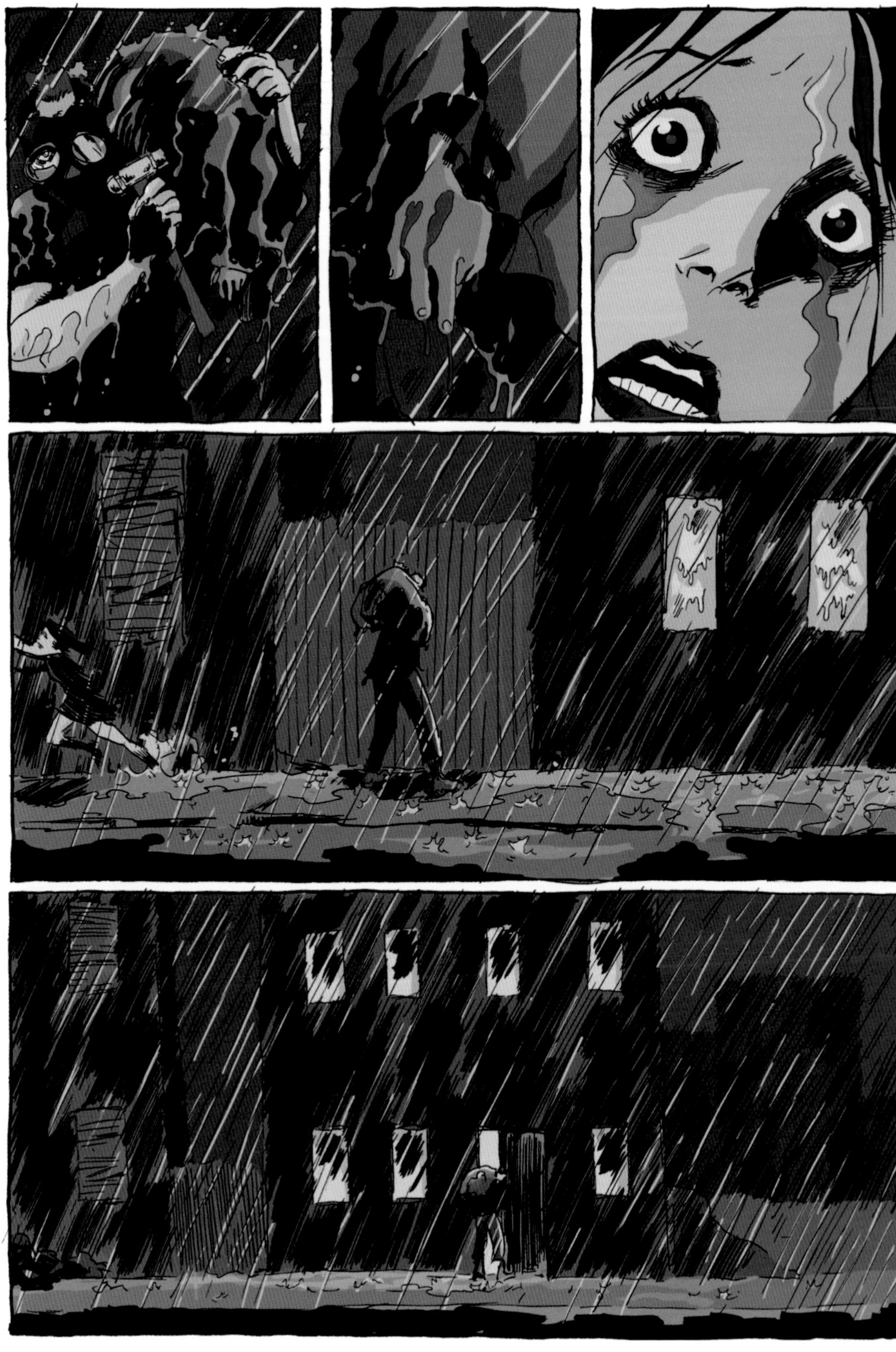

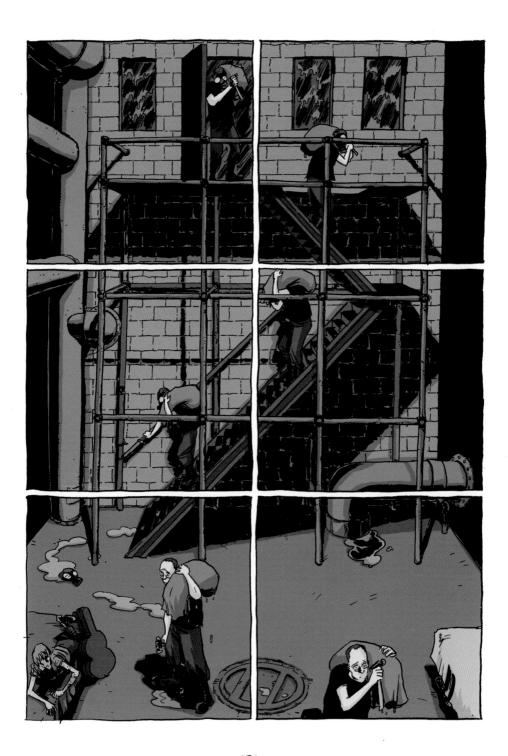

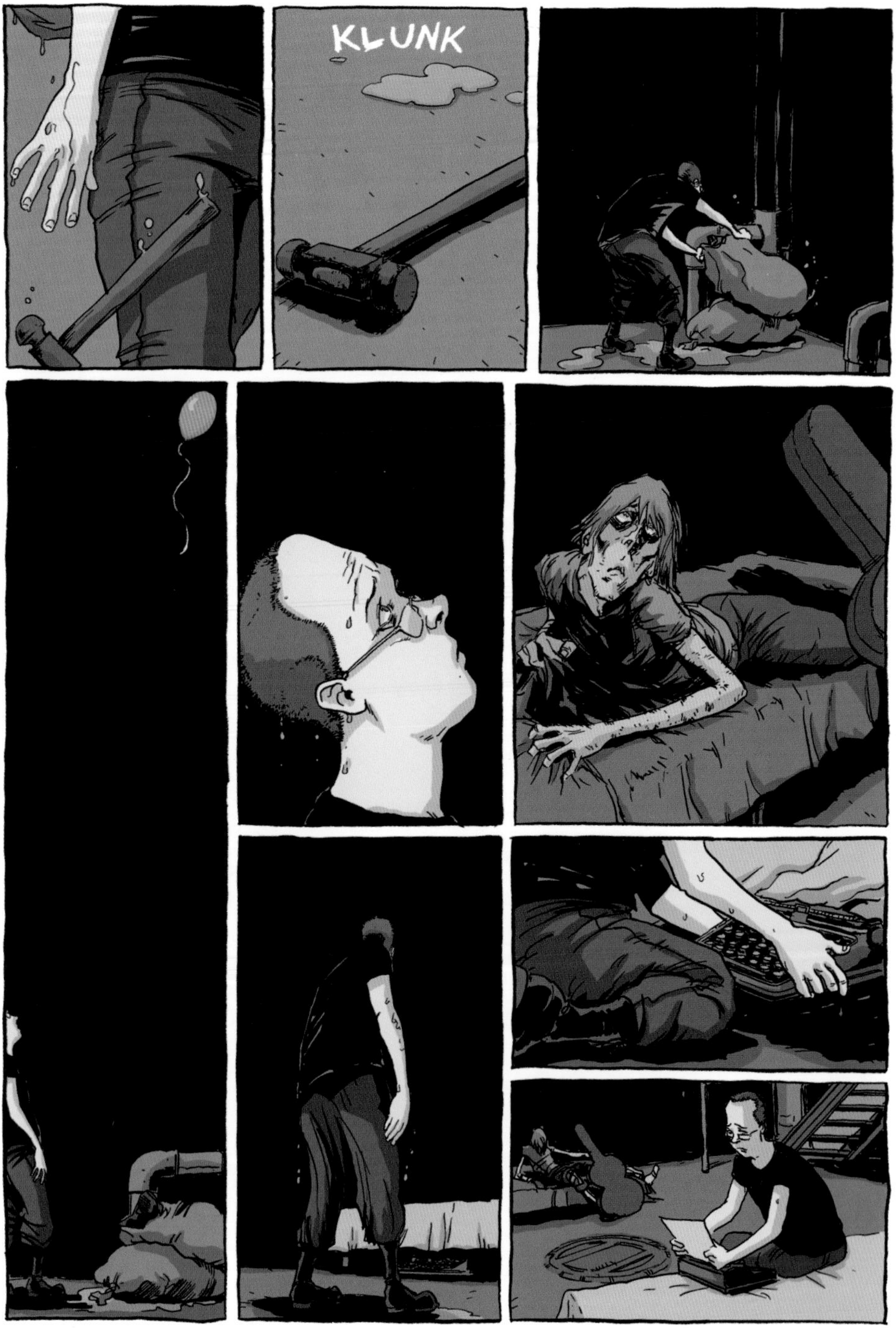
KLUNK

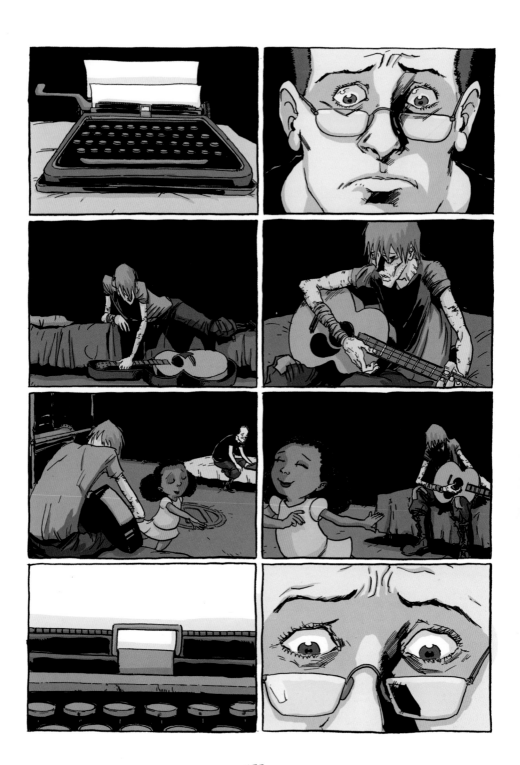

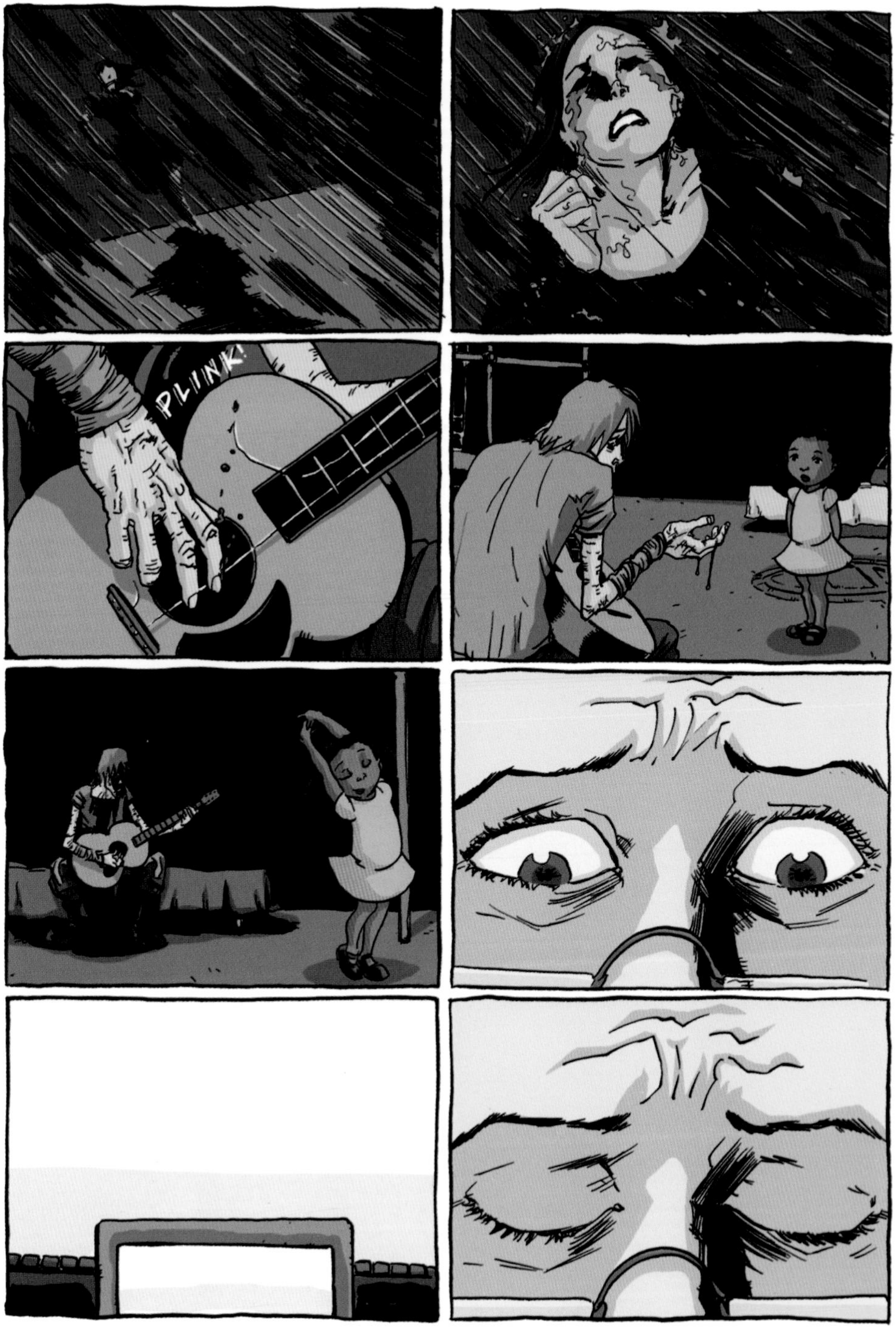
PLINK!

From George O'Connor's sketchbooks

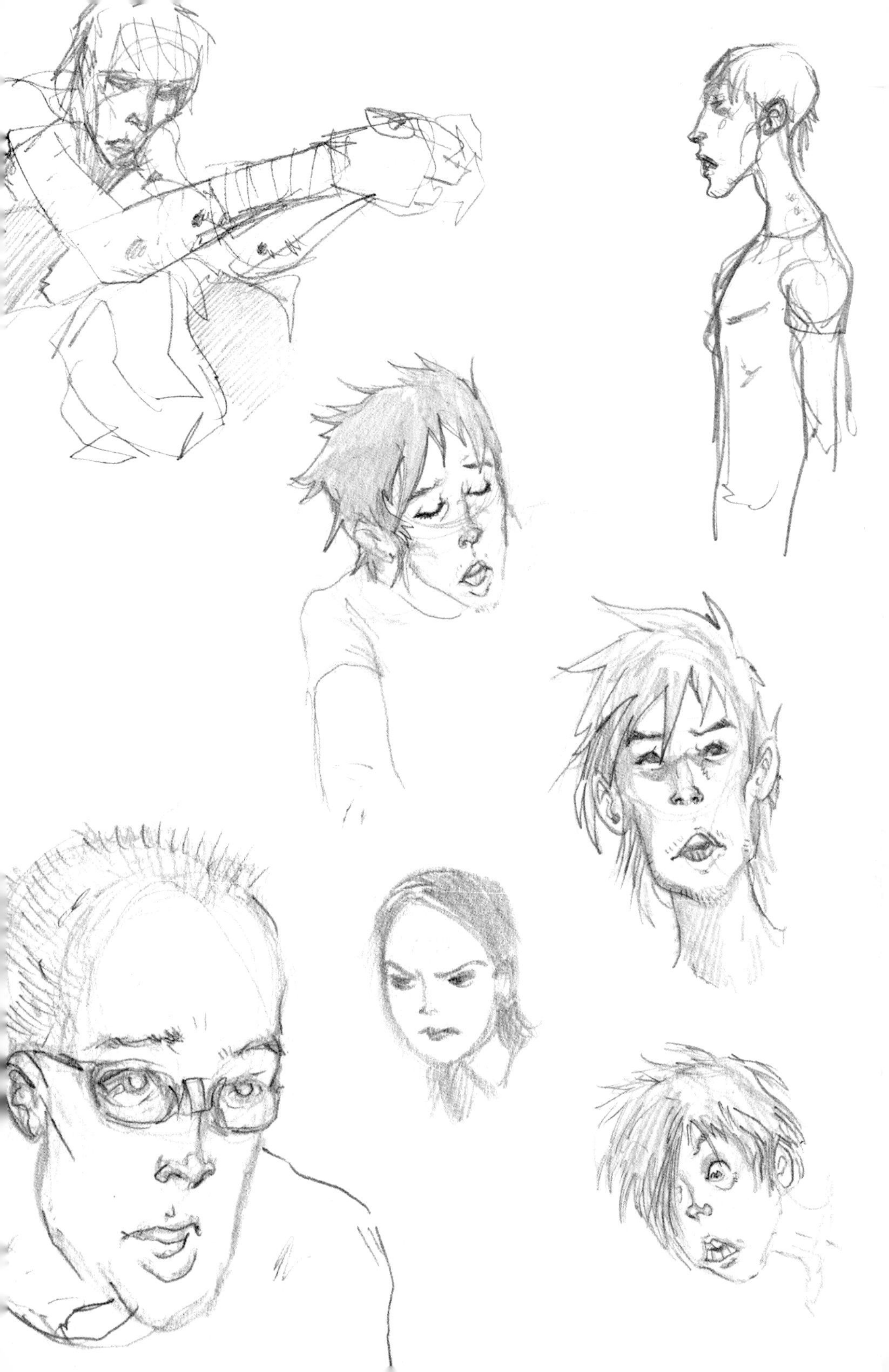

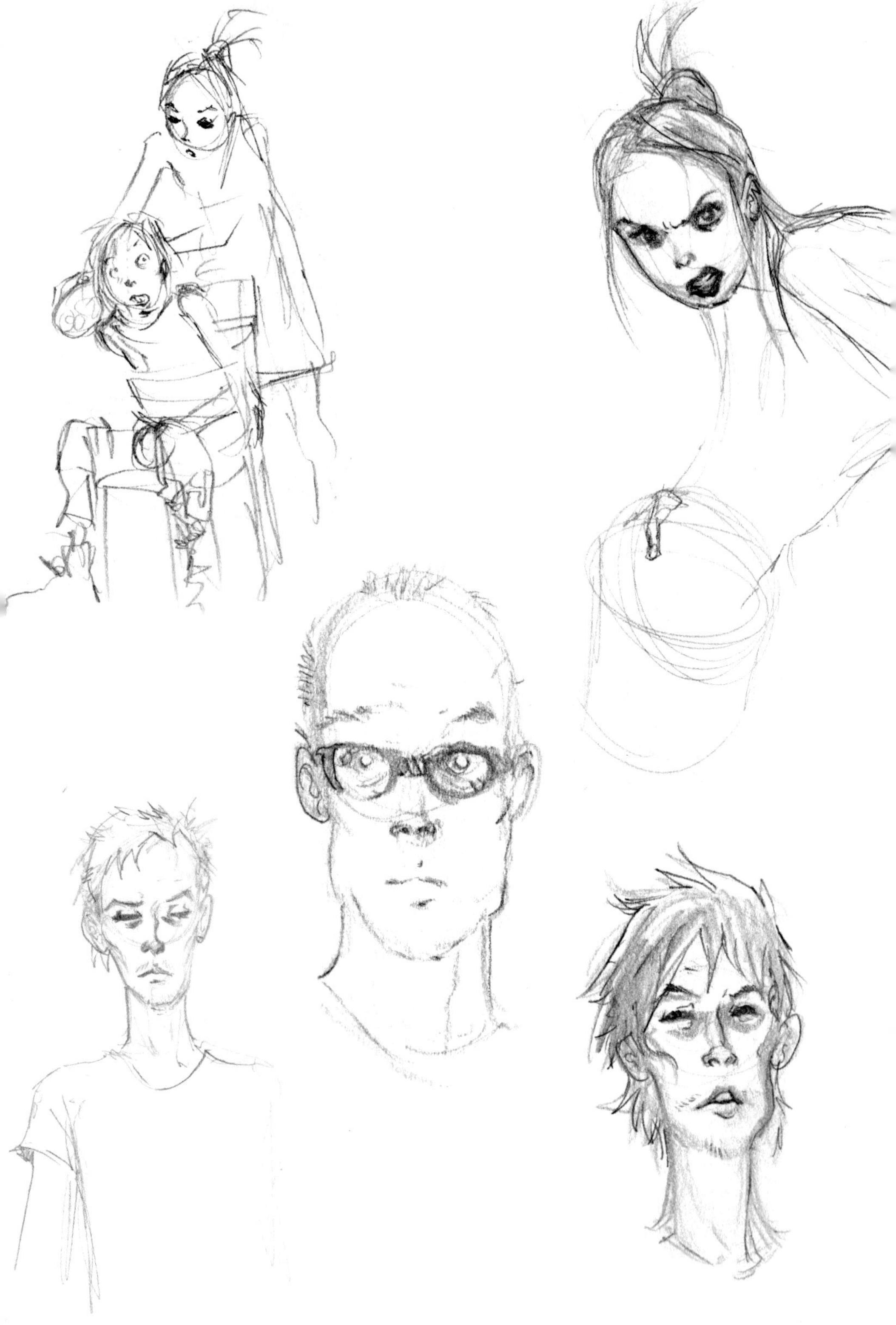

The :01 Collection

EMMANUEL GUIBERT
ALAN'S WAR
THE MEMORIES OF G.I. ALAN COPE

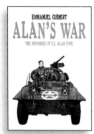

ALAN'S WAR by Emmanuel Guibert
"A story about a man whom war transformed into something better: tolerant, cosmopolitan, observant, and humane." – Cory Doctorow on *boingboing.net*

STASSEN
DEOGRATIAS
A TALE OF RWANDA

DEOGRATIAS by J.P. Stassen
★ "The importance of the story and the heartbreaking beauty of its presentation make it an essential purchase." – *Kirkus*

Refresh Refresh

REFRESH, REFRESH by Danica Novgorodoff, Benjamin Percy & James Ponsoldt
A powerful story about sons, fathers, and the war that comes between them.

EDDIE CAMPBELL
THE FATE of THE ARTIST

THE FATE OF THE ARTIST by Eddie Campbell
★ "Playful and wise, Campbell's latest report from the art front continues to demonstrate his mastery of the comics medium." – *Booklist*

JOANN SFAR
KLEZMER

KLEZMER by Joann Sfar
"Deeply suffused with Jewish religious and ethnic identity, the book is profane, messy, jagged and wildly enthusiastic, much like klezmer itself." – *Publisher's Weekly*

JOURNEY
into
MOHAWK
COUNTRY

JOURNEY INTO MOHAWK COUNTRY by George O'Connor
"A groundbreaking effort that will earn praise as an unusual comics work and as a work of history." – *Publisher's Weekly*

Notes for a War Story
Gipi

NOTES FOR A WAR STORY by Gipi
"[A] story about disassociated youth and the bonds of friendship." – *Booklist*

Three Shadows
Cyril Pedrosa

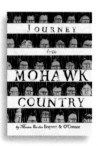

THREE SHADOWS by Cyril Pedrosa
"Pedrosa's intriguing, poignant fable unfolds beautifully in both words and pictures." – *Booklist*

MISSOURI BOY
by Leland Myrick

MISSOURI BOY by Leland Myrick
"The words outline the stories in minimal dialogue and lyrical captions, making each section a visual poem." – *Publisher's Weekly*

Appollo · Lewis Trondheim
BOURBON ISLAND 1730

BOURBON ISLAND 1730
by Appollo & Lewis Trondheim
"[A] swashbuckling tale of 18th-century piracy and colonial tension on a small French Island." – *Kirkus Reviews*

ORPHANS! MAYHEM! TERROR!
THE BLACK DIAMOND
DETECTIVE AGENCY

THE BLACK DIAMOND DETECTIVE AGENCY by Eddie Campbell
"A visually stunning graphic narrative with all sorts of complicated plot twists." – *Kirkus*

GUS

GUS by Chris Blain
"This one-two punch of all-out energy and rigid formalism hurtles the reader through the stories." – *Publisher's Weekly*

Slow Storm
Danica Novgorodoff

SLOW STORM
by Danica Novgorodoff
"What stands out about Novgorodoff's book are the artistry of its pages . . . and the human themes of loneliness, spiritual meaning and connection to the landscape of one's home territory." – *Louisville Courier Journal*

ABEL SORIA PLEECE
Life SUCKS

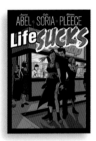

LIFE SUCKS by Jessica Abel, Gabriel Soria & Warren Pleece
"Hilarious. . . . Abel and Soria hit their mark with plenty of attitude and just enough snark to let their characters come to life." – *Booklist*

The Photographer

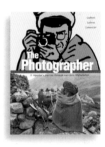

THE PHOTOGRAPHER
by Emmanuel Guibert, Didier Lefèvre & Frédéric Lemercier
"A work of stunning originality and power." – Sebastian Junger, author of *The Perfect Storm*

THE ETERNAL SMILE
BY GENE LUEN YANG
& DEREK KIRK KIM

THE ETERNAL SMILE
by Gene Luen Yang & Derek Kirk Kim
American Born Chinese creator Gene Yang in collaboration with indie comics genius Derek Kirk Kim in a collection of three stories where reality and fantasy collide – for good or for ill.

STUFFED!

STUFFED by Glenn Eichler & Nick Bertozzi
When a normal, middle-class family inherits the remains of a taxidermied African warrior, they are faced with some uncomfortable questions about the nature of family–and race. From *The Colbert Report* writer Glenn Eichler and *The Salon* creator Nick Bertozzi.

For everyone who we lost while I was working on this book.
— George O'Connor

First Second

New York & London

Text copyright © 2009 by Adam Rapp
Illustrations copyright © 2009 by George O'Connor

Published by First Second
First Second is an imprint of Roaring Brook Press,
a division of Holtzbrinck Publishing Holdings Limited Partnership
175 Fifth Avenue, New York, NY 10010

Distributed in Canada by H. B. Fenn and Company Ltd.
Distributed in the United Kingdom by Macmillan Children's Books,
a division of Pan Macmillan.

Design by Danica Novgorodoff
Color by Hilary Sycamore and Sky Blue Ink; lead colorist Alex Campbell

Library of Congress Cataloging-in-Publication Data is on file at the Library of Congress.

ISBN: 978-1-59643-300-7

First Second books are available for special promotions and premiums.
For details, contact: Director of Special Markets, Holtzbrinck Publishers.

FIRST
EDITION

First Edition September 2009
Printed in China
1 3 5 7 9 10 8 6 4 2

BY ART
WE LIVE